Coastal Sage

The publisher and the University of California Press Foundation gratefully acknowledge the generous support of the Ralph and Shirley Shapiro Endowment Fund in Environmental Studies.

Coastal Sage

PETER DOUGLAS AND THE FIGHT
TO SAVE CALIFORNIA'S SHORE

Thomas J. Osborne

UNIVERSITY OF CALIFORNIA PRESS

University of California Press, one of the most distinguished university presses in the United States, enriches lives around the world by advancing scholarship in the humanities, social sciences, and natural sciences. Its activities are supported by the UC Press Foundation and by philanthropic contributions from individuals and institutions. For more information, visit www.ucpress.edu.

University of California Press
Oakland, California

Library of Congress Cataloging-in-Publication Data

Names: Osborne, Thomas J., 1942– author.
Title: Coastal sage : Peter Douglas and the fight to save California's shore / Thomas J. Osborne.
Description: Oakland, California : University of California Press, [2018] | Includes bibliographical references and index. | Identifiers: LCCN 2017028639 (print) | LCCN 2017031282 (ebook) | ISBN 9780520958913 (Ebook) | ISBN 9780520283084 (cloth : alk. paper) | ISBN 9780520296657 (pbk. : alk. paper)
Subjects: LCSH: Douglas, Peter, 1942–2012. | Conservationists—California—Biography. | California Coastal Commission. | Coastal zone management—California.
Classification: LCC HT393.C2 (ebook) | LCC HT393.C2 O83 2018 (print) | DDC 333.72092 [B]—dc23
LC record available at https://lccn.loc.gov/2017028639

Manufactured in the United States of America

26 25 24 23 22 21 20 19 18
10 9 8 7 6 5 4 3 2 1

This book is dedicated to my wife, Ginger Tredway Osborne,
the love of my life,

and

to our grandchildren, Evangeline Harper Osborne and
Graham Thomas Osborne, to whom I promise to do all I can
to care for our oceans and beaches and ensure a sustainable
Earth for the coming generations

The ebb, flow, and perpetual beat of wave and tide against a shifting shore; the bounteous generosity of a nurturing Earth; the treasured, amazing variety of life at all scales nested in Nature's home.

PETER DOUGLAS,
"A Celebration of Life," June 9, 2010

CONTENTS

ILLUSTRATIONS

FIGURES

MAPS

PREFACE

"The coast was spectacular. . . . I travelled slowly, stopping often just to let the essence of Nature's artistry seep into my bones. . . . Cool clear, even foggy mornings, warming piercing light mid-day, and waning winds as a kaleidoscope of colors pull the falling light of sunset over the far horizon where imagination takes me on mythic travels. Then there's the canopy of countless stars pulled up from the darkening East like some gossamer blanket hitched to the sun coming down, sinking below the Western sky. How primal, grand and awe-evoking such visions of an endless sea edged by rugged land."[1] So rhapsodized Peter Douglas later in life recalling his drive along a stretch of California's coast in 1971 while advocating passage of a bill to protect the Golden State's shore. His words resonate with me, seeping into my bones and launching travels of my own imagination. They helped draw me into this writing project nearly four years ago.

Douglas's words drew me for reasons rooted in the provenance of this book. The idea for it emanates from my nearly lifelong love of the Pacific world coupled with forty-some years of living along the Orange County coast, swimming in its coves, and surfing Southland beaches. I have been an activist, testifying in civic forums for public access to Table Rock Beach in south Laguna, for shuttering the San Onofre nuclear power plant, and for stopping the State Route 241 Toll Road project that would have bisected a state park and endangered wildlife and habitat; chairing the citywide work group that wrote Laguna Beach's Climate Protection Action Plan; and advocating restoration of an estuary that once existed at Aliso Creek in Laguna Beach. In all of these instances I have found myself on the side of ocean activists and have counted on help from the California Coastal Commission in protecting our shore.

So though I am an academic, full disclosure requires me saying I am not, in writing about coastal issues, a disinterested party. In other words, the following excursion into environmental history was written by an environmental activist. Still, my training and career as a professional historian compel me to look at the complex issues discussed in this book from more than one side, to use a range of sources that are at times conflicting, and to reach evidence-based conclusions. This said, has the book been written from an environmentalist point of view? Yes. However, that does not exempt me from the standards just mentioned. Where I may not have met those exacting standards, I trust critics will—with good reason—point that out.

Moreover, I do not believe that, in the controversial issues discussed in this book, any one side has a monopoly on truth, sincerity, and virtue. Doing the research on this volume has convinced me that in many instances where property rights clashed with what I treated as the public interest, both sides had valid concerns that the historian in me must address. Being a supporter of the Coastal Commission does not absolve me of the responsibility to be fair-minded. I have witnessed, studied, and participated in enough environmental battles to neither seek nor expect praise for this book from either end of the spectrum of opinion on the controversial matters addressed. The most I hope for is acknowledgment from my peers in academia, and all discerning, open-minded readers for that matter, that this book constitutes an honest, credible attempt to tell a little-known story about a person I never met who arguably has done more than anyone else to protect California's storied coast from overdevelopment and for public access.

How should a book about such a person be titled? The appellation *Coastal Sage* has a double meaning. In a literal sense it conveys the sagelike, wise-elder qualities of Peter Douglas, especially during the later years of his executive directorship of the agency he cofounded and led. In a more figurative sense, the title evokes the image and qualities of the coastal-sage-scrub plant so common to California's littoral region. Like Douglas, the plant is hardy (adaptive to drought and other stresses), hospitable to wildlife (providing habitat for endangered California gnatcatchers), and emblematic of a coast both viewable and accessible to the public.

The title *Coastal Sage,* like so many titles, is merely suggestive, leaving more to be said here about the nature of this book. Some have asked: Is this a biography of Peter Douglas, the long-serving, recently deceased executive director of the California Coastal Commission? The answer is no. Well, then, does this account purport to be a comprehensive history of the commission he led? Again, no. I hope other writers will pen works on those deserving yet—at the time of this writing—neglected subjects. With those clarifications in mind, I can say that the selected biographical elements and episodes of Coastal Commission history incorporated into this book are integral to the narrative in order to give it coherence. This book, then, is best described as a study of Douglas's changing roles over the thirty-four years he worked for the commission. During those nearly three and a half decades, as the broader environmental movement peaked and then lost momentum, he received a remarkable education and seasoning, evolving into a coastal sage. By telling that story I hope to help fill a gap in California's and the nation's environmental history and to entice readers into thinking about and acting on coastal issues.

As the above suggests, I wrote the work with several audiences in mind. Academicians, policy makers, and journalists were foremost in my thinking. As researchers, writers, educators of the next generations, and public servants, they are especially influential in shaping public thinking and implementing policy. But I have also aimed this study at laypersons: citizen-activists, voters, and others who care about the state and fate of California's coast.

In numerous discussions I have had with informed voters and a good many self-identified environmentalists, knowledge of Peter Douglas's work on behalf of California's coast has been sketchy at best. In fact, before embarking on this book project, I would have had to count myself among this group. After searching and finding that very little had been published (and assuredly no book-length monographs) on either the history of the Coastal Commission or Peter Douglas's role in shaping that history, I decided to undertake the present study. In part, then, I wrote this volume to educate myself.

While I conducted more than thirty in-depth recorded interviews and consulted with others who had expertise, the conclusions I reached in the book do not necessarily reflect the opinions of any agency, group, or individuals with whom I spoke. Moreover, in my use of these interviews, consultations, and other materials, I alone am responsible for whatever deficiencies may be found in this volume.

Organizationally, the book contains seven chapters of various lengths, all of which are accompanied by endnotes appended for the purposes of scholarly documentation and referring readers to additional sources for further investigation. Chapter 1 offers the most biographical information about Douglas, connecting his early experiences with a later development of his environmental consciousness. Chapter 2 provides, figuratively speaking, a panoramic view of California's coast, focusing on its geomorphology and diverse physical attributes—which Douglas knew in detail—and its earlier development. Chapter 3 traces the rise of coastal activism in the 1960s, set against the backdrop of California's countercultural movement, a Bay Area conservation effort, public insistence on beach access at the Sea Ranch development along the Sonoma coast, and the Santa Barbara oil spill. Chapter 4 narrates the emergence of environmental politics in the 1960s and 1970s, focusing on the creation of the California Coastal Commission and Douglas's early involvement with that agency. Chapter 5 concentrates entirely on Douglas's executive-director years, highlighting his role in the commission's handling of twelve salient and controversial issues. Chapter 6 chronicles Douglas's last months in office, his declining health and visits with the people and to the places that mattered most to him, and his final thoughts on nature and the cosmos, California's coast, what owners of beach property owed the larger community, purposeful living, and death. Chapter 7 treats his legacy as a coastal manager and historical figure. "A Selected Time Line" (appendix A), "A Selected List of Peter Douglas's Accomplishments and Honors" (appendix B), and a bibliography appear at the end of this book.

ACKNOWLEDGMENTS

No undertaking of this kind is the solitary work of its author; without help from others this book would not have been completed. Still, I alone am responsible for whatever errors of fact or interpretation are found in this work.

During the years spent researching and writing this account, I have incurred debts to many people who contributed to this project in various important ways.

Douglas family members and friends of Peter provided needed biographical information and insights into the values that animated him and the ways he inspired others. In that regard I wish to acknowledge first and foremost Christiane M. Douglas, sister of the famed executive director, who generously offered information on Peter's early years, furnished me with useful documents and photographs, and most of all encouraged this project from beginning to end. Peter Douglas's sons, Vanja and Sascha, provided me with a number of insights and revelatory anecdotes regarding their father. Jeff Staben, executive assistant to Peter Douglas, helped with obtaining California Coastal Commission photos and permissions. Consultation with Dr. Gary Griggs, director of the Institute of Marine Sciences at UC Santa Cruz and an acquaintance of Peter Douglas, was indispensable in my writing of chapter 2, which focuses largely on coastal geology. He also provided an important photograph appearing in this book. Former state legislator Alan Sieroty, Douglas's mentor and longtime confidante on coastal politics, was the first person I interviewed for this project, and in him I could see the skill set, breadth of vision, and warmth that many have attributed to his protégé. Dr. Charles F. Lester, an exemplary coastal steward and Douglas's handpicked successor as commission chief, generously consented to my interviewing him and sent me an electronic copy of his article in the journal *Coastal Management* (41, no. 3

[2013]). Dr. Chad Nelsen, CEO of the Surfrider Foundation, spoke to me tellingly about how Douglas mentored and inspired him to become a coastal activist and leader. Janet Bridgers, cofounder of Earth Alert! and environmental educator, sent me a copy of her filmed interview of Peter Douglas and shared with me her interactions with him on other occasions.

Librarians, archivists, and other information handlers guided me expertly through labyrinths of materials, both digitalized and printed, which are not always easy to access. Dean Rowan, reference librarian at the UC Berkeley School of Law, downloaded and put on disc for me a seminal law review article that I needed. Michelle Morgan, an archivist at UC Berkeley's Bancroft Library, helped me do a difficult computer search of Sierra Club materials dealing with Coastal Commission matters. Conversations with noted historian Todd Holmes, an interviewer and associate academic specialist at that library, deepened my understanding of the structural tensions between panelists and staff that have dogged the Coastal Commission since its founding. Pauline Manaka, reference librarian at UC Irvine's Langson Library, emailed me otherwise hard-to-access articles in scholarly journals. Librarians at the State Archives in Sacramento went out of their way to accommodate my research visits and numerous requests for documents and copying. Renee L. Pieschke, who works with the U.S. Geological Survey, put extra time into helping me with usage of an important map.

Highly skilled editors kept me aware of the need and ways to communicate subject matter more clearly and effectively and helped keep this project moving forward. Merry Ovnick, masterful editor of the *Southern California Quarterly,* put me through the rigors of answering her tough questions with sound evidence and reasoning before publishing my article (a distillation of this book) "Saving the Golden Shore: Peter Douglas and the California Coastal Commission, 1972–2011," appearing in the winter 2014 issue of that publication. The University of California Press, publisher of that academic journal, granted permission for me to include portions of the article in my book. Kate Marshall, acquisitions editor at that press, offered wise counsel and helped in other important ways with this project, as did editorial assistant Bradley Depew. Dore Brown, production editor, helped clarify my writing of several passages and did an excellent job of keeping this project on schedule. Copyeditor Bonita Hurd saved me from making numerous errors of commission and omission; her eye for compositional detail accounts in no small measure for whatever polish this book may have. Similarly, Janet Fireman, former editor of the journal *California History,* saved me from making some embarrassing compositional errors, prompted my rethinking of chapter titles, and provided me with encouragement.

Friends and academic colleagues offered support and invaluable perspectives on matters of substance and exposition. My longtime dear friends Flossie and Paul Horgan, who were among the cofounders of the Bolsa Chica Land Trust, agreed to be interviewed, secured a photo for the book, and, over many laugh-filled potluck meals and fun hiking excursions, helped educate me on the effort to save Bolsa Chica Wetland from development. My friend and a distinguished historian of the Golden State, Glenna Matthews, read the manuscript in its entirety and helped me see the subject matter within a larger historical context. Scholar Angie Frederickson sent me an electronic copy of her informative article on ports, environmental justice, and the California Coastal Act, which appeared in the same issue of the *Coastal Management* journal mentioned above.

Finally, and with deepest gratitude, my wife and muse, Ginger Osborne—to whom this book is dedicated (along with our grandchildren)—read and listened to me read countless passages and made many suggestions that helped clarify my writing. Her unwavering support, as always, sustained me.

TJO
Laguna Beach, California

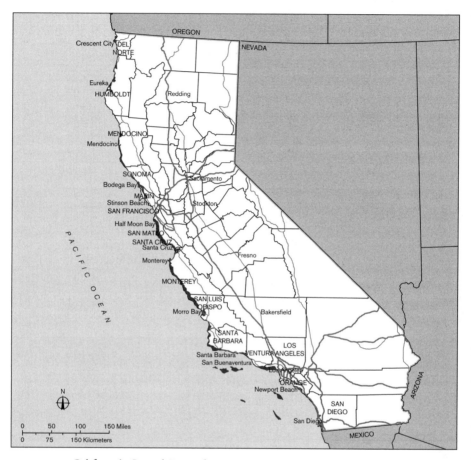

MAP 1. California's Coastal Zone, showing major counties, cities, and rivers. Source: California Coastal Commission.

ONE

Few Safe Harbors

PETER M. DOUGLAS'S FORMATIVE YEARS

THE FIRST THREE DECADES of Peter Douglas's life brimmed with traumatic wartime struggles to survive, followed by adventures along the California coast and exotic, low-budget overseas travel. Memories of a precarious childhood amid the horrors and devastation of Nazi Germany in World War II remained etched in his mind long after that conflict ended.

Leaving his native country and coming to the United States in the war's aftermath gave rise to a whole new range of peacetime experiences and opportunities that would further shape the youth's unfolding life. Specifically, growing up in coastal California placed the Golden State's imprint on a boy who early on was smitten and awed by the Pacific shore of his adopted home. Later, his pathway toward entering a career in coastal management was filled with twists and turns in both his personal and his early professional life.

WAR'S CHILD

Peter Michael Ehlers was born in Berlin, the capital of Adolph Hitler's fantasized Third Reich, on August 22, 1942. Maria Ehlers, the infant's mother, was Jewish, making her son and daughter, Christiane (born in 1941), Jews in accordance with German law. That meant life-threatening danger in a city where Jewish shops and synagogues had been earlier vandalized and set ablaze on Kristallnacht, the "Night of Broken Glass," in November 1938. Though some Jews had fled the city, in 1942 Berlin still had Germany's largest Jewish population, making these Berliners prime targets for mass deportations to ghettoes and extermination camps in Poland and elsewhere.

That Peter, his sister, and their mother survived the war was due largely to family connections, Maria's resourcefulness (enhanced by a limited use of English), and, especially, the ingenuity of a devoted nanny, Paula Elisabeth Vetter. Peter and Christiane's gentile father, Reinholt Claren, was a well-connected prominent industrialist and patent lawyer. Peter said he was assured his father was not a member of the Nazi party. Their father, with whom Peter and Christiane had little contact, used his ties with officialdom to protect his vulnerable family from persecution. Hoping to provide an added layer of religious cover for her children, Maria had Peter and Christiane baptized Catholic.[1] On December 5, 1944, an Allied bomb destroyed much of the family home, landing Peter (who had sought cover in the family's self-built air raid shelter) in a hospital for hernia repair surgery. Thus began, upon his release from the hospital, what Peter described much later as "our desperate flight from the Russians,"[2] whose armies were invading Germany from the east and despoiling nearly everything and everyone along the way to Berlin. By then Peter's parents had separated permanently, and he, his sister, his mother, and Paula scrambled literally from one sanctuary (often the urban home or farmhouse of a friend or acquaintance) to another. "Traveling by tractor and train, by foot and horse-drawn wagon, we joined a desperate flood of refugees and ran for weeks, stopping only upon reaching relative safety just inside the American zone of control in Bavaria."[3] Looking back on this "fear-filled, harrowing period of our lives," Peter attributed their survival largely to the "incredible resourcefulness" of Paula, whom he and his sister referred to reverentially as their "soul mother."[4] Christiane recalled how Paula, when food had become increasingly scarce, fed Peter and her by cooking two batches of potato soup: the first using a peeled potato, and the second using only the skin. Hunger, disease, terror, and death stalked them and other German refugees on the move, and not every family had a Paula.

Maria, whose art world connections gave her some measure of influence, not only struggled to protect her children and Paula but also worked to undermine the Nazi regime. An example of Maria's risky, pro-Allied efforts was her resistance activity in the Bavarian town of Mitterteich near the end of the war in early May 1945. As American troops were approaching, the Nazi mayor of the town, wrote Douglas, planned a last-ditch stand against incoming U.S. forces by furnishing rifles to boys and old men while overseeing the positioning of a small detachment of German SS soldiers behind city hall.[5] When the mayor learned that Maria had stirred up the townspeople to protest the German war effort, he tried to have her hanged. The citizenry quickly came to her aid, forcing the mayor to flee.

Next, something remarkably fortuitous happened. As American troops entered the town, Maria walked out to meet them "waving a white handkerchief." "Hello, boys!" she said, and then warned them about the SS detachment behind city hall. The American soldiers surrounded the small German force, which surrendered quickly. Shortly thereafter, Maria was brusquely asked for her identification papers by the U.S. officer in charge, who was on the lookout for Nazi sympathizers among the townspeople. Such documents had been lost in the family's harried flight from the Russians, she replied. Sensing the urgency to prove her support for the Allied cause, Maria handed the officer photographs of her sister and brother-in-law (in U.S. Navy uniform) who had been living in Southern California. "What's his name?" demanded the officer. "Chapman Wentworth." The interrogator paused, stood, "took mother's hands and embraced her," said Douglas. As fate would have it, the American inquisitor— Special Agent Bert H. Dreebin—had gone through Officer Training School with Chapman Wentworth and, like his comrade-in-arms, lived in Los Angeles![6] Officer Dreebin then sent telegrams to Alice Ehlers (Peter's maternal grandmother, residing in Southern California) and Christina Wentworth (Maria's sister, also living in the Southland), telling them that Maria and her children were safe and how they could be reached by mail. Shortly thereafter, care packages from Mrs. Ehlers in America began arriving in Mitterteich, and Special Agent Dreebin saw to it that these parcels reached Maria and her family. The packages included chocolate, sugar, powdered milk and eggs, puddings, biscuit mix, and sometimes U.S. dollars. Highly beneficial at the time, the chance occurrence of Maria meeting Officer Dreebin in May 1945 would be of even greater importance five years later.

In the aftermath of the war, Maria actively helped the town of Mitterteich recover from the carnage. She aided the Red Cross in reuniting families in the town that had been separated by the chaos of hostilities. According to Christiane Douglas, their mother worked with the American officers in that town as a "liaison" between them and the citizenry, thereby fostering a less problematic postwar occupation. Maria's involvement in Mitterteich in the years 1945–1950 did not go unnoticed and would soon stand her family in good stead.

With Germany in ruins in the late 1940s and welcoming relatives living in Southern California, Maria, Peter, Christiane, and caretaker Paula were more than ready to try their luck in America, a land relatively unscathed by

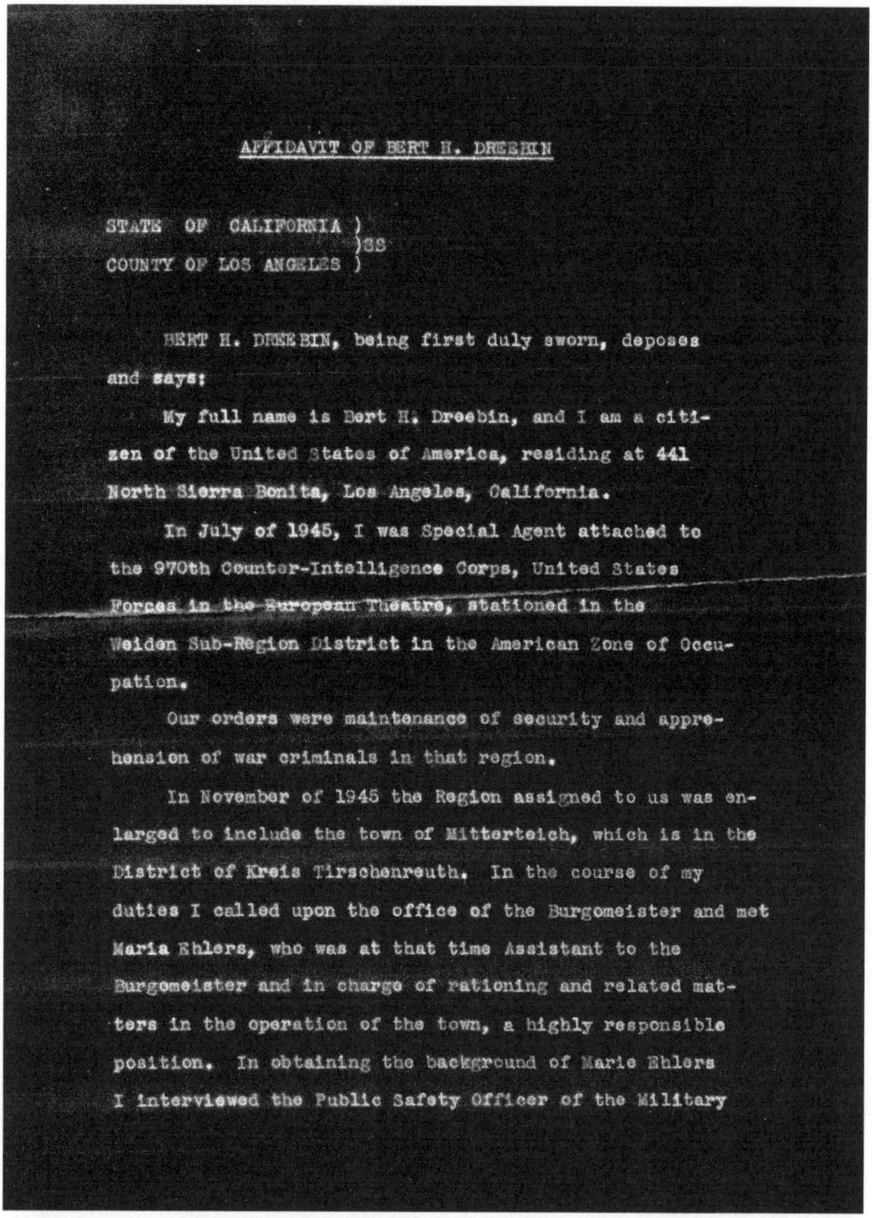

AFFIDAVIT OF BERT H. DREEBIN

STATE OF CALIFORNIA)
)SS
COUNTY OF LOS ANGELES)

BERT H. DREEBIN, being first duly sworn, deposes
and says:

My full name is Bert H. Dreebin, and I am a citizen of the United States of America, residing at 441
North Sierra Bonita, Los Angeles, California.

In July of 1945, I was Special Agent attached to
the 970th Counter-Intelligence Corps, United States
Forces in the European Theatre, stationed in the
Weiden Sub-Region District in the American Zone of Occupation.

Our orders were maintenance of security and appre-
hension of war criminals in that region.

In November of 1945 the Region assigned to us was en-
larged to include the town of Mitterteich, which is in the
District of Kreis Tirschenreuth. In the course of my
duties I called upon the office of the Burgomeister and met
Maria Ehlers, who was at that time Assistant to the
Burgomeister and in charge of rationing and related matters in the operation of the town, a highly responsible
position. In obtaining the background of Marie Ehlers
I interviewed the Public Safety Officer of the Military

FIGURE I. Letter written by Bert H. Dreebin, special agent, 970th Counter-Intelligence Corps, United States Forces, dated August 13, 1946, attesting to Maria Ehlers's assistance in the American-occupied town of Mitterteich, Germany. Photo courtesy of Christiane Douglas.

Government Detachment in the aforementioned town. I found that Marie Ehlers had materially assisted the American Military Government in the administration and enforcement of the law at the time when the Americans first occupied the town and through-out the balance of this occupation.

Marie Ehlers was of great assistance to the Counter-Intelligence Service of the United States Government in obtaining the names and background of Nazi leaders, and in one instance advising us of the return of a high Nazi party official and as a result of this information this person was apprehended by the United States authorities.

In my opinion, Marie Ehlers was most helpful to the American cause and as a result I would like to recommend that every assistance be given her in again visiting the United States.

Subscribed and sworn to before me

this 13 day of August, 1946.

Notary Public in and for the
County of Los Angeles, State of
California.

the late war, where, seemingly at least, opportunity for those willing to work hard abounded. With high hopes for a better future, the little band of war-weary refugees sailed across the English Channel to Dover, England, in early August 1950, and then, after a brief stay with the children's maternal grandfather in the Devon County town of Bovey Tracy, boarded a transatlantic ocean liner bound for New York City.

The voyage across the Atlantic made an indelible imprint on eight-year-old Peter—a highly positive one. Late in life he reminisced: "I spotted my first whale and giant manta. . . . My soul was drawn into the ocean as one given over entirely, without resistance, to the Siren's song. . . . It was there on that journey an intangible, unbreakable, lifelong bond between Ocean and me was forged."[7] This bond was strengthened and extended to the Pacific Ocean in the years that followed. Sailing past the Statue of Liberty, Douglas later recalled, brought tears to his young eyes. Some problems at the port's immigration office were resolved "after my mother's work with the Allies during and after the war became known." Specifically, Maria carried with her a letter signed by Special Agent Dreebin attesting to her recent status with the U.S. military in occupied Germany and her work with the Red Cross in reunifying refugee families during the last few months of the war. Thereafter, "we were given the VIP treatment."[8] Soon Maria, her children, and Paula flew to California, with a stopover in snowbound Chicago, arriving at the Los Angeles Airport just before Christmas.

They were met and picked up by well-to-do relatives of his mother in "a convertible automobile and [driven] along South Bay beaches to our new home in Palos Verdes."[9] Seeing tall palm trees swaying in balmy breezes and feeling the sun on his face, Peter closed his eyes, knowing "without doubt, if paradise exists on Earth, this had to be it."[10]

GROWING UP IN COASTAL CALIFORNIA

While the new environment may have been paradise for the new arrivals, Peter and perhaps the others with him continued to feel the traumatic effects of war. Much later in life he reflected on how, after having settled in California, his boyhood might have been influenced by the cataclysm of World War II. "My drawings in class [second grade] were filled with fiery scenes of violence, death, and destruction. Mostly I drew depictions of diving airplanes firing cannons and dropping bombs on running people, hapless animals, and harmless homes. I apparently also drew mangled bodies strewn across the page, occasionally pressing hard on my pencil until it broke." He sought and enjoyed solitude, looking on himself as somewhat of a loner "in constant transit." During World War II and throughout his life, he saw himself as "always being uprooted, of never belonging to a fixed place." In addition to producing nightmarish depictions and carrying memories of collective violence and of being alone and on the move, Douglas "learned to be observant and noticed many things around [himself] that others missed."[11] His powers of observation would serve him well much later when, as head of the California Coastal Commission, so much depended on his ability to master mountains of legal minutia and read the roiling, complex, ever-shifting Sacramento political landscape.

Peter's change of surname in 1954 perhaps bespoke a newfound sense of agency, even happiness, for the California transplant on the cusp of adolescence. When Peter was twelve and living in affluent Rolling Hills with his sister and other relatives, the siblings became U.S. citizens. At the urging of an adult family member, Peter and his sister were encouraged to think about taking an American-sounding surname. The siblings' oldest cousin, Peter Douglas Wentworth, lived in the Palos Verdes area, providing a familial connection to the name *Douglas*. Meanwhile, a neighbor in Rolling Hills—the CEO of McDonnell Douglas (Donald W. Douglas Jr.)—spent time with young Peter, taking him for helicopter rides. Drawn to their cousin, and to their neighbor, who may have become somewhat of a father figure to the boy, Peter decided to adopt the surname Douglas and talked his sister into doing likewise.[12]

At that time, Peter and Christiane attended the private Chadwick School in Palos Verdes, where they learned English by immersion while working on campus to pay some of their expenses. Afterward, their mother enrolled Peter as a working scholarship student at the Robert Louis Stevenson School, an all-boys college preparatory academy located on the Monterey Peninsula, in upscale Pebble Beach. A boarding student who worked on campus to defray part of his tuition, he "lived happily in a converted tool shed behind the kitchen." These Spartan quarters meant that he was left pretty much to himself. "Often on moonlit nights," he arose and followed "animal tracks through thick woods to the rocky shoreline near Bird Rock." There, he recalled much later, he first ruminated on life's big questions: "Sitting for hours, searching star-filled heavens for clues to the essence of being, moved by the mystery and wonder of it all, I wrestled with grand, confounding questions. And I found some answers on that ancient seashore bathed in moonlight." Mostly, though, he concluded "there are no answers to the universal 'why.' It was there I determined that what matters most to me is living the questions I asked, and making my life . . . a worthy expression" of the search for whatever the natural world could teach an inquiring person. Overwhelmed by the beauty and rhythms of tides washing across rocky shores, he felt "harshness leave my life."[13] Both time and the alluring California seascape seem to have coalesced into a healing balm, salving the boy's wartime hurts, allowing him to more fully pursue the adventures of youth.

Another healing agent, as well, operated in Peter's boyhood years. His German-born, Jewish grandmother on his mother's side, Alice Ehlers (called "Mima" by family members), formed a strong bond with him while becoming "the greatest adult influence in my life." A prominent harpsichordist, she had left her German homeland in the mid-1930s to concertize and thereafter remained abroad, first in England and then in the United States. A Johann Sebastian Bach specialist, Ehlers performed at venues in the Soviet Union, Israel, and South America, among other places internationally; she also performed at Pomona College (Claremont, California) and held a professorship of music at the University of Southern California. She had been a friend of the world-renowned organist, medical missionary, and Nobel laureate Dr. Albert Schweitzer.[14] Ehlers imbibed Schweitzer's "reverence for life" philosophy, along with his pacifism. These teachings she instilled in her grandson, Peter, who saw them as forming the root of his ethical/environmental thinking throughout the rest of his life.[15] Simultaneously, the ties between the mentor-grandmother and her protégé-grandson—both of whom spoke English and German—deepened, to the satisfaction of both.

When not being schooled and mentored in the 1950s and early 1960s, young Douglas embraced an ocean-and-beach-going lifestyle; occasionally, though, he camped in the desert and Sierras. "I spent most of my free time on the beach or in the water," he later recalled. Serving as a junior lifeguard at Redondo Beach spoke to his proficiency as an ocean swimmer. Surfing and diving brought him great joy. Douglas surfed on handcrafted balsa boards just as the wave-riding craze was sweeping Southland beaches. "I also did a lot of diving in those days and remember pounding hundreds of abalone steaks and eating fish caught in the rich nearshore waters just south of Torrance Beach." Much later he would lament, "The sea of plenty is no more."[16]

Beginning in his late teens, Douglas held a number of maritime jobs working "long hours" on tugboats, garbage haulers, and passenger craft. His nascent sense of environmental ethics had not yet taken hold. Crewing on a converted transpacific racing sloop, he and his coworkers picked up garbage from ships in Los Angeles Harbor and dumped it in the ocean off the east end of Catalina Island. Sometimes they came upon barrels of floating "gunk" from U.S. Navy vessels; he and fellow crewmen shot holes in the metal drums, making sure they sank. Such "gunk" may have consisted of chemical weapons waste.[17] In hindsight, referring to the above incidents, Douglas told an audience of surfers in 1999: "Out of ignorance and an unthinking, foolish urge to dominate, I scarred the earth a few times in my youth."[18]

THE EDUCATION OF A POLITICAL ACTIVIST

Douglas's maritime employments continued, as time permitted, even after he went off to college. He studied for a year at UC Berkeley in the early 1960s, during which time he grew uneasy about protesters and hippies on campus. Their drug usage and criticisms of his adopted country offended his immigrant, Republican, pro-American sensibilities.[19] Consequently, he transferred to the less politically volatile UCLA, living off campus with his grandmother, Mima, to save on expenses. His conservatism still intact, Douglas graduated in 1965 with a bachelor's degree in psychology.

Upon graduating, Douglas briefly entered the merchant marine world, gaining work and passage on a Norwegian chemical tanker crossing the Atlantic. The tanker job was a means toward achieving his twofold aims: to pursue further studies at the Philipps University of Marburg, Germany, and reconnect with a young German woman, Rotraut Schmidt. He had first met Schmidt, a recent pharmacy school graduate who was on vacation, at a puppet show in a beer garden in Salzburg, Austria, in 1959 while Douglas was on a European trip with his American relatives. Subsequently, the two had become pen pals. Later, in the medieval town of Marburg, finding his classes at Philipps University "excruciatingly boring," Peter stopped attending and sought further education elsewhere: at a German tavern in the town. On one such visit, he met "an amazing curmudgeon," Henri Lohrengel, "a retired high school teacher, concert violinist, linguist (he read, spoke, and wrote twenty-three languages!) . . . simply the most knowledgeable person I had and have ever met." During the next six months the teacher and his pupil became close friends. They studied the Greek classics, Roman writers, Hermann Hesse, Buddhism, ancient religious texts, geopolitics, and humankind's despoliation of the global environment. In addition to supplying Peter with this rich tutorial in the liberal arts, Lohrengel nurtured the seeds of ecological thinking that earlier had been planted in Peter's mind . "His words of wisdom got me thinking about Earth and environment in ways I had not explored before."[20]

While Douglas's environmental thinking had been nudged forward during the year of self-directed study in Germany, he still needed to figure out how to make a living given his aptitudes and values. Though he was not particularly drawn to law, he valued what legal studies might teach him regarding how society functions and enforces norms through the justice system, and so he entered the UCLA School of Law. In hindsight, he remarked, "Little did I know then, how valuable my legal training would be."[21]

In his second year at the School of Law in the late 1960s, Douglas became what he called "a newborn activist": "My activism focused on social justice, civil and individual rights and liberties, antipoverty and antiwar activities, prisoner rights, fair housing, and student counseling (focused on resistance to a horribly misguided war in Asia)." Looking back on this turning point in his political life, Douglas affirmed: "I am a child of the sixties and proud I never grew up. I have worked consciously and continuously at maturing my idealism and commitment to service on behalf of people and nature."[22] He had not yet explored the field of environmental law. At that time Douglas served as chairperson of the Community Participation Center (CPC), a political activist group composed of law students who went into Watts and other impoverished neighborhoods to help residents organize and battle for fair housing and improved social services. CPC members also counseled young men on draft resistance. Fellow CPC organizers included John Lovell, Wally Walker, and Ralph Ochoa. Peter's classmate and fellow CPC member Robert H. Burnham, who went on to become Newport Beach's city attorney, recalled Douglas's passion for social issues and the latter's skill in facilitating the group's meetings at his apartment near campus.[23] Douglas's wife, "Roe" (he and Rotraut Schmidt had married in 1966), served as CPC executive secretary. She had been instrumental in liberalizing Douglas's politics, including his party switch from Republican to Democrat.[24] Before long, she decided that the CPC's reform efforts were futile and told Peter she planned to return to her German homeland.

Though Peter believed his CPC involvement worthwhile, his disillusionment about his adopted country waging war in Vietnam and sense of burnout mounted.[25] So after graduating with his law degree and passing the California State Bar examination in 1969, he was ready to set out with Roe in search of greener pastures—that is, a place or country on the globe where they could live peacefully and happily. Perhaps there existed a utopia or Camelot or Shangri-la that would meet their needs. Thus began the young couple's roughly yearlong odyssey abroad.

A YEAR ABROAD: GOING OUT AND GOING IN

When recounting a long journey as a young man, environmentalist John Muir reflected, "I only went out for a walk" and found that in going out he "was really going in." That is, ultimately Muir learned about himself and the general direction his life would take. This was in certain ways similar to the experience of newly minted lawyer Peter Douglas as he and Roe went in search of a new place to live outside of America. For him, at least, that exploration helped clarify where they would settle and work for progressive societal change.

In writing about this search for a place to call home, Douglas did not identify all the countries they toured while "living out of our VW van for less than $2.50 a day." After six months on the road, traveling slowly across North Africa, the pair made it to southern Tunisia en route to Morocco. By then, in February 1970, the realization struck Peter that they had been "searching for a place we discovered didn't exist. I came to understand that no country is or could ever be all I wanted it to be."[26]

This pivotal point in their wanderings came when they reached the "low-lying island of Djerba, off the coast of Tunisia." Relaxing on a deserted white sand beach beneath "a clear cerulean sky," Douglas recalled Homer's tale of *The Odyssey*. Perhaps drawing on his tutorial with Henri Lohrengel several years earlier, Douglas identified with the mythical Odysseus who resisted the Sirens' call to bask in the seeming utopian land of the lotus-eaters and instead returned to his home. For all of America's faults, he realized, law school had taught him to "appreciate the freedoms individual citizens have" in his adopted country. "There we have the right and ability to get involved and bring about actual social change. Indeed, I began to see it as a citizen's responsibility in a democracy, such as it is." Then, too, he felt he owed something to America for the opportunities and skills it had provided him: "I was grateful for what I had received and wanted to give something back."[27] Douglas saw that "the fire of activism" still burned brightly within him. Disdainful of armchair activists, which he saw himself becoming, this American Odysseus decided he must return to California and work to build the just society he envisioned. He told Roe of his decision, and now "the choice was hers. Thankfully, she decided to return with me."[28]

The two then voyaged, with their van, on "an ancient rust bucket freighter" across the Atlantic, with stops in the Canary Islands, Curacao, Venezuela, Santo Domingo, and Puerto Rico. After disembarking in Vera Cruz, Mexico, they began the last leg of their long journey, "driving slowly north through Mexico from the Yucatan Peninsula." Crossing the border into the United States, they learned from the radio that little had changed in America in the thirteen months they had been away, except that "now protests against the Viet Nam war had escalated" as casualties grew. Racial discrimination "against non-white Americans still ran rampant across the land"; and on the environmental front, a huge oil-well blowout in the Santa Barbara Channel "was still much in evidence." Last on his list of recollections from their journey: on the morning of February 9, 1971, the day after they arrived at his mother's home in Redondo Beach, a 6.6-magnitude earthquake struck, centered in the San Fernando Valley. "It felt like we never left."[29]

EMPLOYMENT: RIGHT PLACE, RIGHT TIME, RIGHT JOB

Their savings exhausted, Douglas hit the pavement in search of work, knocking on doors of law offices known for their progressive practices. While he was well received, none "could afford to pay me," he remembered. Other firms showed interest in him but required that he bring a group of clients to their businesses. Because he was new to the profession, he had no client base to offer an otherwise interested prospective employer. Douglas's job prospects did not seem hopeful.

Then instead of him finding a job, a job found him. "Out of the blue," said Douglas, he received a phone call from a former law school classmate, Rowan Klein, who had heard that Peter had returned from his travels and needed work. At the time Klein was working for liberal Democratic state assemblyman Alan Sieroty, who represented the Fifty-Ninth District, located on the west side of Los Angeles. Klein told Douglas that Sieroty needed to hire an aide to work primarily on environmental legislation, "specifically a bill to protect California's coast."[30] Douglas greatly distrusted the legislative process, convinced that it was controlled by special interests and irredeemably

FIGURE 2. *Left to right:* Tom Zanic, Mike Upson, Alan Sieroty, Evan Kaizer, and Peter Douglas, 1982. Zanic, Upson, and Kaizer were legislative assistants to Assemblyman Sieroty at that time. Photo courtesy of Alan Sieroty.

corrupt. Yet he was broke and needed a job. So he agreed to meet Sieroty and Klein for breakfast at a Santa Monica restaurant.

"I liked Alan [Sieroty] the moment we met," recalled Douglas. The large, gentle, intelligent assemblyman struck the young job-seeker as a person with "high ethical standards, ... progressive ideals and an endearing twinkle in his eye." After an exchange of biographies, they discussed Sieroty's broad legislative agenda: abolishing the death penalty, prison reform, consumer protection, accessible health care, the protection of artists' royalties, and the need to safeguard California's coast. Particularly important, Sieroty said that he probably would be championing a bill (not yet written) for coastal protection that he and a coalition of environmental organizations wanted badly. The aide he hired would be involved in drafting the legislation and "shepherding" it through the legislature. Douglas had not considered environmental law as a career path for himself until that moment. The prospect of protecting the coast that had been such a source of his comfort, inspiration, and sheer fun while growing up appealed to him. But what Sieroty said next dampened Douglas's enthusiasm measurably: the person hired had to relocate to Sacramento. The applicant told Sieroty that he was not interested in moving to Sacramento, "an unsophisticated backwater." The assemblyman would not budge on this; if Douglas wanted to be considered for the job, said Sieroty, he had to agree to make the move to the state capital. After a few days of thinking the matter over, Douglas and Roe decided he would take the offer and agreed to relocate. The job was now his, and it was the right job. "Little did I know then," Douglas reflected much later, "that this fateful decision would launch me on a lifelong labor of love and in a direction I had not dreamed of even a few weeks earlier."[31]

What about the new employee's salary and work space? Because Sieroty had not supported Democrat Robert Moretti in his successful bid to become Speaker of the assembly in 1971, Douglas's new boss had been "punished" by having to settle for a small office, staff, and budget. Salary-wise Douglas's position was classified as "Second Girl," and it paid $350 a month. Sieroty agreed to match that amount out of his pocket, which meant that the talented new hire would earn a yearly income of $8,400. As to work space, Douglas performed his labors in "a coat closet with its door removed." His desk was old and chipped and took up nearly the entire floor space of the cubicle. Atop the desk sat "piles of papers and reports."[32]

He and Roe packed their few belongings into Zorba, their trusty VW van, and headed north to Sacramento. On the road north, Douglas was, in effect, leaving behind his status as political outsider and critic of governmental processes; whether he realized it or not, he was en route to becoming one of the most effective coastal policy makers and managers in the America of his time.

TWO

California's Coast

ITS ORIGINS AND PRE-COMMISSION DEVELOPMENT

"CALIFORNIA'S COAST IS A MARVELOUS place to behold," exulted Peter Douglas.[1] The primordial birth throes of this "marvelous place," this crenulated seascape, had been violent and epic. Since that distant time, nature and humans have seen to it that the Golden State's shoreline, including seaward islands, remains ever-changing. By the 1970s this strip of sand, cliffs, estuaries, and developed properties was subject to increasing habitat loss while becoming off-limits to the public in more and more places. To a lesser extent, insular California, too, experienced environmental changes, resulting in the loss of native plant and animal species.

In their physical features, California's coast and offshore islands (all but two of which are within Coastal Commission jurisdiction) have been shaped and reshaped by Pacific geologic, oceanic, and climatic forces. These features and forces—such as plate tectonics, currents, tides, waves, winds, and weather—in turn, have largely determined the course of human history along California's storied eleven-hundred-mile shoreline. Until the arrival of Europeans in the area with Juan Rodríguez Cabrillo's historic voyage for Spain in 1542, the human footprint along the coast and offshore islands had left scarcely a lasting trace. Before European contact, numerous maritime Indians had, like their Paleolithic forbears, lived for millennia off the bounty of sea and tidelands in a veritable Eden. Subsequently, much of the coast has undergone ever-increasing development. Franciscan missions, cattle and sheep ranches, ports and harbors, military installations, railroads, factories, urban centers, oil rigs and refineries, highways, housing, power plants, parks, hotels, educational/research complexes, and beach recreation facilities have altered the seaboard dramatically in the past nearly 250 years. By the early 1970s, when Douglas began his lengthy governmental service in coastal

conservation, the human imprint along the littoral had become so discerna-
ble, encroaching, and problematic as to arouse public concern about what
seemed to many a beleaguered, vanishing coast.

A PACIFIC-BIRTHED AND -SCULPTED LANDFORM

Not only was Peter Douglas interested in all things coastal, his work throughout a lengthy career in shoreline management necessitated at least a rudimen-
tary knowledge of the geology of potential building sites, the flow of sand
along the shoreline, weather patterns, and the nesting and foraging habitats
of critters in and near tidal zones. Accordingly, he praised a book by scientists
Gary Griggs, Kiki Patsch, and Lauret Savoy, *Living with the Changing
California Coast* (2005). In a back-cover blurb he told prospective readers:
"California's coast is a living landscape endlessly besieged by waves and tides,
upland erosion, seismic forces, and human efforts to secure land's edge in
place." The book was a "must-read for property owners, developers, investors,
public officials, and activists who care about our coast's future." Given
Douglas's stress on the need for a basic understanding of the landforms and
other physical aspects of the state's tidelands and offshore islands, a few words
on these matters seem in order.

California's coastal mountains originated on the floor of the mid-Pacific
Ocean millions of years ago. While researchers have found rocks well over a
billion years old in southeastern California, the shape of the coast took most
of its present form fairly recently in geologic time, about 25–30 million years
ago. The creation of our present coast resulted from a major shift in plate
motions. The head-on collision between the massive North American Plate
to the east and the much smaller Farallon Plate to the west changed to a
sliding motion along the San Andreas Fault. After the geological formation
of California's coast, Pacific forces began the ongoing process of shaping the
littoral and insular landmasses the ocean had birthed. These landmasses, in
turn, have interacted with climate, ocean currents, and other natural forces
to provide habitat for marine and terrestrial life in seaboard California.

In the late 1960s, the revolutionary plate-tectonic theory, comparable to
the paradigmatic shifts in thinking ushered in by revelations about biological
evolution and about the structure of the atom, commanded the attention of
earth scientists worldwide. Bolstered by the discovery of the oceanic source
of ophiolite rocks,[2] plate tectonics led scientists to the deep-Pacific origins of

California and its coast. Ophiolites include chert, pillow basalt, serpentinite (also called serpentine, and designated the state rock in 1965 by the California legislature), jade, and other deep-sea rocks forming what geologists term the Franciscan Complex. More than a century ago, this mélange of rocks was so named by renowned UC Berkeley geologist Andrew Lawson for its presence in and around San Francisco and beneath its bay. Lawson also first recognized and named the San Andreas Fault and led a major statewide effort to study the effects of the great 1906 San Francisco earthquake.[3]

What do plate tectonics, ophiolites, and the Franciscan Complex reveal about the birth, geological composition, and shape of California's coast? More than 100 million years ago the relatively small Farallon Plate (one of the gigantic, sixty-mile-thick slabs of Earth's crust and upper mantle known as the lithosphere)[4] repeatedly collided with the much larger North American Plate. These collisions, unleashed by the hot, fluid material beneath each of these plates, forced the Farallon Plate to plunge downward beneath the heavier North American Plate, after which the former plate vanished. This geological process, known as subduction, left in its wake a deep sea trench that filled with marine sediments. As the plate collisions and subduction continued, massive quantities of these seafloor sediments, as well as large fragments of ocean crust (the ophiolite sequence), were scraped off and added to the growing edge of California. As a result of that subduction process and ensuing new collisions between the Pacific Plate and the North American Plate, huge ophiolite fragments from the ocean floor scraped against the overhead North American Plate, forming an accretionary wedge on the western rim of the continent. According to an apt maritime metaphor of one writer: "In California was the prow of the North American Plate."[5] The seminal scientific thought undergirding that metaphor was the work of many researchers. Among them, Eldridge Moores, professor of geology emeritus at UC Davis, attained particular distinction for demonstrating, in 1969, the links between California's ophiolites and plate tectonics.[6]

About 15 million years ago another dramatic, consequential geologic event occurred, one that has spawned calamitous, coast-contouring earthquakes ever since. For reasons not fully understood, the west-to-east thrust of the Pacific Plate stopped, and a southeast-to-northwest movement began. Rather than colliding as before, the now side-by-side Pacific and North American Plates have repeatedly scraped against one another laterally ever since. In effect, the subduction and accretion that had occurred for millions of years and given us an offshore trench, the Sierra Nevada, and the volcanoes of the

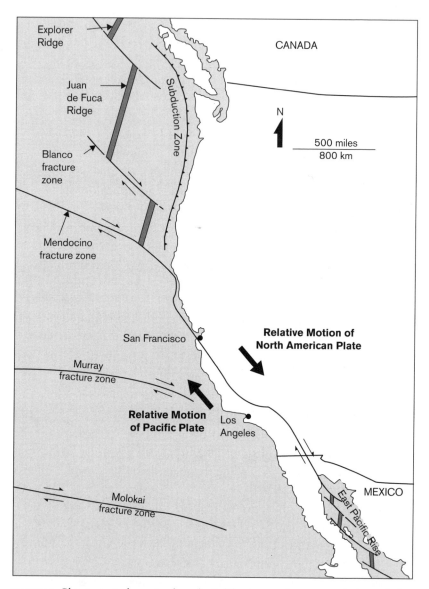

FIGURE 3. Plate tectonic dynamics along the California coast. Large arrows indicate the lateral movement of the Pacific Plate with respect to the North American Plate and landmass. Photo courtesy of the U.S. Geological Survey.

Cascade Range, ended along the stretch of coast from San Diego to Cape Mendocino, as these two leviathan plates began to slide and scrape alongside each other. The resulting friction resists motion or slippage for decades at a time. As Griggs puts it: "With the Pacific Plate stretching all the way to Japan, and the North American Plate extending to the middle of the Atlantic, there is a lot of real estate converging where these two plates meet."[7]

The Pacific Plate is moving northwest about an inch and a half each year, but friction keeps the San Andreas Fault locked until the accumulated stress is overcome, and then the plates slip five, ten, fifteen, or more feet, triggered by a large earthquake. While most temblors are small and may be barely noticed by people, the colossal nearly one-minute-long earthquake that leveled much of San Francisco in 1906 was one for the history books, with an estimated magnitude of 7.8.[8]

Situated on the Pacific Ring of Fire—an extensive network of fault zones, trenches, and volcanoes extending around the Pacific Rim clockwise from New Zealand to Chile—California's temblor-prone coast is likely to be ever-changing. Sometimes earthquakes and major shifts in the ground have been instant and dramatic. In the 1906 San Francisco disaster, for example, land along the San Andreas Fault at Point Reyes National Seashore was displaced twenty-one feet, as indicated by part of a fence that was shifted that distance. For good reason, a National Park Service website notes, "Geologically, Point Reyes National Seashore is a park on the move."[9] Highly interested in nature's doings, Peter Douglas possibly visited the site of the frequently photographed land-and-fence displacement, since he and his family once lived in Inverness Park, located immediately adjacent to Point Reyes National Seashore's Earthquake Trail.

The Golden State's littoral will be affected in another way by plate tectonic readjustment. As a result of the directional shift in plate motion during the past 15 million years, that part of California west of the San Andreas Fault, from San Diego to Cape Mendocino, has been moving steadily northwestward at the rate of one and a half inches per year relative to the remainder of the state. This migrating strip of coastal land, known as the Salinian Block, or all of California west of the San Andreas Fault, will arrive at the Aleutian Trench off Alaska in about 60 or 70 million years. That strip of the Golden State, including San Diego, Los Angeles, Santa Barbara, Big Sur, and Monterey Bay, will become the Madagascar of the Pacific as it slowly drifts northwestward away from mainland California. For more than a century after Juan Rodríguez Cabrillo explored the California coast for Spain, some

FIGURE 4. The displacement of a picket fence located along the Earthquake Trail at Point Reyes National Seashore, California, 1906. Photo courtesy of the Point Reyes National Seashore Museum, catalog #HPRC 053790.

European cartographers mistakenly portrayed Spanish California as an island;[10] however unlikely, that mythologically based belief might yet be reified by plate tectonics!

These same tectonic forces shaped the state's lengthy shoreline. That shoreline generally faces west from the Oregon border southward, down to the Point Conception headland in southwestern Santa Barbara County. From there the coast makes a "right-angle turn to the east,"[11] forming an inward curve or arc down to the Mexican border. Because that arc constitutes a bend in a coast or shoreline (defined in dictionaries as a "bight"), scientists refer to it as the Southern California Bight. The oceanographic conditions along that stretch of coast are notably different from those of the shoreline to the north of it.

"How so?" the curious reader might ask. According to oceanographer-geologist Keith Heyer Meldahl: "The water in the bight is warmer, and wave behavior more complex, than north of Point Conception."[12] This is largely due to ocean currents and the situation of the Channel Islands in the bight. The wide, cold, sluggish California Current flows southward along most of the state's coast, close to shore above Point Conception, and farther from the mainland (sometimes 150 miles from shore) when it reaches the waters off San Diego. Gray whales, whose annual migrations Douglas occasionally watched, follow this current en route from higher latitudes down to Baja California's warm calving lagoons, afterward returning to the frigid Arctic waters.[13] Since oxygen-producing and nutrient-rich kelp flourishes in cold water, the beds along the coast north of Point Conception are plentiful and abound with fish, which find protection in kelp beds. However, within the coastal waters of the Southern California Bight, bypassed by the California Current, the warmer ocean is much less conducive to kelp ecology and the marine life dependent on it. Even with this variation, according to marine ecologist Elna Bakker, "the state shares with the west coast of North America the distinction of having one of the world's richest seaweed floras . . . , comparable with those of Japan and Australia in both diversity and luxuriance."[14] The protection of marine resources and habitat, which includes kelp forests, is a Coastal Commission responsibility. Located offshore at the edge of the bight, the Channel Islands somewhat shield Southern California's beaches from the most towering of the west swells, the sort that crash along the state's north coast at surf breaks such as Maverick's, located near the town of Half Moon Bay. The rollers at Maverick's, generally ridden only by a handful of elite surfers, at times dauntingly top out at above fifty feet. The warmer water and more manageable waves along the bight—at Santa Barbara, Malibu, Palos Verdes, Huntington Beach, Laguna Beach, San Onofre, and San Diego—draw many more surfers and other ocean recreationists.[15] Douglas, as noted earlier, surfed, dove, and crewed in these waters as a young man.

Far more visible and wondrous to our eyes than most of the geomorphic processes and features just sketched are the spectacular results of those processes, in particular the California marinescapes wrought by plate tectonics, earthquakes, waves, tides, and winds. High-relief, steep cliffs, often crowned by majestic coastal redwoods, predominate along the north and central coasts, while a more gradually sloping topography with a different constellation of plant life characterizes the shore of the Santa Monica Mountains along the southern coast.[16] The dramatic precipices and outcroppings, especially but not only of the north and central coasts, are embedded with granite, volcanic rocks, shale, sandstone, chert, and serpentinite, all of which attest to the numerous primordial subduction and accretion processes. In Big Sur one sees, touches, and marvels at the high, near-vertical cliffs, coastal slopes, and headlands composed of Franciscan Complex rocks and granite. The latter migrated seaward (to points north and south of San Francisco and to the Farallon Islands) from the Sierra Nevada range as a result of earthquakes and motion along the San Andreas Fault over the past 18 million years.[17] Steep cliffs and headlands can also be found in Southern California, along the Santa Monica Mountains from Point Magu to Malibu, at Palos Verdes, and at Point Loma in San Diego. About 790 miles of the state's coast consists of low cliffs and bluffs eroded into uplifted marine terraces. The hardy coastal sage scrub growing in such places often provides habitat for California gnatcatchers and coastal cactus wrens, as at Newport Beach's Banning Ranch—where protection of their habitat from development is a key issue in a major ongoing dispute before the Coastal Commission. Most marine terraces are composed of five to twenty-five feet of layered and unconsolidated younger sediment resting on older bedrock.[18] In addition to high and low cliffs, bluffs, and marine terraces, some three hundred miles of sand dunes, wetlands, and lagoons are interspersed along the coast from San Francisco to parts of San Diego. Wetlands and lagoons, which comprised some three hundred thousand acres of California's shore (not including San Francisco Bay) before Spain's arrival in the mid-1500s,[19] offer needed habitat for both marine and terrestrial creatures, from fish and shellfish to raptors, whereas sand dunes can serve as buffers protecting back-dune areas from wave attack.

While tectonic forces account for the origins and physical outlines of the coast, winds, waves, rain, landslides, and river drainage subsequently altered the shape and look of California's littoral zone. Westerly winds from out in the Pacific buffet the entire shoreline, slowly wearing away the coast's jagged outcrops, sculpting its sand dunes, and shaping Monterey pines and cypress trees that stand as iconic sentinels, many of them captured in the works of photographers, painters, and poets.[20] Such natural beauty and art lay at the heart of Peter Douglas's thinking and work, as evidenced in his writings and the large, stunning photograph (presumably) of the Big Sur coast prominently displayed on the wall of his San Francisco office. He understood how Pacific storms with accompanying high waves alter California's shoreline, sometimes destroying expensive beach real estate in the process. According to UC Santa Cruz oceanographer Gary Griggs, wave heights in California

FIGURE 5. El Niño–caused slide damage, temporarily closing Highway 1 through Big Sur, winter of 1982–1983. Photo courtesy of Gary Griggs.

have been increasing since the 1980s. "When increasingly large waves are combined with a gradually rising sea level, we can expect more frequent flooding and inundation of low-lying areas and an increased rate of coastal cliff and bluff retreat."[21] The most impactful of all the above occurrences are the El Niño Southern Oscillation events,[22] which attacked the coast, causing cliff erosion and damaging homes, businesses, and public infrastructure in 1978, 1980, 1982–1983, and especially 1997–1998. For example, El Niño–related heavy rains in the winter of 1982–1983 caused a massive slide of rock and soil in Big Sur, resulting in the state's closure of scenic Highway 1 for about eight months.[23] Because waves transport beach sand (usually southward, or downcoast, along most of California's shore), a phenomenon called "littoral drift," homeowners along the coast historically have installed revetments (such as large rocks positioned in front of oceanfront houses) to protect their property. Accordingly, owing to a loss of beach sand, homeowners at Pajaro Dunes, located along central Monterey Bay, turned to a revetment to save their exposed homes during the El Niño winter of 1982–1983.[24]

The "Pineapple Express" rainfall phenomenon, another force of nature affecting the California coast and its hinterland, is so called because it arises near the Hawaiian Islands, where that fruit is grown. Pineapple Express winds carry huge aerial flows of water, an estimated ten to fifteen Mississippi Rivers' worth, to the California coast, where they descend in torrents of rain. Resembling massive rivers in the sky, these sporadic storms can deliver up to half of the state's precipitation between the months of December and February. Researchers have found that Pineapple Express storms "have broken 40% of California droughts since 1950."[25]

As the Pineapple Express phenomenon suggests, occasionally the precipitation pendulum has swung from drought to deluge. Catastrophic flooding has sometimes resulted, as in December 1861, when the Central Valley became so thoroughly flooded after weeks of downpour that the state capital was temporarily moved from Sacramento to San Francisco.

Heavy rains often coincide with landslides and other coastal cliff and bluff failures along California's shore. This is particularly the case in areas where high winter waves have eroded the bases of cliffs, resulting in unstable overhangs that eventually collapse onto beaches. For example, in 2011, Point Fermin, San Pedro, suffered the loss of parkland and property, as well as the destruction of six hundred feet of an abutting street (Paseo del Mar), which tumbled into the Pacific owing to a rain- and wave-action-induced landslide.[26]

Another major force affecting the shape and look of the coast, in this case beaches, is river and creek drainage. Carried by wind, rain, and gravity, the rock and soil eroded from coastal watersheds travels downslope to stream channels. Rivers and creeks in these watersheds transport much of the sand and other sediments to the shoreline, where they nourish beaches. Some of the widest stretches of beach in the state are in Southern California. There, the Los Angeles, San Gabriel, and Santa Ana Rivers, as well as Aliso and San Mateo Creeks, for example, are instrumental in supplying sand at their mouths. This is a natural process that replenishes the sediments regularly

FIGURE 6. The collapse of Paseo del Mar onto the beach below Point Fermin in San Pedro, 2011. High waves had eroded the cliff. Copyright 1981–2016, Los Angeles Times. Used with permission.

swept downcoast by littoral drift. Damming, blockage by debris basins, and extensive channelization of these and other waterways in more recent times greatly impede this replacement of beach sand. As a result, the volume of sand along California's beaches is constantly being altered by both natural processes and the built environment.

Finally, sea-level rise—which was much on the mind of Douglas later in his career—must be considered a formidable force in the ongoing shaping and reshaping of the coast. As Gary Griggs notes, "The elevation of the ocean ... determines the location of the shoreline." A warming ocean, resulting mainly from climate change (which melts the polar icecaps and thermally expands ocean water volume), has led to rising sea levels around the planet.[27] Griggs cites a 2008 study conducted by the San Francisco Bay Conservation and Development Commission that mapped areas along the city's shoreline that would be submerged by a 16-inch sea-level rise by 2050. While this was at the higher end of projections at the time, still the study found that the runways of San Francisco International Airport would be underwater in that circumstance. The same is true for Oakland International Airport, which was built on former tidelands.[28] In 2009, five California state government agencies funded a study, *The Impacts of Sea-Level Rise on the California Coast,* which projected that, by 2100, the state's coastal waters would rise between 1.0 and 1.4 meters, thereby accelerating shoreline recession and changing the footprint of the littoral zone. These are conservative figures, since the study did not take into account the ongoing melt of the Greenland and Antarctic ice sheets.[29] Similarly, a more recent study by the National Academy of Sciences projected a mean sea-level rise of one meter by 2100 along the coasts of California, Oregon, and Washington.[30] To its credit the California Coastal Commission has been tracking sea-level rise and factoring it into its planning and regulatory actions, as indicated in the agency's 2015 *Sea Level Rise Policy Guidance* document.[31]

The physical contours of, and forces shaping, mainland California's coast have been sketched, but what about the state's offshore islands? As with the mainland, insular California's geological origins can be traced back to the primordial past. Most of the state's generally recognized fourteen coastal islands (this does not include those in San Francisco Bay and the hinterland Sacramento–San Joaquin Delta region, which are not within Coastal Commission jurisdiction) came into existence largely as the result of volcanic action.[32] Volcanism, in turn, was triggered by heat and pressure arising from the subduction of the Pacific Plate beneath the North American Plate, as described earlier.

If one were to visit a sampling of these coastal islands today, what would one likely see in terms of terrain, coasts, vegetation, and animal life? Most importantly, one would glimpse a modern-development footprint much lighter than that found on the mainland. Generally, to say that these islands resemble California as it looked on the eve of the gold rush of 1849 would not be far off the mark. Before that time and shortly afterward, Native American Chumash and Gabrielinos, like their distant Paleo-Indian ancestors, lived on, or traveled by watercraft to, various Channel Islands.[33]

Geologically, the islands feature numerous marine terraces created by wave erosion, some as high as two thousand feet in elevation. Granitic rocks constitute much of the South Farallon Islands, a major rookery for seabirds and seals as well as a great white shark habitat; San Onofre breccia (a hard, expensive, prized building material in California) is abundant on Santa Catalina, Santa Cruz, and Santa Rosa Islands; volcanic rocks compose most of San Clemente Island. Serpentine—a hard, waxy, green material—is plentiful on Santa Catalina, as is steatite, or soapstone, which Indians used to carve bowls, pipes, and other objects.

MAP 2. California's islands. Source: Allan A. Schoenherr et al., *Natural History of the Islands of California* (Berkeley: University of California Press, 1999), 6.

For a dramatic view of an offshore island's topography and coastline from both towering cliffs and the sea, ninety-six-square mile Santa Cruz Island, the largest of eight such landforms in the Channel archipelago, is hard to match. The endemic and endangered Santa Cruz Island fox makes its home amid the bluff-top coastal sage scrub and Santa Cruz Island pine. Ocean kayakers enjoy paddling over emerald water through the island's stunning sea caves carved into volcanic rocks along the north shore; seals and sea lions haul out on nearby boulders. From Santa Cruz Island, a nesting ground for bald eagles, one can view the three prominently vertical, rock-studded islets comprising Anacapa Island. San Miguel Island is known for its sand dunes, created largely by strong offshore winds, and treacherous reefs that have made the surrounding waters a graveyard for ships. Navigator Juan Rodríguez Cabrillo landed on this island and, according to some accounts, died as a result of a fall and was buried there in 1543.[34] Santa Rosa Island features a suite of topographies and sceneries: high cliffs, white sandy beaches, dunes up to four hundred feet high, and rolling hills carpeted with dense grass. Southward, Santa Catalina Island, also visited by Cabrillo (who described his interactions with Indians there), is the only Channel Island with any significant development; it is dryer and its beaches are overlain with small cobbles and gravels rather than white sand. The most recognized trees on the island are nonnatives imported from throughout the Pacific world, including mainland California: blue gums from Australia; the tree-of-heaven from China; and Monterey pines native to the mainland. Santa Catalina is the only Channel Island that has snakes, including the western rattlesnake. Arboreal salamanders, Pacific tree frogs, and a number of bird species make their homes there, along with nonnative bison, pigs, goats, rats, and mule deer. Seals and sea lions visit the island but are not present in large numbers, since they do not breed there given the extensive boat traffic and human presence on the island. Yellowtail, white sea bass, and barracuda once abounded in the surrounding waters, but because of fishing their numbers have declined.[35]

Two of California's seaward islands are largely but not entirely outside Coastal Commission jurisdiction. Presently, both San Nicholas and San Clemente Islands are owned by the U.S. Navy, which uses them for staging military operations, including Navy Seal training and weapons-targeting exercises. For national security and personal safety reasons, civilian tourists and recreationists are not allowed on either island.

COASTAL DEVELOPMENT: HARBORS, HOTELS, HOUSES, AND MORE

Before the 1849 gold rush rocketed San Francisco to international prominence as a port city, there was little visible evidence of development along California's coast. After the gold rush and up into the early 1970s, flurries of insufficiently regulated construction occurred.

Aside from some Spanish missions, presidios, and pueblos located near the shore, and a Russian fort (decommissioned in 1839) near Bodega Bay, there were few signs of the built environment that, throughout the twentieth century at least, would intrude increasingly on bluff tops, coves, and beaches along California's coast. While the built environment remained slight until the gold rush era, nonindigenous humans still left their mark on sea and land. Sea otter hunting initially by the Russians and conscripted native Alaskans, and later by the Spanish, Mexicans, and Americans, resulted in the near extinction of the furry marine mammal. Cattle ranching, along with farming and the introduction of nonnative plant species, also negatively affected ecosystems.[36] Compared to what took place in the late 1800s, these human-made alterations of the littoral were minimal.

The last two decades of the nineteenth century, by contrast, witnessed substantial seaside development that was but a harbinger of what would follow. In addition to a number of smaller hotels, two luxury megaresorts appeared on California's coast in the 1880s: Hotel Del Monte in Monterey and Hotel Coronado on San Diego's Coronado Island. The former drew such guests as President Theodore Roosevelt and writer Ernest Hemingway, among other notables. Visiting Monterey when Hotel Del Monte opened in 1880, Scottish writer Robert Louis Stevenson lamented, "The Monterey of last year no longer exists. Monterey is advertised in the newspapers, and posted in the waiting-rooms at railway stations, as a resort for wealth and fashion. Alas for the little town! It is not strong enough to resist the influence of . . . the millionaire vulgarians of the Big Bonanza."[37] A building bonanza, indeed. Similarly, Hotel Coronado hosted monarchs and millionaires from around the world who came to enjoy the surf, sun, and sand.

In the early decades of the twentieth century, the pace of coastal development accelerated, fueled by urbanization. Monterey was becoming America's most important fishing port, and the first of what would grow into dozens of sardine- and salmon-processing plants was built on its Cannery Row waterfront, later immortalized by novelist John Steinbeck.[38] In 1909–1910, Union Oil built what then was reputedly the world's largest oil pipeline; it extended more than two hundred miles from the San Joaquin Valley to Avila Beach near San Luis Obispo, where the viscous "black gold" was transferred to oceangoing tankers.[39] Contemporaneously, the building of Los Angeles Harbor, the completion by Henry Huntington of a light rail (Red Car) system from the City of Angels to Redondo Beach and other seaside towns, the appearance of shoreline fun zones, and the introduction of surfing and tent camping along beaches mainly in the Southland—all set the stage for rapid growth. Coastal towns, like Venice and Laguna Beach, were incorporated between the turn of the century and the 1920s. Millionaire land developer Abbot Kinney, for example, created Venice-in-America (later simply called Venice) in 1905 by draining marshland and building gondola-traversed canals, a twelve-hundred-foot pier, and an amusement park—all of which were connected by the Red Car rail system to metropolitan Los Angeles and Santa Monica.[40] In that same period, developers reprised the canal-gondola trope in Naples, Long Beach. Asilomar, a thirty-acre beachfront conference center run by the Young Women's Christian Association and featuring Julia Morgan–designed buildings, opened in Pacific Grove in 1913. Less than a decade later the YWCA added twenty more acres to the compound, which by then included a cluster of structures: Grace Dodge Chapel-Auditorium, Phoebe Apperson Hearst Social Hall, Visitors Lodge, Guest Inn, Health Cottage, Class Hall, Crocker Dining Hall, and more.[41] Nearby, between Monterey and Carmel, the Pebble Beach golf course opened in 1919, soon to become world renowned for its fairways and greens overlooking picturesque, jade-colored headlands along California's Central Coast. Large amusement parks featuring giant roller coasters, arcades, and in some cases Ferris wheels and carousels were operating along the coast in Santa Cruz and Playland in San Francisco by the 1920s.[42]

Similarly, along Pacific Coast Highway in south Orange County, development was rife. Standard Oil had built a forest of derricks in Huntington Beach in the 1920s, followed by pumping operations for oil and gas in the Bolsa Chica lowlands, defiling much of the once existing salt marsh.[43] A few miles south, the Thompson Company leased 1,750 acres that later became an oil drilling site at the Banning Ranch in Newport Beach.[44]

Even in the Depression-ridden 1930s, when funding was scarce, and during World War II, development along the coast continued. Two mammoth engineering projects, the San Francisco–Oakland Bay Bridge and the Golden Gate Bridge were completed in 1936 and 1937, respectively. In the former year a harbor at Newport Beach opened, servicing Balboa Yacht Club members and other recreational boaters. Also in that year the Balboa Fun Zone, including a forty-five-foot Ferris wheel and arcades, began operating. The nearby Balboa Pavilion (in use since 1906) provided a venue for band music and other popular entertainment. In World War II, San Francisco's Presidio served as the command center for U.S. Army operations in the Pacific Theater, and after the Pearl Harbor attack the Long Beach naval base and shipyard provided the major anchorage for the U.S. Pacific Fleet. Elsewhere along the seaboard as well, military installations abounded. Monterey County's Fort Ord, for example, doubled in size, from 15,000 acres in World War I to 30,000 acres in World War II, and the Marine Corps' Camp Pendleton in San Diego County grew into purportedly the world's largest military post, occupying some 123,000 acres.[45] Meanwhile, the San Diego Chamber of Commerce partnered with navy and defense contractors to build new docking facilities and dredge the city's bay to accommodate three new aircraft carriers. Aside from the military infrastructure added to San Diego's coast on the eve of World War II, the U.S. Navy's huge displacement of millions of cubic yards of dredged sand and the transfer of the granular substance to nearby beaches assuredly altered the shoreline.[46]

An overview of the postwar era of the late 1940s to the early 1970s must stress that the Golden State saw its fastest growth to date in population, tourism, and development along the coast at that time. For, example, the population in sparsely inhabited Mendocino County in Northern California nearly doubled between 1940 and 1960,[47] and in the Southland city and county of San Diego easily doubled during that period.[48] With more than 17 million inhabitants, California surpassed New York in 1962, becoming the most populous state in the Union.[49] Development, depletion, and degradation of coastal resources resulted. Most of the burgeoning population lived on or near the coast and needed sufficient electricity, which led to the building of nuclear power plants along the Central and Southern California shore. A housing boom required lumber; the original North Coast redwoods, which had been logged since gold rush days, underwent increased cutting; by the 1960s, 90 percent of the older trees had been taken for construction. Containerization (the use of portable, tamper-proof compartments to store and ship goods) at the ports of Los Angeles and Oakland in the 1950s greatly enhanced the state's transpacific trade while further industrializing and polluting the coast.[50] Illustrative instances of this astounding growth in the middle decades of the twentieth century are numerous.

One such instance figured into the personal life of Peter Douglas himself. As history would have it, the private preparatory academy he attended in adolescence—the Stevenson School (named after writer Robert Louis Stevenson)—opened in 1952 along the Central Coast at Pebble Beach on 17 acres of land. By 1970, according to the school's website, "16 new buildings had been built, 21 more acres had been acquired, 312 boys were enrolled, [and] the famous Spyglass Golf Course had been built abutting the campus."[51]

Though a comparatively minor development, Douglas's school and the adjacent golf course exemplified an expanding built environment along some of the most scenic stretches of California's shore.

In 1960, wealthy homebuyers were settling into the upscale, gated community of Monarch Beach, just north of Dana Point (it was later annexed by that city) in Southern California. Some 214 houses were being built. The living space in many of these ran between 2,500 and 10,000 square feet; some had five-car garages, maid's quarters, swimming pools, racquetball courts, and home offices.[52]

The city of San Diego at this time was growing in population, housing, and infrastructure by leaps and bounds, as noted earlier. Perhaps the clearest sign of the city's dynamism was the establishment in 1960 of the San Diego campus of the University of California, which included Scripps Institution of Oceanography. Situated originally on 63 acres of land on a scenic La Jolla bluff overlooking the Pacific, UCSD rose immediately to international academic prominence in the biological and marine sciences. In 1962, President John F. Kennedy committed the federal government to transferring 436 acres of Camp Matthew land to the campus. By the end of the decade the university's three college campuses occupied 1,900 acres and housed forty-four hundred students.[53] Quickly the institution became an incubator for the booming biotechnology sector that contributed greatly to the city's and county's economic growth.

Anticipating the military's growing need for potable water in 1961, the federal government built one of California's earliest seawater desalination plants for the U.S. Navy, at Point Loma, San Diego.[54] The plant was dismantled in 1964 and shipped off to Guantanamo Bay, Cuba, to furnish water for the American naval base there. Still, the Point Loma facility exemplified the further industrialization of Southern California's coast and was a harbinger of similar projects that would be aimed at meeting the water needs of thirsty Californians in the decades ahead.

A year later Ben Brown began developing land abutting his nine-hole golf course near the mouth of Aliso Creek in South Laguna, at that time an unincorporated coastal community immediately south of the city of Laguna Beach. To the golf course, Brown added his home and rental apartments. Soon afterward, he rebranded his expanded links-apartment complex, all of which was located in a floodplain, as the "Aliso Creek Inn."[55] The entire development was cradled within one of the most scenically exquisite coastal canyons in Southern California, through which a once meandering Aliso

Creek emptied into the Pacific. Within a decade contaminants in the creek issuing from new housing subdivisions inland pooled in an estuary where the watercourse met Pacific Coast Highway.[56]

During this period, the Sea Ranch was one of the earliest major developments along the rugged, wild, and thinly populated Sonoma County coast about a hundred miles north of San Francisco. In 1963, Oceanic Properties, a subsidiary of Hawaiian developers Castle & Cooke, purchased for an estimated $2.7 million the fifty-two-thousand-acre Rancho Del Mar owned by the Ohlson family. The ranch's boundaries enveloped ten miles of spectacular coastal bluffs and beaches, as well as groves of redwood and fir trees. Noted Bay Area landscape architect Lawrence Halprin designed what became an internationally prominent, award-winning project, by far the largest of its kind on California's North Coast. Halprin's guiding ethos was "living lightly on the land."[57] In applying this ecological principle, he oversaw the building of a community whose modern, angular, wood-and-glass structures nestled inconspicuously into the redwood forest and windswept headlands. Moreover, Halprin envisioned residents of the new community engaging with the sea and sharing a lifestyle of connectivity with the coastal environment and each other.[58]

The best of ecological intentions, however, did not immunize Sea Ranch's designer and builders from the wrath of similarly conservation-minded outlying neighbors. The construction phase was prolonged and acrimonious owing to Oceanic Properties' effort to cut off existing public access to the ten-mile ribbon of coastline fronting the development. The resulting protracted dispute between the property owner and non–Sea Ranch locals demanding continued public access to the beach became a major factor (discussed in chapter 3) leading to the establishment of a governmental agency authorized to manage California's entire coastline.

While the Sea Ranch dispute raged, Monterey, beginning in the 1960s, regained the media spotlight as burgeoning tourism replaced the virtually defunct fishing-and-cannery economy of the city. Historian Connie Y. Chiang noted that between 1959 and 1969, "tourist dollars spent on the Monterey Peninsula more than doubled from thirty-two to sixty-seven million dollars." Cashing in on nostalgia for the waterfront setting in writer John Steinbeck's *Cannery Row,* city planners opted for preserving, renovating, and repurposing Cannery Row's old, deteriorating fish-processing factories into trendy shopping venues and tourist attractions evocative of the area's romanticized industrial past.[59]

In 1963, a very different, ethereal type of facility was built and began operating on a high cliff overlooking the Pacific in Big Sur, the Esalen Institute. Located about 140 miles south of San Francisco on scenic Highway 1 and named after the Esselen Indians, who had earlier inhabited the area, the retreat center offered paying guests a tableau of seminars that included Asian and Euro-American psychologies, Gestalt therapy, yoga, and more. Its teachers included such international luminaries as double Nobelist, chemist, and peace advocate Linus Pauling; psychologist B. F. Skinner; historian Arnold Toynbee; poet Gary Snyder; physicist Fritjof Capra, and futurologist and inventor Buckminster Fuller. The facility and grounds, featuring natural hot-spring baths, occupy approximately 150 acres of some of the most photographed coastline in the world.[60] Though pristine coastal land was being developed, little, if any, public opposition to the construction of the retreat center materialized.

In June of that same year a small-craft harbor opened in the city of Oceanside. The harbor came to occupy seventy-five acres of water and twenty-five acres of land, enough space to accommodate 954 boat slips.[61] While boaters were happy, sunbathers and swimmers very soon became disgruntled and outspoken about the loss of sand on abutting beaches caused by littoral drift—that is, the movement of fine beach sediment owing to the interaction between waves and harbor jetties. Moreover, concern mounted throughout the city about the fact that displaced beach sand was swept by this interaction into the mouth of the harbor, causing extreme shoaling. By 1964, the water depth at the harbor entrance had been reduced from twenty to ten feet, rendering it impossible for some of the Marine Corps' craft to enter at low tide. Three years later a tropical storm near the southern tip of Baja, California, "sent strong upcoast waves to unprotected Oceanside, quickly transporting fine-grained beach sand to the harbor entrance channel."[62] As it turned out, nourishing or replenishing the sand supply at Oceanside beaches became a costly, controversial, and too frequent endeavor. Because there was no statewide coastal authority yet, Oceanside residents and their officials had to work with the Army Corps of Engineers, who had built the small craft harbor, to cobble a plan for keeping the mouth of the harbor open and the city's beaches blanketed with sand.

About that same time, several miles north at San Onofre Beach in San Diego County, surfers encountered another infrastructure intrusion, this time one with a perceived health threat: the building of the San Onofre Nuclear Generating Station. Rapid population and housing growth in and around San Clemente pointed to a need for a local, presumably more affordable source of electricity. The plant was owned by Southern California Edison, San Diego Gas & Electric Company, and the City of Riverside Utilities Department. Construction of this commercial power plant, situated on an eighty-four-acre site, began in 1964. The first of its three units began operating in 1968.[63]

Similarly, to meet the electricity needs of the growing population and commercial sector along and near the Central Coast, Pacific Gas & Electric began construction in 1968 of the Diablo Canyon nuclear power plant near Avila Beach in San Luis Obispo County. The plant, sited on about nine hundred acres nearly atop the Hosgri earthquake fault, was completed in 1973, eventually producing electricity for nearly 3 million people from two reactor units. In 1969, the Sierra Club, California's leading citizens' environmental advocacy group, divided over the controversial issue of locating a nuclear power plant virtually on or near an earthquake fault. David Brower, president of the organization, resigned owing to his board's support of the Diablo Canyon project and formed Friends of the Earth, which began a vigorous campaign to shut down the plant and prevent the commissioning of any more such facilities along California's coast.[64] The anti-nuclear-power movement helped direct Californians' attention to the link between shoreline development and public safety.

While nuclear power plants were industrializing parts of California's seaboard, the Irvine Company built the posh, sprawling Newport Beach Fashion Island Shopping Center, which opened in 1967, on the suburban south Orange County coast. The first four buildings housed department stores: Buffum's, J. W. Robinson's, the Broadway, and J. C. Penney. Later the entire complex, which the Irvine Company owned, expanded greatly in terms of the number of high-end department stores (Nordstrom's, Bloomingdale's, and Neiman Marcus), and shops and gourmet eateries, all of which became fringed by expensive hotels, offices, financial services institutions, and cultural venues. As the shopping mall grew larger and upgraded its stores, appealing to an ever-wealthier clientele, the value of residential real estate near the vast commercial complex soared.[65] Given the historically conservative political bent of much of coastal Orange County, which championed property rights, the public, not surprisingly, welcomed virtually every addition of shops and office space to Newport's premier marketplace.

Not far south of Fashion Island, affluent residents of Monarch Beach and other nearby communities would soon be able to moor their yachts at Dana Point Harbor, located on the south Orange Coast about halfway between Los Angeles and San Diego. Construction began in the late 1960s. Rock breakwater jetties were built and then boat slips were installed. On July 31, 1971, the harbor was officially dedicated. Eventually, the harbor would accommodate more than twenty-five hundred pleasure craft, and numerous restaurants and shops would go in, assuring a steady stream of visitors and customers. Many surfers were not thrilled by this project, given that the jetties had eliminated the legendary break at what had once been heralded in the wave-riding world as "Killer Dana," so-called because of the risk of powerful waves tossing surfers and swimmers headlong into boulders on the shoreline.[66]

Meanwhile, some thought San Diego's downtown historic plaza needed a major renovation to restore historic buildings, stimulate commerce, and generally keep up with the times. Thus, after years of study, which had begun in the 1960s, the city council in 1972 approved developer Ernest W. Hahn's project for a large, multilevel shopping center branded Horton Plaza, plus a major redevelopment of adjoining property, all of which occupied 41.5 acres, encompassing fifteen city blocks. According to the *New York Times,* this "architecturally stunning" redevelopment project was one of "the most ambitious retail structures ever built in a single stroke in an American city."[67] All of this growth, coupled with new high-rise waterfront hotels (including a twenty-one-story luxury condominium development in La Jolla Village near the cove, built in 1968), affected San Diego's shoreline. These impacts and those along the rest of California's seaboard went largely unmanaged in the absence of a statewide coastal regulatory agency.

PUBLIC ACCESS TO BEACHES:
THE 1960S AND EARLY 1970S

As described, the post-World War II explosion of California's population, especially in the 1960s, resulted in a housing boom in many parts of the state, while private and commercial development along the coast threatened public use of some beaches. Gated residential beach developments and fences blocking public foot traffic along the shoreline were becoming more common. Add to this growing restrictiveness the dramatic rise of surfing, which brought board riders, like Peter Douglas, in droves to breaks up and down the coast, and the public's growing insistence on beach access during this decade seems virtually inevitable. With reference to the Atlantic, Gulf, and Pacific coasts, one legal scholar noted, "Public demand for beach access has continually increased since the 1960s."[68] Earlier I mentioned the local citizenry's concern regarding the loss of public access to the coast in Northern California. A few examples focused on the more heavily visited Southern California shoreline should prove illustrative of the growing statewide insistence on the public's right to use beaches.

Unarguably the most protracted struggle between residents and beachgoers over public access to the shoreline has taken place in Malibu, a coastal community in north Los Angeles County known for its celebrity homeowners, who include some of Hollywood's wealthiest and most notable figures. Development there, like in other parts of coastal California, included gated communities and brought in its wake many claims to private beach enclaves by affluent homeowners. The battle lines drawn there after the mid-twentieth century became only more fixed and contentious in the subsequent half century.

Beginning in the 1950s, Malibu's name became emblematic of sun and fun. Surfers in increasing numbers frequented its beaches, which had not yet become earmarked as the exclusive preserve of the Hollywood set and other wealthy homeowners. The 1959 film *Gidget,* a teen coming-of-age surfing movie set in Malibu, and surf music referencing beaches there further swelled Malibu's young beach crowd while signaling the coming of a California-based youth/surfing culture that would sweep much of the nation by the early 1960s.[69] Lighter and smaller surfboards, designed especially for young females, resulted in Malibu becoming the launch site of what writer Simon Winchester called "girl surfing." Simultaneously, Hobart "Hobie" Alter and his friend George "Grubby" Clark invented, produced, and marketed their new lightweight polyurethane foam boards that revolutionized the sport while making the two entrepreneurs a fortune.[70] The music of California's Brian Wilson and the Beach Boys, especially their 1963 hit "Surfin' U.S.A.," provided an anthem of the times that called out Malibu's famed County Line Beach, a favorite of wave riders.[71]

As Malibu's surfing reputation was taking off in the mid-twentieth century, population growth and development there similarly bounded. From a sleepy coastal village of 2,328 residents in 1950, Malibu had morphed into a hot-property, celebrity-surf community of 6,486 in 1960, and it grew to 12,376 by 1969.[72] Development projects completed in the 1960s include the Outrigger condominiums on Carbon Beach, Malibu Park Junior High School, Malibu West Homes and Beach Club, Malibu Mesa Homes, and the forty-eight-unit Maison DeVille condominiums. Along Pacific Coast Highway, real estate offices, gas stations, banks, and restaurants mushroomed.

Amid this rapid population growth and development, fueled largely by the emergent youth/surfing/celebrity culture, Malibu real estate values skyrocketed and beaches once accessed by the public began disappearing behind private gates and fences. Local residents figuratively and literally drew lines in the sand that the beachgoing public dared not cross. Homeowners posted signs reading "PRIVATE PROPERTY NO BEACH ACCESS," "PRIVATE BEACH no Trespassing—NO Boats."[73] Looking back, Los Angeles Times reporter Philip L. Fradkin recalled, "Los Angeles County had done nothing to open new or enforce existing beach access paths to the Malibu beach. The phone calls and mail I received from outraged Malibu residents, who wanted to protect their special enclave from outsiders, surpassed in quantity and vitriol the responses I received to more significant stories."[74] Regarding public access to the shore, Malibu was simply a worst-case scenario of what had been happening along the California coast from Sea Ranch to San Diego in the 1960s and early 1970s.

Similarly, public access and use of beaches became an issue in Orange County, where a 1965 grand jury report called attention to the "overcrowding of our parks, beaches and harbors" even as that county worked to acquire more public recreational areas. One such area was a swath of shoreline at Niguel Beach, better known as Salt Creek Beach, a spot that was and remains popular with surfers and swimmers. Land abutting the beach was owned by the Laguna Niguel Corporation, which proceeded to sell it to AVCO Community Developers. In 1968, AVCO set the beachfront property aside for building single-family houses, condominiums, and apartment complexes. With the prospect of the beach becoming a private enclave of homeowners, citizens quickly launched a "Save Salt Creek" movement aimed at ensuring public access to the ocean. The Orange County Board of Supervisors responded by negotiating with AVCO for a public right-of-way to the water. On February 2, 1971, the developer agreed to provide the county with acreage for beach parking and the beach itself. These developer concessions came with a price tag of $2.6 million for the county.[75] In July of the following year, nearly one mile of beach was opened to the public, while the parking lot had not yet been completed. If the Orange County public agencies had not decided to push for public use of Salt Creek, the beach there would have served only nearby wealthy homeowners. Absent a statewide coastal authority, battles like this one would have been fought repeatedly, and outcomes would have depended entirely on the discretion of local (including county) government officials and developer influence in policy making.

While the Salt Creek imbroglio played out, another struggle for public access erupted at Trestles Beach in San Onofre, located at the northern edge of San Diego County. Usually referred to simply as "Trestles," so called because two railroad bridges cross San Mateo Creek, which empties onto the beach, the break there is one of the most coveted by surfers along the entire California coast. Though Trestles is situated on the Camp Pendleton Marine Corps base, and entry to the beach was restricted to military personnel, members of the San Onofre Surf Club disregarded, and at times destroyed, parking and other regulatory signs, sometimes using the signage for firewood.[76] Knowing that that area had been earmarked for designation as a state park, surfers in the 1960s (including this writer) risked trespassing on federal property to gain access to the storied break. Then, when Richard M. Nixon was elected president in 1968, he located his hacienda-styled Western White House—which he sonorously dubbed La Casa Pacifica—at nearby Cotton Point, thereby delaying the opening of Trestles as a state park. This occurrence resulted in federal screening checks at Trestles in order to augment the security of the chief executive's sprawling compound. Unhappy surfers had to await the end of Nixon's presidency in the early 1970s to gain legal use of that wave-riding beach.

Simultaneously, another beach battle was being waged in La Jolla, an upscale area of San Diego, where students and local hippies campaigned against moneyed homeowners claiming exclusive rights to secluded Black's Beach. This beach, which is frequented mainly by surfers and nudists, is located just below the Torrey Pines bluffs. Assuredly, La Jolla Shores, located just south of Black's Beach, was public and included parking, lifeguard service, and picnic tables. Black's Beach, on the other hand, was private; UCSD used the beach for research and maintained an access road, shared by well-fixed neighborhood residents. University personnel controlled traffic on the access road through use of a barrier chain and lock.[77]

By the summer of 1969, San Diego hippies had begun enjoying Black's Beach. They parked their vehicles in the residential community on the bluff and walked down the access road to the beach. Alternatively, they parked at La Jolla Shores and walked or went by sea northward to Black's Beach. They saw themselves as liberators of what they called "the people's beach."[78] Their open defiance of what the homeowners regarded as their inviolable property rights kept the beach-access controversy there in the spotlight of media attention into the early 1970s.

So when Peter Douglas began working in Sacramento for Assemblyman Alan Sieroty in 1971, California's iconic coast had been undergoing rapid development, and public use of many beaches could no longer be taken for granted. In the state and nationwide, citizens were awakening to the environmental and other consequences of seemingly limitless, underregulated economic growth. Grassroots stirrings for governmental action to preserve and ensure public access to California's and the nation's natural heritage— especially beaches—were under way.

THREE

Sea Change

CALIFORNIA'S ENVIRONMENTAL SURGE

IN THE 1960S AND EARLY 1970s a profound shift in the Golden State's history was taking place. The convergence of California's countercultural movement, a Bay Area conservation effort, public insistence on beach access at the Sea Ranch development along the Sonoma coast, the Santa Barbara oil spill, and the struggle to pass environmental legislation in Sacramento catalyzed a robust, grassroots ecological consciousness.[1] This new consciousness became resident in Peter Douglas. This convergence and the emergent ecological thinking transformed politics and would profoundly influence the next half century and more.

These happenings and this consciousness emerged out of a broad historical context. What had begun in the late nineteenth and early twentieth centuries as a national wilderness conservation effort to set aside parklands for public use and natural resources for commercial utilization began transitioning in the 1960s into a broader environmental movement that focused on energy regulation, pollution control, public health, and social equity, among other things.[2]

During this decade of societal change and its spillover into the 1970s, activists in California and elsewhere formed coalitions that entered the political arena. Amid concern that the Golden State's shore was disappearing largely because of rampant, haphazardly regulated development,[3] the idea of a statewide coastal authority was conceived. Peter Douglas embarked on his lengthy career in coastal management at this singular, pivotal moment in environmental history.

Oxford Dictionaries online defines *left coast* as: "The West Coast of the US, especially California." Whether voiced or not, usually there is a presumption in discourse, printed and otherwise, that the West Coast states, particularly California, are left-leaning politically. Aside from important exceptions to this sweeping presumption, it is largely accurate. For that reason, coastal California was not merely receptive to the counterculture of the sixties but instead was, in many ways, ground zero for the rise and spread nationwide of the values of free speech, nonmaterialism, gender and racial equality, nonviolence, and environmental protection that influenced politics during this time of profound social unrest and change.

That said, in most respects California's environmentalism in the 1960s had little to do with hippies and rebelling youth; with the important exception of some avant-garde nature writers/philosophers and surfers, it was only tangentially a part of the countercultural movement of the times. A middle-aged, gainfully employed Sierra Club member would have been far more representative of the emergent environmentalism than a member of the antiestablishment Youth International Party (known as Yippies). Environmentalists often referred to themselves as conservationists and, like progressives in early-twentieth-century America, tended to be college-educated, white professionals, Democrats or Republicans, and members of the middle and upper-middle classes. Rather than condemning "the Establishment," corporate America, and technology, they, again like turn-of-the-century progressives, worked for reform within the existing socioeconomic system. Instead of being categorically opposed to development, they labored to ensure it did not overwhelm the natural environment or reduce public access to wilderness areas and beaches. Many if not most of them opposed, for public safety reasons, the siting of nuclear power reactors along the coast, such as at Bodega Head, where in 1962 an aroused public succeeded in stopping the erection of a nuclear facility on or near the San Andreas Fault. Some opposed the siting of nuclear power reactors anywhere. In their appearance, politics, and demeanor, at least, they were engaged citizens, not radicals, dropouts, or outliers.[4] So while a global countercultural youth movement provided the historical context out of which the environmentalism of the sixties arose, those who worked for the preservation of nature and public access to it were for the most part mainstream Californians who worked (very effectively) through the existing political system.

Apposite to a left-leaning state with a strong progressive tradition, Democratic governor Edmund G. "Pat" Brown convened a conference, "California and the World Ocean," in Los Angeles from January 31 to February 1, 1964. Scientist Roger R. Revelle, head of UCSD's Scripps Institution of Oceanography, was a principal speaker. Few at that time saw more clearly than he the challenges that would confront those charged with coastal management in the near future. He declared, "The most critical region of the sea from the standpoint of forward planning . . . is the coastal zone, from the beach out to perhaps ten or twenty miles. . . . Without access to the shoreline, the land-based population cannot make use of the resources of the sea. . . . [Moreover, we] . . . must find ways to accommodate the requirements of fishing, public recreation, vacation housing, agriculture, industry, business, highway transportation, and permanent residences and we must create the tools to carry out a rational plan."[5] Following the conference, Brown established the Governor's Advisory Commission on Ocean Resources. The commission met six times in two years. Its somewhat reorganized successor in 1967, under Governor Ronald Reagan, met three times. Management of marine resources much more than coastal conservation was the focus of these two commissions.

In March of that year the Los Angeles Regional Water Quality Control Board conducted a symposium in the city, "The Marine Environment in Southern California's Changing Ecology." The 350 attendees hailed from the professional, corporate, and civic-sector worlds. They included government administrators, aerospace personnel, industrialists, scientists, engineers, and representatives from the League of Women Voters, Sierra Club, Audubon Society, California Federation of Women's Clubs, and similar citizen's groups.[6] This assemblage reflected the growing environmental consciousness among mainstream Californians who were beginning to realize that the pollution of coastal waters had to be addressed by effective public policy.

While California's environmentalists were overwhelmingly mainstream on the political spectrum, there were, as noted, at least two components of that cohort that in many ways challenged the dominant capitalistic, consumptive, development-driven culture: adherents of so-called Deep Ecology, and surfers. While the environmental views of these two groups were compatible, the former seemed to be more philosophically oriented and the latter more athletically/kinetically inclined. The two groups were certainly not mutually exclusive, as Peter Douglas, for example, albeit at different stages of his life, had a foot in each camp.

With roots in ancient Buddhism and the nature writings of Henry David Thoreau, John Muir, Rachel Carson, Aldo Leopold, Barry Commoner, Barry Lopez, Gary Snyder, and others, the Deep Ecology movement emerged in the countercultural 1960s. Humboldt State University, where sociologist Bill Devall taught the principles of Deep Ecology, was a California center of this spiritual-istic, Earth-centric thinking that stressed the interdependence and sanctity of all life, not just human life.[7] As noted (chapter 1), Peter Douglas read and said he was influenced by the books of Carson and Lopez, and to the end of his days (see chapter 6) he adhered to many of the values and ideals associated with Deep Ecology. Carson, Lopez, and other Deep Ecology proponents emphasized long-term, holistic thinking about humankind's relationship to the environment, as opposed to short-term technological fixes, and embraced an ecologically informed politics, nonmaterialism, environmental justice, and simple living.[8]

As suggested, such an outlook resonated with a contingent of wave riders, too. While surfing had a presence in California going back to the 1880s, not until the 1950s did the number of its enthusiasts begin to expand dramati-cally. Commercialization assuredly made inroads in the advertising and sale of boards, board shorts, surf wax, music, films, the promotion of contests, and more. Yet a core of wave riders remained purists. Sometimes called "soul surfers," they eschewed the competitions and commodification of the sport and instead focused on a Zen-like oneness with and reverence for the ocean. Mickey "Da Cat" Dora, a well-known surfer, decried the professionalization and corporate sponsorship of the sport. He warned against selling out to corporate interests who, in his opinion, did not appreciate the transcendent, individual experience of wave riding.[9] A good many soul surfers frequented Southern California's beaches, especially at San Onofre and Malibu, the early meccas of a surfing subculture that did not look favorably on the intru-sion of harbors and housing developments along the recreational coast. Yet 1960s wave riders remained slow to organize and get active politically.[10] Meanwhile, other, more mainstream environmental groups led the way in mobilizing their supporters for the purpose of shaping public policy.

THE SAN FRANCISCO BAY CONSERVATION AND
DEVELOPMENT COMMISSION, 1965–1969

In the 1960s, citizens in the Bay Area and along the North Coast were the first to organize for governmental action concerning the shore. Local activists played a central role in the creation of the San Francisco Bay Conservation and Development Commission (BCDC), which Peter Douglas dubbed "the first coastal management program in the world."[11] It served as the prototype for a future statewide coastal regulatory agency. Some of the commission's leaders were instrumental in the effort to create and guide such a statewide body.

Activists created BCDC in response to the bay's deteriorating condition. The post–World War II boom in Bay Area housing and development along the shores of the largest estuary on the West Coast of the Americas resulted in the continued infilling of San Francisco Bay. Put starkly: by 1960 the bay was about one-third smaller than during the 1849 gold rush. A U.S. Army Corps of Engineers study released to the media in 1959 documented the shrinkage and projected further loss of size in the decades ahead. Eventually, according to this study, the entire estuary would be reduced to little more than "a broad river." The announced plans of the Crocker Land Company to work with other developers to decapitate Mount San Bruno, located south of San Francisco, to obtain the fill they intended for parts of the southern portion of the bay alarmed a number of influential area residents.[12] More development meant more pollution. Three reform-minded Berkeley faculty wives—Kay Kerr (wife of UC president Clark Kerr), Sylvia McLaughlin, and Esther Gulick—who were friends, sprang into action. They assembled a small group of concerned citizens who in 1961 created the Save San Francisco Bay Association, better known as "Save the Bay," a citizens advocacy organization whose purpose was to protect "the Bay from pollution and reckless shoreline development and make it cleaner and healthier for people and wildlife."[13] By the end of 1962, Save the Bay had twenty-five hundred members.[14]

What started as a concerned citizens' environmental movement eventuated in the creation of a government agency with jurisdiction over the bay and its shoreline, which, in turn, provided a template for the later public effort to secure statewide management of California's entire coast. After persuading the City of Berkeley to shelve a plan to double the city's size by infilling part of its waterfront, Save the Bay leaders took advantage of Kay Kerr's political connections and involved powerful state senator Eugene McAteer in the campaign to protect the estuary. Assemblyman Nick Petris joined forces with McAteer, and the two coauthored, and in 1965 secured passage of, a bill setting up a study group that evolved into BCDC that same year.[15] The McAteer-Petris Act, however, stipulated that the commission was to be a temporary state agency, slated to expire in 1969. In that year an amendment to the law was passed that conferred permanency on BCDC. Similarly, when statewide coastal regulation was established in the early 1970s, the agency entrusted with that task would be temporary until it could develop a program that would be duly approved by the state legislature and governor.

Significantly, the McAteer-Petris Act empowered the commission to issue permits for development. Not surprisingly, this displeased builders. The rationale for permitting, according to McAteer, was that commissioners "needed to be able to protect the bay while . . . planning for it or the risk was you wouldn't have much left."[16] Here was a critical precedent for a future statewide coastal management agency exercising power to issue or deny development permits. Peter Douglas attested to the importance of BCDC's example in this matter when the state Coastal Commission was later being established.[17]

In addition to its issuance of permits, BCDC was a prototype coastal regulatory body in another way as well—namely, it wrestled with the perennial and difficult issue of balancing the interests of a conservation-minded public with those of developers. Said Democrat Joseph E. Bodovitz, a newspaper reporter and the first executive director of the commission: "The more development-minded people [commissioners] had to take a look at marshlands, but similarly the absolute conservationists . . . had to understand there was an economy in the bay area, and that shipping after all, did depend on ports, and ports did depend on dredging and deep water areas. People had to confront the legitimate interests of both conservation and development."[18]

A very close connection would develop between BCDC's leaders and those who would guide a yet-to-be-created statewide coastal regulatory agency.[19] Democratic governor Pat Brown appointed Melvin B. Lane, a Republican and the publisher of *Sunset* magazine and Sunset Books, as the founding chair of BCDC. Lane skillfully oversaw the development of a plan for the future of the bay that incorporated the interests of ports, waterfront cities, recreationists, and environmentally concerned citizens. This foray into regional coastal management and planning was thought by some to be "the first of its kind in the world."[20] When the California Coastal Commission was formed in the 1970s, Governor Ronald Reagan appointed Lane as that agency's first chairperson.

What Bodovitz would learn as the executive director of BCDC about coastal matters—about balancing the interests of fractious and demanding groups and managing a new bureaucracy with major responsibility and inadequate financial resources—would serve him well in the future when he headed the state Coastal Commission. As all of the above examples indicate, if that soon-to-be-created public agency had a progenitor, it was BCDC, which Peter Douglas saw as "the model for the California coastal protection program that was [later] enacted by a vote of the people of California."[21]

SEA RANCH, COAAST, AND THE COASTAL ALLIANCE

Like the founding of BCDC, the Sea Ranch development controversy along the Sonoma coast engaged the public and played an important role in the establishment of the state Coastal Commission. In this case, it was the local citizenry's response to news that the developer was closing off public access to ten miles of beach, which had previously been open, that led to a popular demand for a statewide governmental authority to oversee coastal matters.

William (Bill) Kortum, a Petaluma veterinarian, led the public fight to regain the people's right to use what had become ten miles of privatized beach along the Sonoma coast at the Sea Ranch development, owned—as mentioned previously—by Oceanic Properties, an affiliate of the Hawaiian-based firm of Castle & Cooke. The developer's privatization of the surf and sand resulted from the county supervisors' granting of building permits without insisting on public access to the beach. Local residents tried working with county officials to reopen public access but got nowhere. In 1968, frustrated and by now convinced that local government would be of little help, Kortum and others formed Californians Organized to Acquire Access to State Tidelands (COAAST).[22] As the name indicates, the organization was committed to achieving statewide access to beaches so that California's citizens would not be dependent on the public-mindedness of local officialdom, which too often seemed beholden to developers. COAAST mounted an initiative campaign aimed at passage of a measure guaranteeing public beach access whenever coastal property was being developed. According to the *Santa Rosa Press Democrat* newspaper, one Sonoma County official, on learning of the petition drive to get the initiative on the ballot, roared that the measure was "the stupidest thing I've ever heard of."[23] On behalf of its Sea Ranch project, Castle & Cooke pumped massive amounts of money, including funds used to hire a San Francisco ad agency, into a successful effort to defeat the Coastal Access Initiative, as the measure was called.

Meanwhile, California assemblymen Alan Sieroty and John F. Dunlap had been following the COAAST initiative effort. The two legislators had gone to Sonoma County, where they conducted assembly hearings on the Sea Ranch project. They asked COAAST to bring into its network organizations throughout the state that were committed to littoral protection. Influenced by the thinking of citizen-activist Ellen Stern Harris of Beverly Hills, Sieroty, Dunlap, and a growing number of others realized that coastal management needed to be statewide and no longer left to the discretion and whims of local governing entities. Up and down the entire coast, public access and amenities, habitat protection, parking, water pollution, and myriad other issues arose, yet no statewide mandates existed for addressing these problems. Instead, at that time in the late 1960s, balkanization reigned as fifteen counties, forty-five cities, forty-two state units, and seventy federal agencies made piecemeal decisions about these coastal issues with virtually total disregard for the state's coastline as a whole.[24] In the face of this fragmented, haphazard management and hodgepodge of mostly local government policies, Sieroty's and Dunlap's efforts to pass legislation aimed at creating a statewide coastal planning commission stalled in Sacramento. The stall was due to concerted opposition from oil companies, the California Real Estate Association, the County Supervisors Association, the League of California Cities, and other groups.

Meanwhile, COAAST expanded its fold in 1969 to include a dozen environmental groups, assembled under the banner of the California Coastal Coalition, which in 1971 morphed into the California Coastal Alliance. The goal of the Coastal Alliance was "to secure an effective state coastal program."[25] Momentum for such a program was gathering, fueled by citizen concerns about locating nuclear power plants along the coast and by the outcry of northern Californians against being shut off from beach access at the Sea Ranch. By 1972, 110 groups comprised the Coastal Alliance.[26] All that remained in order to galvanize the broader public to insist on governmental action to protect and manage the coast was for an environmental catastrophe to occur in a scenic, oceanfront, resort community.

THE SANTA BARBARA OIL BLOWOUT OF 1969

"I am always tremendously impressed at the publicity that the death of birds receives versus the loss of people in our country in this day and age.... [T]he fact that we have had no loss of life from this incident is important."[27] So misspoke Fred L. Hartley, president of the Union Oil Company of California, in the wake of the 1969 blowout of his company's Platform A, located in the Santa Barbara Channel, six miles offshore from Summerland. If the ensuing environmental disaster were not enough, Hartley's insensitive words, coupled with his denunciation of environmentalists, reverberated across America, assuring a tidal wave of public demand for protecting coasts and inland areas from desecration and pollution. Up to the eve of the twenty-first century this was, in the words of environmental historian John Opie, the "most publicized offshore oil rig release" in American history.[28] Some media and conservationists portrayed the blowout as "the environmental shot heard around the world."[29]

Really bad news sometimes serves as the catalyst to bring about reform, as when revelations that radioactive strontium-90 was found in milk pregnant women drank helped lead to the U.S. Senate's passage of the atmospheric test-ban treaty in 1963.[30] Similarly, decades after the Santa Barbara spill, Peter Douglas observed how the "public psyche suffers from a serious attention deficit. . . . Absent galvanizing events such as . . . the 1969 Santa Barbara Channel oil well blowout, the public tends to ignore environmental protection."[31] While that seems largely true, that particular galvanizing event has held the public's attention for decades and is not likely to be forgotten any time soon.

On the afternoon of January 29, 1969, a natural-gas blowout occurred at an oil drilling site that extended thirty-five hundred feet below the ocean floor. Rig workers labored to cap the hole from which gas and oil spewed. Their initial efforts succeeded, but pressure blew through the cap they had put in place. During the next eleven days, after which the malfunctioning rig was capped, some two hundred thousand gallons of crude oil rose to the ocean surface and, carried by incoming tides, spread to beaches from Rincon Point to Goleta. Thirty-five miles of scenic coast was mired in black tar and goo, while some eight hundred square miles of ocean near the shore was covered with an oil slick.[32] One writer at the time lamented that "the beaches were black . . . , and reblackened every day as the tides came in. The odor of crude oil reached us like the whiff of a decaying future."[33] Winds and swells also spread the slick seaward, defiling beaches, coves, and marine habitats on picturesque Anacapa, Santa Cruz, Santa Rosa, and San Miguel Islands.

Marine life had received a devastating blow. Dead seals and dolphins washed ashore; the blowholes of dolphins were clogged by oil, causing massive lung hemorrhaging. Seabirds, particularly those that dove into the ocean for food, became soaked in tar and died in large numbers. Citizen volunteers worked ceaselessly to clean the feathers of sick grebes, cormorants, and other seabirds; fewer than 30 percent of the treated birds survived. Those birds surviving the oil slick often succumbed to the chemical agents used to disperse the viscous black substance. Some thirty-six hundred seabirds are known to have died owing to contact with the oil.[34]

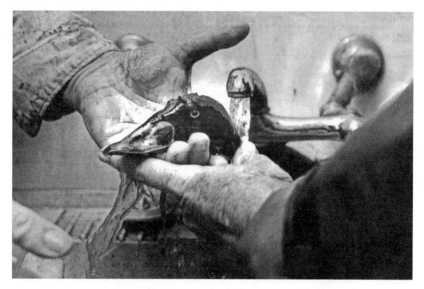

FIGURE 7. The plight of an oil-soaked bird in Santa Barbara, 1969. Copyright 1981–2016, Los Angeles Times. Used with permission.

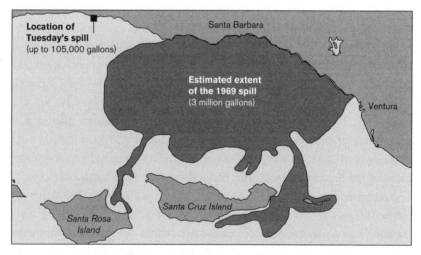

MAP 3. The extent of oil-polluted waters and beaches resulting from the 1969 Santa Barbara blowout. Source: Copyright 1981–2016, Los Angeles Times. Used with permission.

What caused the blowout? Investigators found that inadequate protective casing inside the drilling hole was responsible for the rupture that spewed and spilled an estimated 3 million gallons of oil (including seepage from the explosion-induced cracks on the ocean floor near the blowout) over a period of months onto the shores of Santa Barbara and nearby communities. They concluded that the insertion of more steel-pipe sheeting inside the drilling hole would have prevented the blowout.[35] Naturally, the state and federal governments had standards for offshore drilling of wells, with California's requirements being the more stringent. Since Platform A was located beyond the state's three-mile jurisdictional limit, the less rigorous federal standards applied. In January 1969, just before the blowout, the U.S. Geological Survey exempted Union Oil from the five-hundred-feet-below-the-ocean-floor standard for drill-pipe casings. So to cut costs, the oil company opted for a mere 15 feet of such casings. So-called secondary casings were reduced from 861 feet to 238 feet, thereby undercutting what would have been additional protection from blowouts.[36] To many, underregulation was the culprit, and the public's response was instantaneous.

In and around Santa Barbara people reacted with shock, grief, outrage, and the determination to see to it that there would be no more oil spills along their coast. One writer, who himself volunteered to rescue birds, commented, "I had been impressed by the way energetic college students, shopkeepers, surfers, parents with their kids, all joined the beach clean-up. I saw a Montecito society matron transporting oily birds in her Mercedes."[37] Media news depicted bird and marine mammal lovers weeping openly at seeing the oil-laden, dying creatures. *Santa Barbara News-Press* editor Thomas Storke captured the local response well: "Never in my long lifetime have I ever seen such an aroused populace at the grassroots level. This oil pollution has done something I have never seen before in Santa Barbara—it has united citizens of all political persuasions in a truly nonpartisan cause."[38]

The anguish felt and expressed by Santa Barbarans registered with officials at the highest level of government in Washington, DC. Said President Richard Nixon: "It is sad that it was necessary that Santa Barbara should be the example that had to bring it to the attention of the American people. What is involved is the use of our resources of the sea and of the land in a more effective way and with more concern for preserving the beauty and the natural resources that are so important to any kind of society that we want for the future. The Santa Barbara incident has frankly touched the conscience of the American people."[39] The American body politic, and especially its

California contingent, was now mobilized for action to save and assure public access to the endangered coast.

Only days after the beginning of the Santa Barbara calamity, citizens there organized Get Oil Out. Founder Bud Bottoms urged people to reduce their driving, destroy their oil company credit cards, and boycott service stations representing corporations engaged in offshore drilling. The organization's volunteers gathered one hundred thousand signatures on a petition drive aimed at banning offshore drilling. Restrictions on new drilling in California waters were soon tightened.[40]

The reputation of Union Oil, and by association of an entire industry, was tarnished. While the company spent a fortune on the cleanup, including compensating local businesses for lost revenue and fishermen for lost catches, costly lawsuits as well had to be settled. Moreover, frightened by the disaster, other California coastal cities, like Laguna Beach, prepared to battle the oil industry, if necessary, to keep drilling rigs from operating off their shores. Meanwhile, environmentalism in California's and the nation's politics in the late sixties and early seventies turned a corner; thereafter, its role in government at all levels increased appreciably.[41] The celebration of the first Earth Day, on April 22, 1970, signified, among other things, that a new era of international environmental politics had arrived.[42] The Golden State would be in the forefront of this paradigmatic shift in thinking and policy making.

THE CALIFORNIA ENVIRONMENTAL QUALITY ACT (1970)

Especially in the aftermath of the Santa Barbara oil blowout, state politicians— particularly Republicans—registered the voting public's awakening to the need for government protection of the environment through regulation. Republicans had attained a slim majority in the state assembly in the 1968 elections. As the 1970 elections approached, they wanted to augment that majority by being able to wave environmental credentials at voters. Consequently, the Republican assembly Speaker, moderate Bob Monagan of Stockton, established a Select Committee on the Environment, whose charge was to draft proposals for legislation aimed at safeguarding the environment.[43]

Congress's passage of the National Environmental Policy Act in 1969 supplied Monagan and his Republican colleagues with somewhat of a template for a similar measure tailored to California's needs.[44] The Republican strategy of casting the party as a protector of the environment failed, as Democrats regained their majority in the Sacramento legislature as a result of the 1970 election, placing them in an advantageous position to craft the content and language of what became the California Environmental Quality Act (CEQA) of that year. Some of the language of the National Environmental Policy Act was used in the measure. Oddly, the terms *project* and even *environment* were not defined in the law.

Odder still, legislators seemed to assume the measure would apply only to public works, as no debate took place on whether private development projects fell within the regulatory reach of the CEQA review process. Governor Ronald Reagan shared that assumption. In 1972 the California Supreme Court, in the landmark *Friends of Mammoth* case, held that CEQA unequivocally included within its purview private development projects subject to government approval.[45]

With CEQA's legal purview having been clarified, lead public agencies had the responsibility, under the terms of the law (drafted mainly by Democratic Assemblyman John Knox), to prepare environmental impact reports on projects likely to have consequential effects on natural surroundings, such as air and water quality as well as animal habitats. These reports would inform citizens about the quality of the air that would be breathed, the water that would be drunk, and the health of riparian habitats likely to be affected by projects under consideration for permits. Moreover, EIRs would have to consider both the ways to avoid or mitigate damaging effects, and the range of alternatives to a given project. Before permits could be issued by cities, counties, or the state, the public had to be given an opportunity to respond to an EIR.

Knox's bill had passed with widespread public support; and in early April 1973, CEQA began to be applied uniformly throughout California. According to the Golden State's Planning and Conservation League, CEQA is "California's premier environmental law."[46]

THE IDEA OF A COASTAL COMMISSION

CEQA constituted a striking example of statewide governmental action to safeguard the environment; simultaneously, coastal activists and a few legislators in the late 1960s and early 1970s set about the task of protecting California's entire shoreline from overdevelopment and for public access.

Regarding the latter, the inadequacy of government policies prevailing at that time is evident in the fact that only about 260 miles of California's 1,100-mile shore was legally accessible to the public. In other words, the citizenry was denied access to about three-fourths of the state's coastline. This mattered in California, where, in the 1970s, 85 percent of the state's population of 20 million people lived within 30 miles of the Pacific edge.[47] Geographical proximity to that shoreline heightened public awareness of what was happening to it.

The provenance of the idea of a statewide coastal commission prefigured much about how such an agency would eventually look and function. Seemingly, the idea evolved in steps. When the development at Sea Ranch spawned a local movement that aimed to assure public access to the Sonoma coast, residents in the area had not yet envisioned the establishment of a statewide regulatory agency to handle such matters. The seed of such an idea took time to form and germinate. The unresponsiveness of county supervisors to their residents' pleas for reopening routes to the shore assuredly helped that germination by moving the public to envision calling for a statewide authority.

Known for her outspokenness, Ellen Stern Harris claimed credit for the idea of a statewide commission to manage California's coast.[48] Peter Douglas agreed the credit was hers.[49] While this was largely so, Harris was not the only environmentalist calling for such an agency in the late 1960s. Either independently of Harris or in concert with her, Sierra Club officer and scientist Dr. Richard H. Ball, chairman of the Conservation Committee of the Angeles Chapter, declared in 1968: "There is a need for a statewide, or at least regional, coastal commission that could objectively evaluate coastal utilization priorities and coordinate planning, with the power to veto projects."[50] Harris, however, did more than anyone else to flesh out the idea of a statewide coastal regulatory body and suggest a way of structuring it so as to balance state power with regional concerns.

An environmental activist from Beverly Hills with political connections in Sacramento and Washington, DC, Harris watched closely the struggle of citizens in Sonoma County. Having served on the Los Angeles County Regional Water Quality Control Board, she recalled how concerned she became about each newly permitted project that piped effluent from a sewage plant, or thermal pollution from a power plant, or waste from an oil refinery, into the ocean. Each of these permitted discharges meant that "we were giving up another scenic and recreational piece of our coast."[51] Added to this, she said, was her experience of driving her kids through Malibu in the late 1960s and hearing them say they "could not see the ocean anywhere," because, said Harris, "it had been blocked off like a Chinese wall with a whole bunch of houses."[52] At the meeting of a 1968 subcommittee (of the Assembly Committee on Natural Resources, Land Use and Energy) on beaches, Harris stated, "There is a growing awareness among the public that their treasured shoreline, along with the rest of their irreplaceable environmental heritage[,] has been squandered through indifference and inaction."[53] The coast and access to it seemed to be vanishing, not just in the Southland but elsewhere in California as well. She was saddened and upset by the thought that future generations of children would not have the pleasurable beach experiences that she had had growing up.

Harris's Los Angeles water board tenure provided the seed of an idea: perhaps the statewide administrative structure under which that panel operated might be adapted to a coastal regulatory body for California. This meant that just as California had a State Water Resources Control Board with subordinate regional boards, a statewide coastal management agency should be set up with underling regional commissions. A state coastal board would do the planning and take appeals from the local boards. The latter would mostly interact with local citizens and hear why a given action should be taken or prohibited.

Seeding this idea while getting nurturing feedback from trusted friends and officials was the next step for Harris. She broached it to her friend William T. Davoren, a high-ranking official overseeing Region 9 (the western states and across the Pacific to Guam) with the U.S. Department of the Interior. He suggested that Harris look at the structure and functioning of the San Francisco Bay Conservation and Development Commission (BCDC), which might provide part of the model for the statewide agency she wanted to see created. Driving up and down the seaboard, she met with other leaders as well about the idea of a statewide coastal authority, receiving input and encouragement from Democratic state senator Fred Farr, California State Parks commissioner Margaret W. Owings, and Democratic assemblyman Alan Sieroty.[54]

Based on the positive feedback she had received, Harris entrusted the embryonic idea to state legislators and their aides, who then set about the process of framing legislation to protect the Golden State's entire coast. A major struggle in Sacramento loomed as more than a dozen bills—calling for a study of the coast and for the establishment of a statewide commission and/ or regional coastal commissions—were written and defeated between 1967 and 1972.[55]

Into this maelstrom of sixties-generated countercultural drama, estuary infilling, Bay Area activism, beach closings, a catastrophic oil blowout, a rising chorus of public demands for environmental safeguards, and an incipient idea for statewide coastal regulation landed twenty-seven-year-old legislative aide Peter Douglas. The year was 1971. Arguably, the most propitious moment in California and possibly U.S. environmental history had been ushered in by a combination of Bay Area matrons, profit-hungry coastal developers, a cost-cutting oil company, and an electorate mobilized for governmental action to save the Golden State's endangered shore. In the field of coastal management, here was a rare convergence of crisis, opportunity, and leadership (or more accurately, leadership-in-the-making). Granted, Douglas was inexperienced with governance and not yet proficient in environmental law. By his own admission, he had, up to that point, "never considered work in environmental law."[56] This would soon change.

After relocating with his wife, Roe, in Sacramento, his first order of business was to learn as quickly as possible the intricacies of the legislative process and who the relevant players were with respect to passage of a coastal protection law. Regarding his first encounters on the job, Douglas recalled meeting Ethan Wagner, Sieroty's onetime chief of staff, who stopped in to talk about the matter of coastal legislation. Douglas remembered having been previously warned by Rowan Klein, a UCLA law school classmate also working for Sieroty, that "drafting a good coastal protection bill would be easy, but getting one passed and signed would be nearly impossible and could take years."[57] Ronald Reagan was governor at the time, and most Republicans adamantly opposed governmental interference with property rights while favoring local "home rule," meaning they believed that city councils and county supervisors should have paramount authority in matters affecting their respective jurisdictions. Not yet fully appreciating this political reality, Douglas naively asked Wagner why, "given the iconic status of California's coast, Democrats and Republicans could not simply agree on a protection plan for this irreplaceable geographic treasure." Looking incredulous, Wagner laughed and rolled his eyes to the ceiling, responding, "You'll see."[58] Wagner was right. Very soon afterward Douglas learned for himself why passage of such a law was most difficult: "Corruption, ideological entrenchment, hypocrisy, ignorance, special interest lobbyists, [and] corporate power ruled the political roost."[59]

As Douglas gained a deeper understanding of how and why measures were passed, or rejected, in the state legislature, he was visited in his office by O. James (Jim) Pardau, chief consultant to the Assembly Committee on Natural Resources and Conservation (known at another time as Natural Resources, Land Use, and Energy). After saying hello, Pardau shoved a large folder into Douglas's hands, saying, "Here's the first rough cut at a coastal bill. It's all yours now. Good luck!"[60] The draft, Douglas learned, had been the work of E. Lewis (Lew) Reid, a brilliant attorney and Republican from the Bay Area who had helped with the organization of the California Coastal Alliance.

Before laboring on the rough draft of Reid's work, and with the failure of a coastal protection bill in 1970 in mind, Douglas held an all-day working session in February 1971 in which he met with a group of coastal activist leaders at the Napa home of Assemblyman John F. Dunlap. Alan Sieroty was there, as were Bill Kortum, Lew Reid, and Janet Adams, head of the Coastal Alliance. Adams was resourceful, indefatigable, and—with more than a hundred organizations comprising the Coastal Alliance under her leadership— powerful. Lew Reid aptly described Adams as "a hurricane with a heart."[61] She was particularly skillful in matters of campaign strategy, working with legislators, pursuing media relations, and organizing activists. Ray McDevitt, a partner with Reid in their San Francisco law firm, also attended. His head brimming with ideas after the meeting at Dunlap's home, Douglas sat down and, in consultation with Reid and McDevitt, drafted Assembly Bill 1471, one of the more salient coastal protection measures among nearly a dozen others.[62] Sieroty introduced the bill; its cosponsors included the assembly Speaker, Bob Moretti, and Assemblymen Dunlap and Edwin Z'berg.[63]

AB 1471 provided statewide jurisdiction for a new coastal management agency, coordination of this agency with six regional subagencies that would be created, the granting of permit-review power for development projects in the Coastal Zone, adequate funding, authority to impose fines on violators of the law, and the development of a statewide coastal plan that listed land use priorities.[64] As Douglas had been warned, securing passage of this bill would not be easy.

Working with Janet Adams, Douglas drove throughout California to meet with environmental activists and others who seemed likely allies in the campaign to gain passage of AB 1471. Organizing free-spirited activists in such a campaign, said Douglas, was "truly like herding cats."[65] He learned fast that he needed to exercise patience, listen carefully, rein in egos, lower expectations, be empathetic, and hone his communication skills.

While on the road, Douglas explored in detail various coastal sites. Evidencing the heart of a poet, he waxed lyrical about what he was seeing and experiencing: "[Shores] in perpetual motion, pushing, pulling, pulsing with winds, tides and currents hiding a deepness we were just beginning to understand. My bonding with coast and ocean on these forays to the front forged forever links never to be broken. Saving the sundown coast became my cause akin to a crusade for god—only this god was a goddess called Gaia."[66] Erato, the ancient Greek muse of poetry, could not have penned these sentiments more lyrically and poignantly than Douglas.

On this occasion, however, the sundown coast of Douglas's adoration was not to be saved, though Democrats had a majority in both houses of the Sacramento legislature. Despite this partisan advantage in Sacramento, AB 1471 was strongly opposed by local governments (the League of California Cities and the County Supervisors Association of California, for example) and by commercial real estate interests, utilities, oil companies, and trade unions. Still, the measure—encumbered with new amendments strengthening local prerogatives—passed (fifty-five to sixteen) in the assembly on September 22, 1971, and went to the senate.[67] That chamber was much less conservationist-minded and more solicitous of municipal interests than the assembly. In the senate the Natural Resources and Wildlife Committee, which had just rejected four other coastal bills, had charge of AB 1471's fate. On November 16, the final day of that committee's deliberations on the measure, one member was a no-show, Democratic Senator James Q. Wedworth (a resident of Hawthorne), who had promised his support of AB 1471. Wedworth, Douglas later learned, "had decided on his way to Sacramento that he needed to take delivery of a purebred colt." Such chicanery must have scoured away another layer of Douglas's naïveté about the legislative process. The animal, he found out, had been a gift from a racetrack lobbyist who had represented big oil companies opposed to the coastal bill, *which, in the senate committee tally, was one vote shy* of the five needed.[68] Television crews camped outside the gate to Wedworth's house. On camera the errant senator claimed he "had personal obligations and rent to pay!" Newspapers, too, reported the "double-cross."[69]

Not having made it out of the Senate Natural Resources and Wildlife Committee, AB 1471 died, in part, one is tempted to say, a victim of special interest "horse trading." While containing a measure of truth, such an explanation would be too facile. Even had the bill emerged from that committee, it likely would have had to clear the Senate Finance Committee, as well, for a senate floor vote. Passage in the upper chamber would have been problematic owing to the sway of powerful business interests and local government lobbyists in Sacramento. Still, had the measure overcome such formidable opposition and gained senate approval, Governor Ronald Reagan—an opponent of AB 1471—would have been able to block it with a veto.[70] Assemblyman Sieroty, a shrewd analyst of Sacramento's political dynamics, attributed the defeat of AB 1471 principally to Governor Reagan's opposition. A spokesperson for Reagan enumerated seven reasons for the governor's dislike of the measure, of which the first two stressed the extensive land-use controls in the bill and the added layers of regional government. Next in importance, Sieroty traced the defeat of the bill to legislators friendly to land developers and utilities.[71]

Though AB 1471 died in senate committee proceedings, the idea of statewide coastal protection at the heart of the measure remained very much alive. Janet Adams, incensed and more determined than ever, announced that if the legislature failed to enact a coastal protection law in 1972, the Alliance would ensure that the public's voice would be heard through passage of an initiative.[72] Working with Adams and others, Douglas remained resolute and poised to take whatever course was necessary to obtain a statewide coastal law.

FOUR

Coastal Conservation, Politics, and a New Commission

PROSPECTS FOR PASSAGE OF LEGISLATION aimed at protecting the coast had much to do with the political climate in the United States, and particularly California, during the sixties and seventies. At the national level, by 1972, mounting American casualties in a seemingly endless southeast Asian war divided an electorate disillusioned by the unfolding Watergate scandal that revealed a covert attempt involving Republican operatives to subvert the presidential election of that year. Mistakenly anticipating that Maine senator Edmund Muskie—known as an environmentalist— would be the Democratic presidential nominee in that year's election, incumbent President Richard M. Nixon felt the need to not be outdone by the senator on that matter.[1] Thus when Congress passed the Coastal Zone Management Act on the eve of that election, Nixon promptly signed the measure into law. Accordingly, if coastal states adopted comprehensive seaboard management plans protecting resources and assuring public access, then such states could regulate federal activities in coastal areas.[2] In California, meanwhile, coastal activists seized the environmental moment and pushed for enactment of coastal protection legislation. At times the push brimmed with high drama. Vested economic interests and an environmentally awakened public clashed and compromised in the tumultuous process by which two landmark California coastal laws in the 1970s went into effect.

Peter Douglas, still in the early stages of a long career in coastal management, played a major role in framing these state laws, which eventuated in the establishment of the commission he would one day head. Jubilation at the passage of these measures, however, was short-lived, as by the late

1970s the public's honeymoon with coastal protection had begun to lose its glow.

In late January 1972, what turned out to be a final effort at that time to pass a statewide coastal bill was launched. According to Douglas, strong opposition was mounted by oil companies, private utilities (for example, Pacific Gas & Electric and Southern California Edison), land development corporations, and building trade unions—whose members suffered the high 7.2 percent state unemployment rate.[3] Senate Bill 100 and Assembly Bill 200, both of which were modified versions of Alan Sieroty's AB 1471 (see chapter 3), did not pass. Lacking sufficient votes, SB 100 was held in committee in mid-May, resulting in the launch of an initiative campaign at that time. Almost simultaneously, Governor Reagan offered what may have been intended as his alternative to a statewide coastal commission, the California Comprehensive Ocean Area Plan. Many environmentalists viewed the Plan as a fact-gathering endeavor that, while valuable, did not provide the needed force of a law establishing a regulatory authority.[4] Meanwhile, the legislative process regarding AB 200 continued. On July 6 that measure passed easily in the assembly, sixty to eleven, with minor amendments; but afterward a watered-down version of AB 200 was rejected by a four-to-four vote in the Senate Committee on Natural Resources, the graveyard of many of the earlier coastal protection bills. Lobbyists with the building trade unions and the Chamber of Commerce credited themselves for the outcome.[5] "The Legislature has failed," concluded Janet Adams. "We trust the people will not. The coast is still out there, but it won't be there long."[6]

With the state legislature's failure to enact a law establishing a California coastal commission, advocates in increasing numbers turned to the initiative process already under way, cheered on editorially by the *Los Angeles Times.*[7] In accordance with initiative protocol, when 5 percent of the electorate voting for governor in the most recent gubernatorial election signed a petition calling for the enactment of a given measure, the proposition would be put on the ballot in the next general election, in this case November 7, 1972. Between mid-May and the November election, proponents of a coastal initiative would have to work at warp speed to craft the proposition, gather the requisite signatures to qualify the measure for the ballot, and build public support. All of this would have to be done with meager financial resources and in the face of strong opposition from amply endowed vested interests.

Douglas awaited initiative language from the Coastal Alliance but did not receive it. Concerned about the short time frame, in mid-May he phoned attorney Ray McDevitt, a law partner of E. Lewis (Lew) Reid, a Republican who served as the Alliance's legislative director. Within days, Douglas and McDevitt huddled in the latter's San Francisco law office overlooking Market Street. They started on a "crystal clear late spring Saturday morning," recalled Douglas nearly four decades later, and finished that afternoon. Both felt excited and at the same time overwhelmed by the task facing them. The consequences of not getting the language right weighed heavily on the two.[8]

"Getting it right," said Douglas, meant to them adhering to the founding principles of the Alliance's "Save Our Coast" campaign. Douglas laid out those principles,[9] which are designated, in some instances paraphrased, and summarized as follows in accordance with his ordering:

Local versus greater than local interests. Too often local interests prevailed over broader, statewide interests to the detriment of California's coast. No longer would that be the case: where conflicts arose between local and state interests the latter necessarily would trump the former.

The precautionary principle. Rachel Carson's blockbuster book *Silent Spring* underscored the grave environmental threat posed by using DDT, a chemical insecticide. Developers would not be allowed to use technologies that potentially could cause great ecological harm to coastal resources. In the permitting process, when there was doubt about the advisability of using a new technology, the applicant would be denied permission. The inclusion of the precautionary principle (borrowed from Europe) in Proposition 20 constituted either the first instance or one of the earliest instances of the implementation of that standard in American public policy-making.

Failure avoidance. In environmental-protection lawmaking, success was temporary and failure permanent. Narrowly crafted laws had narrow mandates, resulting in the continued ravaging of the coast. Redundancy and overlapping of coastal protection mandates among state agencies was necessary and good.

Strong state land-use policies. Because local land-use decisions were almost invariably parochial, broader public concerns such as public access to beaches, protection of environmentally sensitive habitat, major landform alterations, and the siting of polluting industries would have to be entrusted to a powerful statewide coastal management agency.

Permits and planning. Until a permanent statewide coastal regulatory plan was in place, a temporary coastal commission would need permitting power to prevent developers from subdividing and building on what remained of the state's shore. The authority to plan and issue or deny permits had been critical to the functioning and effectiveness of BCDC. Likewise, this same authority would have to be incorporated into whatever statute established a permanent statewide coastal regulatory agency.

Appointments, representation, and process. On Assemblyman Alan Sieroty's advice, the power of appointing commission members would be divided among the governor, the Speaker of the assembly, and the Senate Rules Committee so that no single ideology, political party, or geographic area would dominate commission decisions. Also, to ensure that regional and local interests would have due input in the making of coastal policy, half (six) of the appointees to regional coastal commissions would be locally elected officials (city council members and county supervisors), and half (six) of the members of a state coastal commission could be but did not have to be locally elected officials.

Burden of proof. To minimize the rapid and too often heedless development of the coast—the sort that had taken place in the 1960s and early 1970s—the pace of coastal construction had to be slowed so a regulatory program could be devised and implemented. Once a regulatory program was in place, the approval of the majority of state commissioners should be required to grant building permits. In the commissioners' decision-making process the burden of proof was to be placed on the applicant to show that the proposed development would not adversely affect the natural environment of the coast. Lew Reid believed that this principle constituted a major departure in land use decision-making in the United States.

An independent quasi-judicial agency. Advocates of a statewide coastal agency feared that governors hostile to a statewide commission would sabotage it through budget cuts, the provision of office space and equipment, appointments, and myriad other ways. Consequently, the agency would not be under the control of any governor, nor of any other single branch of California government, thereby assuring its independence.

Public participation and public support. The failure of the legislature to enact a statewide coastal protection law had assured that advocates of such a measure would turn to voters throughout the state to enact by initiative the "People's Law." Once a statewide coastal regulatory commission was established, maximum public participation in agency decision-making would be facilitated through transparency and noticing commission meetings.

Jurisdictional reach. Coastal commission advocates learned from the BCDC experience that a broad jurisdictional reach would be essential to the agency's effective functioning. Power plant siting and port master plans, in most instances, would fall within the purview of a statewide coastal commission.

Staged implementation. In addition to the aforementioned powers, additional powers might be needed by a coastal agency in the future. Therefore, the foundational statutes for a seaboard commission could not be seen as static and immutable but rather as adaptive and amenable to strengthening should circumstances dictate the need for augmenting agency powers. Coastal management is always a work in progress.

Judicial review. Because a statewide commission's decisions would have consequential impacts, often resulting in lawsuits, it was necessary to incorporate into a coastal protection law a check on the agency's power by rendering its findings subject to judicial review.

Protection of property rights. Though unnecessary because state and federal law protects private property rights, it was important to remind all parties that the prospective statewide coastal protection agency acknowledged those rights and was not above the law.

Douglas affirmed that he and McDevitt kept the above principles in mind while drafting what became Proposition 20, largely a recasting of AB 200.[10] They kept something else in mind as well: the need to retain some of the elements that had been incorporated into the failed coastal bills during at least the preceding three years. Doing so would be necessary, they reasoned, in order to gain newspaper editorial support for the ensuing initiative campaign. These elements included the following:[11]

• One statewide coastal commission and six subordinate regional commissions should be established; they would exist for an interim period of four years, by which time a statewide plan would be prepared and presented (no later than December 1, 1975) by the state commission to the California legislature for adoption in 1976. If the legislature rejected the plan, the commissions would expire on January 1, 1977.

- A split appointment process was retained, whereby authority would be divided between the governor, the state senate, and the assembly, and the statewide panel would include an equal number of public members and locally elected officials.
- A key permitting role for local government was retained; these permits could be appealed to the state commission.
- An interim regulatory jurisdiction was established for all new development in an area extending three miles seaward and one thousand yards landward of the mean high tide line.
- Violators of the act would be subject to a ten-thousand-dollar fine. An additional fine of five hundred dollars per day could be charged for unpermitted development.

Two additional features of Proposition 20 had been incorporated in some of the more than a dozen previously failed coastal protection bills. One was a provision directing that "a hiking, bicycle and equestrian trails system shall be established along or near the coast."[12] Today's California Coastal Trail, a work in progress, is an outgrowth of the coastal initiative. In May 2016, a 2.3-mile section of that hiking route aptly named the Peter Douglas Trail, for his coauthorship of Proposition 20 and other achievements, opened along the southern end of the remote Lost Coast region of Mendocino County.[13] The other feature of that initiative ballot measure provided for $5 million in government funding for the operations of a statewide and several regional coastal commissions for the fiscal years from 1973 to 1976.

The two lawyers completed their draft in the early afternoon, but Douglas was not quite satisfied. A ringing statement of the public's stake in the measure was needed, he thought. He suggested to McDevitt that they add the statement "The People of the State of California hereby find and declare that the California coastal zone is a distinct and valuable natural resource belonging to all the People." McDevitt thought this language too risky in that it could be interpreted as an unconstitutional taking of private property, thereby calling the entire measure into question. Douglas disagreed, saying the language "would be read to be hortative" rather than as a pronouncement negating private ownership of property along the coast. When the language was, indeed, challenged in court, Douglas was proven right in saying that a tribunal would regard the statement as expressive of a yearning or hope rather than as a taking of private property.[14] This anecdote is telling: though Douglas was a meticulous legal draftsman, his sundry writings and speeches

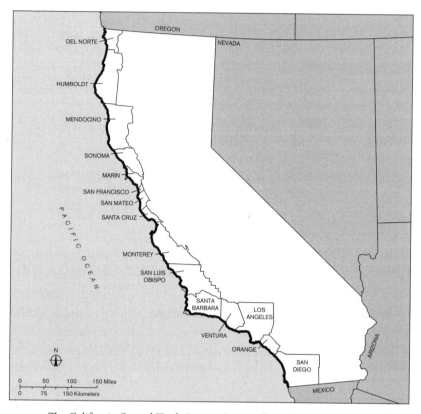

MAP 4. The California Coastal Trail. Source: Coastwalk California/California Coastal Trail Association.

nearly always evinced stirrings reminiscent of a Thomas Jefferson and, on occasion, the high purpose and concentrated fury of a Thomas Paine. A rarity in Sacramento, Douglas, as will be shown, had the head of a consummate lawyer/bureaucrat and the heart of a poet.

CAMPAIGNING FOR THE "PEOPLE'S LAW"

The roughly five-month campaign to gather signatures and garner public support for Proposition 20, the California Coastal Zone Conservation Act of 1972, was characterized by high-energy, large-scale citizen involvement; resourcefulness; and a low budget. Said Douglas, "We had virtually no money. What we had that the opposition didn't is broad-based public support and legions of volunteers."[15] Opponents of the measure, largely from the corporate world, had more than ample financial resources but, as Douglas noted, little in the way of citizen participation in the effort to defeat the initiative.

While Proposition 20 was being drafted, Janet Adams and the Coastal Alliance flew into action, launching the signature-gathering and public-outreach campaign for passage of the measure. The underfunded Alliance spent eight thousand to ten thousand dollars on the printing and mailing of petition materials.[16] Thousands of people participated. Douglas noted that some citizen-volunteers took their vacation time to work full-time for the initiative; others came out of retirement to do likewise. Homes were converted overnight into campaign centers. Young people got involved. "The November 1972 election was the first General Election in which eighteen-year-olds could vote[,] which energized students across the State to register."[17] George McGovern ran for the presidency that year, and generally, "McGovern supporters were our supporters," said Douglas, who, himself, walked precincts simultaneously for McGovern and Proposition 20. Unlike most signature-gatherers for ballot initiatives then and since, those working for Proposition 20 were *unpaid* citizen-volunteers "from all walks of life." Educators and college students were particularly active. Numerous professors, high school biology teachers, surfers, divers, Sierra Club members, lifeguards, airline pilots, and park department employees plunged into the signature-gathering effort. In Los Angeles one young couple "went on leave from their doctoral programs in marine biology to make the initiative drive a success," noted Adams.[18] Professional signature-gathering operatives, on the other hand, had warned that Save Our Coast's unpaid, amateur force could never get the job done, especially given the rapidly approaching thirty-day deadline to gain certification of the 325,000 required signatures in time for ballot printing. They said they could get the job done for between $160,000 and $200,000. These operatives, like opponents of the measure, averred it was "statistically impossible" for unpaid volunteers to round up 16,000 signatures a day and get them validated in time to qualify the initiative for the November ballot.[19]

To stop this effort before Proposition 20 could even get on the ballot, business and labor opponents outspent advocates of the measure nearly one hundred to one.[20] The major funders of the opposition and the amounts they contributed to defeat Proposition 20 were reported as follows to the secretary of state as California law required:[21]

Contributor	Amount of Contribution
Irvine Company	$50,000
Deane & Deane	50,000
Standard Oil Company of California	35,000
Bechtel Corporation	30,000
General Electric Company	30,000
Southern California Edison	27,633
Southern Pacific Land	25,000
Mobil Oil Corporation	15,000
Gulf Oil Corporation	15,000
Texaco	15,000
Occidental Petroleum Company	10,000

Southern California Edison messaged its ratepayers to oppose the coastal initiative. Said Ellen Stern Harris, "During the campaign [for Proposition 20] I opened my utility bill to discover a letter carrying a similar message to the one anti-Prop. 20 corporations had brought to television and radio." She took her complaint to the California Public Utilities Commission, contending that Edison "had usurped the neutral medium of the bulky envelope to improperly propagandize." When the CPUC turned down the complaint, Harris and the Center for Law in the Public Interest took the matter all the way to the State Supreme Court, which upheld the plaintiffs.[22]

Other opponents of the initiative measure included the following: Citizens Against the Coastal Initiative, the California Chamber of Commerce, the California Real Estate Association, the California Manufacturers Association, the Teamsters Union, the Council of Carpenters, and the Building and Trades Council of California. According to documents compiled by the California secretary of state, these groups collectively contended that the power of a statewide commission to issue permits "would . . . establish a two to four-year moratorium on virtually all building in the coastal area, including development for recreational purposes." Land values would tumble causing a reduction in local tax assessments and revenues. Adoption of the initiative would delay power-plant siting, risking power outages for Californians. Moreover, a state coastal management agency would introduce "supergovernment" and weaken the authority of local polities.[23]

If a genuine citizens group fought against the coastal initiative, its activities and the size of its membership have not been credibly documented. Sierra Club lobbyist John Zierold seems to have been right when he testified on October 10, 1972, at a public hearing on the measure: "There are no citizens . . . in the so-called Citizens Committee Opposed to Proposition 20. There are major corporations with all manner of wealth and resources to confuse and obfuscate the election process."[24] Three days before the November general election, the *Lodi News-Sentinel* ran an article attacking Proposition 20 and listed information regarding Citizens Against the Coastal Initiative. The group's San Francisco office at 870 Market Street was located in the city's Financial District. Edwin W. Wade, mayor of the city of Long Beach and past president of the League of California Cities, was listed as a cochairman of this "citizens group," as was John F. Crowley, secretary-treasurer of the San Francisco Labor Council.[25] These two cochairs represented entities that had a major economic stake—tax revenues for a city, and jobs for workers—in coastal development. That the opposition claimed or insinuated that these entities were "citizen groups" serving the public may have been clever and legal, but it was also disingenuous and highly misleading. Instead of seeking a greater societal good, they pursued their own narrow economic interests. Such groups were not true civic organizations that sprang from a grassroots citizenry. Regarding this labeling ruse, one historian satirically observed, "Realizing they would not get very far by calling themselves 'Big Businesses Against Coastal Protection,' Proposition 20 opponents instead claimed to be protectors of the public interest."[26]

How did the opposition spend its formidable campaign chest? Whitaker & Baxter, an advertising agency that worked largely for conservative clients, coordinated the opposition's strategies and spending. Their money went to buying radio and television spots, billboard space, and direct mailings—all communicating the dire consequences that would ensue if the measure passed.[27] In a flagrant act of deception, the agency emblazoned the slogan "DON'T LOCK UP THE BEACHES" on hundreds of billboards, followed by the tagline "Vote *No* on 20." By almost any measure, the forces opposing the coastal initiative, particularly large-scale real estate interests, either blocked or tried to block public access to beaches, as had been the case at the Sea Ranch along the Sonoma coast, where for more than a decade the developer closed off ten miles of once open beaches (chapter 2). On the other hand, Proposition 20 did just the opposite by insisting on open beaches. It did this by denying building permits to "any development which would reduce or impose restrictions upon public access to tidal and submerged lands, beaches and the mean high tideline where there is no beach."[28] Similarly, powerful agribusiness interests in 1972 resorted to rank deception in promoting Proposition 22, which would have greatly restricted the freedom of migratory farmworkers to unionize.[29]

Warner Chabot, a young activist working with Janet Adams and the Alliance, organized a quick response to the billboard deception regarding Proposition 20. According to Peter Douglas, Chabot assembled a "large cadre of students" who were given the locations of the billboards, white paint, and brushes. The students apparently supplied their own ladders. At an appointed midnight hour, this "Monkey Wrench" (Douglas's term) team drove to the designated sites, painted out the word *No* and painted in the word *Yes,* so that the billboards read, "Vote YES on 20." According to Douglas, "The students scored a direct hit for truth, justice and the American way." Media statewide covered the caper for days. The opponents were outraged and saw that an arrest warrant was issued for Chabot, who vanished reportedly into the Santa Monica Mountains, remaining out of sight until after the election. Shortly thereafter, Whitaker & Baxter became the focus of legislative hearings. "The Alliance could never, in their wildest dreams, have asked for better free publicity," concluded Douglas.[30]

In addition to the highly mobile, up-for-adventure youth cadre just mentioned, the Alliance supporters of Proposition 20 included such groups as the League of Women Voters, the American Association of University Women, the California Congress of Parents and Teachers, the lobbying arm of the Associated Students of the University of California, the Sierra Club, Californians Organized to Acquire Access to State Tidelands (COAAST), People for Open Space, and numerous other citizen groups. Unlike their adversaries, these groups had no direct, evident, and measurable financial stake in the outcome of this political battle.

Proposition 20 backers fought back resourcefully and, given their relative lack of funds, economically. To counteract the disparity in spending on radio and television ads, the Alliance, on advice from attorneys, investigated the logged airtime of the opposition. The backers then used the information gathered to file a complaint to the Federal Communications Commission. Under the so-called Fairness Doctrine (in force at the time but revoked in 1987), broadcasters with FCC licenses who aired political programming on controversial issues of public importance were required to provide airtime for opposing views.[31] In effect, proponents of Proposition 20 were handed free airtime to make their case for coastal protection. Invoking the Fairness Doctrine provided backers of the coastal initiative with a way to even the playing field, despite their limited funding, in the contest for the minds and hearts of California's electorate.

Hollywood and media notables lent their cachet to the Save the Coast campaign. Movie icon Charlton Heston, who starred as Moses in the blockbuster movie *The Ten Commandments,* urged television and radio audiences to support Proposition 20. Likewise, actors Jack Lemmon, Lloyd Bridges, and Eddie Albert went on the airwaves to endorse the coastal initiative. Californian Hank Ketcham, the popular cartoonist who created the comic strip *Dennis the Menace,* which ran in a thousand newspapers in forty-eight countries and nineteen languages, lent his artistry to the campaign. In one of the cartoons, Dennis's mother explains to a neighbor: "We went to the beach . . . but it was gone."[32] Proposition 20 was not mentioned by name but the cartoon attracted considerable attention, thereby serving the purposes of the Alliance and doubtlessly Ketcham. Poignantly, that cartoon recalls the real life experience (see chapter 3) of prominent coastal activist Ellen Stern Harris in the late 1960s, when she drove her children through Malibu and the youngsters complained they could not see the ocean. The genius of Ketcham was that his strips spoke to families practically everywhere, and, in this instance, particularly to moms who wanted their children to be able to romp in the surf and sand.

The grassroots bona fides of the initiative movement were underscored in the 550-mile bicycle ride along California's coast to build public support for the measure. Beginning on the morning of September 14, 1972, state senate president pro tem James R. Mills led the two-wheeler cavalcade from Land's End in San Francisco southward to Mills's home district in San Diego. Participants camped in state and regional parks, where supportive locals served them hot dogs, hamburgers, and spaghetti. Drawing helpful news coverage, townspeople along the route welcomed the ever-changing hundred or so participating cyclists with "Save the Coast breakfasts, barbecues, wine tastings, and sandcastle contests."[33] Locals also made sleeping arrangements for the bicyclists. Several chauffeur-driven long black limousines trailed the riders. These luxury vehicles were occupied by "utility and development" spokespersons wearing expensive Brooks Brothers suits that presented a sharp contrast with the everyday outdoor attire of the cyclists, recalled Mills, a liberal Democrat, many decades later. At the various press stops these "fat cats" disputed Mills's pro-Proposition 20 arguments.[34] Through media coverage the voting public caught a clear glimpse of the lopsided struggle between environmentally minded citizen bicyclists and seemingly profit-driven limousine caravaners.[35] But while public support was building through the bike ride, the battle for the coastal initiative was not quite over.

A LAST-MINUTE POLITICAL DRAMA

Even when sufficient signatures had been gathered, the drama surrounding the initiative did not end. On June 9, 1972, Secretary of State Edmund G. (Jerry) Brown Jr. informed the Alliance that 418,000 signatures had been received and validated. That was more than enough to qualify Proposition 20 to appear on the November ballot.

Unable to prevent the gathering of sufficient signatures, the opposition found yet another way to possibly derail the initiative. Before Secretary of State Brown could authorize placing Proposition 20 on the ballot, a lawsuit seeking a temporary restraining order (TRO) was filed against the Alliance and had to be surmounted. The plaintiff, Newton Pope, owner of the Firehouse Restaurant near the banks of the Sacramento River, alleged that the jurisdiction of the proposed state coastal agency would reach to the Sacramento–San Joaquin Delta, thereby causing his business to lose value. The Alliance, which had grown to include more than seven hundred groups plus local chapters,[36] countered that the ballot proposition made clear that the proposed statewide coastal agency's jurisdiction *excluded* the entire San Francisco Bay estuary and waters running into the Delta. Nevertheless, a Sacramento Superior Court judge issued a TRO, which could have prevented Proposition 20 from appearing on the November ballot. Stunned and alarmed, Douglas raced to Herbie Jackson's law office on the Capitol Mall, where the order had been drafted, and read a copy of the TRO. Douglas found that the required boilerplate wording for such an order, "now . . . it is hereby ordered," was missing. He then told Jackson the latter had failed to proofread his own document. Jackson fumed that he was an attorney and knew how to draft a TRO. "Well, I am an attorney too," answered Douglas, "and this ain't no order." Furious, Jackson rushed from his office hoping to correct the clerical error and have the issuing judge process another TRO. The judge found that Douglas was right and scheduled a hearing for a new TRO *after* the "drop dead" date for getting Proposition 20 on the November ballot. Later, the Alliance's objection to the TRO was sustained and the plaintiff's lawsuit dismissed.

The point of this last minute drama is that it shows how close at hand defeat was, even after months of hard, effective campaigning for the initiative. But for a clerical error on the part of the opposition, "the Save Our Coast initiative might never have been enacted," reflected Douglas.[37]

VICTORY

On November 7, 1972, voters went to the polls. By then—after months of nonstop traveling, speaking, and answering Proposition 20–related questions from people throughout the state—Douglas, like many of his coworkers, was thoroughly exhausted. Near 11 P.M. election night, the results came in and proponents learned they had won, mustering a 55.1 percent majority of the votes cast on the measure. Even conservative Orange County, where an energetic citizen-volunteer had devised a "phone tree" ensuring that every voter was called twice, had a majority (however slight) in favor of Proposition 20.[38] Thus, for the first time in California and possibly the nation's history, a state agency was created by the people themselves.[39] To Douglas, at least, passage of the landmark law showed that voters regarded the coast as "the geographic soul of California."[40]

Victory parties were held up and down the state. At one of these, Douglas was celebrating with friends in Sacramento when a disquieting thought struck him. Turning to another activist, Douglas muttered, "Oh shit! What do we do now?"[41]

COASTAL MANAGEMENT ON TRIAL

If drafting and passing a coastal protection law proved challenging, no less so was implementing it. The machinery of a new and temporary bureaucracy had to be assembled, and all working parts—an executive director, state and regional commissioners, a state staff and office, regional offices, permitting procedures, and more—had to be tended to so that the new law would work. While all this was happening, the clock was ticking. Applicants for development permits were lined up in December 1972, though permit requirements under Proposition 20 did not go into effect until February 1, 1973.[42] Additionally, each passing day reminded Douglas and others that in accordance with Proposition 20, a statewide coastal plan had to be submitted to the legislature by December 1, 1975, and approved. Otherwise the later-amended 1972 law, along with its commissions, would expire on January 1, 1977.[43] In short, the entire coastal protection project was on trial, and time was of the essence.

To make sure that coastal protection succeeded during the period between 1972 and 1976, Douglas labored practically nonstop largely out of the public eye, seeing to it that the administrative apparatus for regulation and planning was set up. A few days after passage of the initiative, Alan Sieroty called Douglas into his office, asking him what were the next steps in implementation of the measure. The young aide answered that, in short order, a budget, regulations, and a liaison committee—connecting the new state coastal agency with the legislature—needed to be established. After being consulted, the assembly Speaker, Robert Moretti (a Democrat from the Forty-Second District), facilitated the request for such a committee, and Sieroty chaired it. Douglas served as a consultant to the committee while carrying out the task of implementing Proposition 20 assigned to him by Sieroty.

As an early step toward that end, Douglas worked with representatives from the senate and the governor's office (though opposed to Proposition 20, Governor Reagan vowed to make coastal protection work because the people had spoken for it)[44] to hold a two-day conference in Sacramento in January 1973 to decide on implementation steps.

For the sixty-five fledgling regional commissioners, installing state commissioners and administrators in office was the first order of business at the Sacramento conference, because leadership was needed to address all of the other urgent tasks. Governor Reagan selected Republican Melvin B. Lane, publisher of *Sunset* magazine and former chairman of the San Francisco Bay Conservation and Development Commission (BCDC), to serve on the California Coastal Zone Conservation Commission (usually and hereafter also referred to simply as the Coastal Commission). Though Reagan was not a supporter of Proposition 20 or of the new state commission and its regional subsidiaries, he made a good appointment in selecting Lane. Once on the commission, Lane's colleagues elected him chair. He would play a major role, presiding over the state commission's deliberations on the California Coastal Plan and ably negotiating mitigations for siting of the San Onofre Nuclear Generating Station along northern San Diego County's coast.[45] A key to Lane's leadership was his insistence on keeping the commission out of what he called "neighborhood squabbles" that consumed time and were better handled by city and county authorities. "Our job is the statewide thing," he told Ellen Stern Harris.[46] While some environmentalists criticized Lane for being too probusiness, and business leaders faulted him for giving too much to environmental activists, Douglas held that Lane "was the best commissioner ever to serve."[47] The new commissioners elected as vice chair the prominent Los Angeles activist Ellen Stern Harris (an appointee of Speaker Bob Moretti), who, as noted earlier, is largely credited for having conceived the idea of a statewide coastal commission. She was the only woman on the newly formed Coastal Commission.[48]

Harris found that being a woman—especially an articulate, outspoken one in the early 1970s—meant that her inclusion on the panel at times raised a gender issue for both her and the commission. Her fellow commissioners had selected her as vice chair because of her impressive familiarity with coastal issues and her leadership skills; but despite her leadership position and abilities, Harris encountered discrimination simply for being female. At a 1973 commission meeting in Eureka at the historic Carson Mansion owned by the Ingomar Club, an exclusive all-male private group, Harris was denied admission into the facility because of her gender, she was told by a club employee. Shocked, frustrated, and angry, she next pled with the club manager, Charles Yelton, to allow her to join her fellow commissioners. He refused. Harris afterward wrote to California attorney general Evelle Younger about her "humiliating experience which caused me considerable distress." Pointing out the broader dimensions of the incident, she continued: "I consider that what occurred was an infringement on my civil rights and an impairment to fulfilling my duties as an officer of the State of California." Harris asked Younger to represent her in the matter "so that never again will any citizen of the State suffer such an experience."[49] As if the development and beach access issues were not thorny enough, discrimination in this and other instances (chapter 5) presented added challenges to the newly minted agency—challenges that Peter Douglas later would steadfastly meet.

With Lane as agency chair, the state commission, per protocol, elected Joseph E. Bodovitz as the agency's first executive director. Bodovitz, whose tenure extended from January 1973 to March 1978, had been a civic-minded newspaper reporter and previously served as executive director of BCDC. The larger preoccupation of the state commission during his executive directorship was with planning and permits. That meant formulating a California coastal plan intended for legislative approval that would serve as a basis for a new statute making the Coastal Commission permanent and simultaneously fulfilling the agency's permitting responsibility.

Carrying out the permitting responsibility necessitates a mention, at least, of the initial difference between Peter Douglas's and Bodovitz's understanding of Proposition 20. Coming from his executive directorship of BCDC, Bodovitz believed that the new Coastal Commission had a charge to balance both conservation *and* development. Douglas, on the other hand reminded Bodovitz that there was no "and" in the coastal agency's mission. The commission was all about conservation, as the title of Proposition 20 clearly indicated. As Douglas stated, "Proposition 20 . . . rejects . . . exploitation, and the subjugation of concerns for the natural environment and the conservation of its resources to the almighty dollar. . . . By emphasizing conservation and protection of natural resources, the Act represents an effort to shift away from [the] anthropocentric mentality that has dominated American culture."[50] Descending from the lofty plane of philosophy to the operational level of implementing Proposition 20, Douglas saw the agency's charge as preserving, protecting, and where possible, restoring the coast. Ever the pragmatic administrator, Bodovitz, on the other hand, seldom expressed himself in such evocative and categorical language when discussing coastal matters. Characteristically, he remained uneasy about the absence of the word *development* in the name of the commission. "If I had been consulted," he said, "I would have had an *and*. . . . So [the name would have been] the California Coastal Conservation and Development Commission."[51] In short, Bodovitz seemed to see the role of the executive director as primarily that of an arbiter between conflicting sides, while Douglas, who appreciated the importance of an arbiter's skills, envisioned far more of an activist role for that official and the agency he led.

This difference—between Bodovitz, who had not participated in the writing of Proposition 20 nor campaigned for its passage, and Douglas, who had both coauthored and barnstormed for the measure—was important. It anticipated the activist, conservationist approach to coastal management that characterized much of Douglas's eventual executive directorship.

In later years Douglas's views shifted in the direction of Bodovitz's understanding of the mission of the coastal agency and the role of its executive director. While Douglas was rightly perceived as an environmental activist by many, still he became more mindful of the importance of economic growth in the regulation of coastal affairs and came to realize there were times when he would have to concede to developers' demands. On those occasions he usually extracted mitigation funds used for the environment (see chapter 5 for a discussion of Bolsa Chica) in return for granting permits.

Apposite the change in Douglas's thinking, he averred in a later speech: "The real question is 'how can we have economic growth *and* effective coastal protection?' The achievement of *both* is the primary purpose of coastal management."[52] Though Douglas had shifted in the direction of Bodovitz's view, it must be emphasized that the former continued to fight ferociously for the shore's environment.

The dynamic tension between Bodovitz and Douglas aside, openness, transparency, and public involvement in planning and permitting were emblematic of the way Proposition 20 was implemented. Douglas's characterization of that measure as the "People's Law" was not hyperbole; if any law was deserving of this appellation, this one surely was. The designation was apt and pertained as much to how it was carried out as to its grassroots origins. Between 1973 and 1975, thousands of citizens attended the 259 public hearings and hundreds of informational meetings, all devoted to formulating a coastal plan in compliance with the initiative. The citizen attendees were not merely passive listeners to what officials had to say and report; instead, they gave input. Historian Jared Orsi concluded, "Often commissioners altered initial plans to incorporate the public responses."[53] Additionally, the interim state panel encouraged regional commissions to establish citizens' advisory groups whose purpose would be to provide commissioners with information regarding the public interest in coastal matters.

All the while, the commissions carried out their permitting functions, but with what results? A modest increase in building, mainly in semideveloped areas, took place. No new large subdivisions along or near the coast were permitted. The state commission met with little success in opening up public views and access at the Sea Ranch development above San Francisco. Two new nuclear reactors were approved at San Onofre, though utility companies wanted more such plants along the coast. Southern California Edison's attempt to expand San Onofre's nuclear plant was denied in 1973 after the state commission's staff report found that "several square miles of coastal waters" abutting the facility had become "the equivalent of a marine desert."[54] Governor Reagan, chambers of commerce, city councils, and other growth advocates were displeased with the commission's decision. A year later, amid mounting pressure from progrowth interests, and after Edison agreed to modify its San Onofre plans to bring the expansion project into compliance with the state's Coastal Zone Conservation Act, the commission approved it. An application for an oil and natural gas processing plant in Santa Barbara was conditionally approved, though the applicant refused the conditions and, therefore, the plant was not built. Commissioners then apportioned the subdivision of the now available site into parcels of farmland and timberland. Evidencing Proposition 20's regard for coastal agriculture, the state commission rejected a proposed residential project that would have transformed farmland into a large bedroom community. The *Los Angeles Times,* California's largest circulating newspaper, applauded this action.[55] In another instance, the City of Monterey was required to scale back a proposed redevelopment project. Applications, on appeal, for new home construction on undeveloped parts of the coast tended to be rejected. Applicants seeking to build commercial structures abutting beaches were required to provide for public access to the shore.[56]

Disproving the dire predictions from opponents of the new coastal law that its passage would bring building to a virtual halt, from February 1973 to December 1976 the six regional commissions denied fewer than 4.5 percent of the 24,825 permit applications received. During that same period, the state commission turned down 262 of the 800 permits sent up to that panel on appeal.[57] Assuredly, development was taking place in the Coastal Zone, but now it was managed in accordance with standards reflective of the public interest. The new regimen of coastal management, in short, was working.

A VISIONARY PLAN

After Proposition 20 passed, Douglas, still in the employment of Alan Sieroty, began serving as a consultant to the Assembly Natural Resources Committee (at another time called the Committee on Natural Resources, Land Use, and Energy, or Committee on Natural Resources) and the Select Committee on Coastal Zone Resources. In these capacities, while helping with implementation of the coastal initiative, he began working with many others on a coastal plan to be submitted to the state legislature by December 1975.[58] Work on the document, officially titled the California Coastal Zone Conservation Plan, took two and a half years.[59] Thereafter, coastal protection depended on whether a new law permanently embodying the essence of a comprehensive statewide plan could command sufficient votes to pass in the Sacramento assembly and senate.

At Douglas's request, as noted, Speaker Moretti set up a select committee of the legislature to oversee implementation of the coastal initiative. Douglas had a second purpose in mind as well: the ad hoc committee would build needed ties between coastal advocates, like himself, and the legislature. Such ties would facilitate passage of a permanent coastal act when the temporary one expired in four years. This assembly-created group worked collaboratively with a similar one from the senate and with Governor Reagan's office.

To make the coastal initiative work, the ad hoc committee set up an informational meeting in Sacramento, held in January 1973 under the golden dome of the State Capitol. Sixty-five of the recently appointed eighty-four regional commissioners attended to be briefed by legislators and other officials on their new duties. These duties included granting, modifying, or denying permit applications and participating in developing a statewide coastal plan. The state commission would take permit appeals from the regional panels and have the final say about what went into the plan.[60]

The appointment process for the state and regional commissions was similar, but the latter bodies were more accepting of coastal development. Six of the twelve state commissioners were appointed by the governor and the leaders of the assembly and senate. The other six were selected by the regional commissions (which ranged in size from twelve to sixteen members) from their membership. Half of the regional panelists were selected by municipal and county governments and consisted of local officials—that is, city council members and county supervisors; Douglas thought the majority of these local governments' appointments were "bad" owing to the parochialism of such officeholders.[61] The other forty-two regional commissioners were appointed by the governor and the leaders of the senate and assembly. Eleven of the twelve state commissioners had supported Proposition 20; the regional commissioners, by comparison, were much less likely to support coastal conservation, especially when deliberating on local development projects.[62]

State and regional commissioners were not the only parties involved in implementing the coastal initiative: neighborhood residents, as well, entered the permitting process and, in so doing, sometimes decided to remain active in shaping a statewide coastal plan. An example of how local citizen involvement in permitting led to planning is evident in the Barrio Logan dispute. Barrio Logan was a largely Chicano neighborhood located near San Diego Bay. In response to a coastal-permit applicant seeking in the early 1970s to build an industrial truck-loading dock in Barrio Logan, residents there mobilized in 1974 to oppose the project. Wanting to build a park and children's play area and ensure public access to the shore, they contended that their enclave was a unique cultural resource that ought not be degraded by industrial development. Though the regional coastal commission approved the permit, residents appealed the decision to the state panel, which denied the project. Encouraged and empowered by this outcome, some Barrio Logan residents subsequently participated in the framing of a California coastal plan.[63]

Barrio Logan residents constituted simply one segment of a much larger public who attended meetings and gave testimony on what should go into a statewide plan. According to one authority: "At the climactic round of joint state-regional hearings on the preliminary plan, 6,000 people attended 20 hearings in 16 counties in six weeks. . . . The commissioners listened to the equivalent of 8,000 pages of testimony from nearly 1,000 people."[64] In terms of the magnitude of public input in crafting policy in California, the writing of the coastal plan was and most likely remains unprecedented.

While the scope of public input was unprecedented, the organization of the yet-to-be written plan was modeled on similar work done years earlier by BCDC. Accordingly, the incipient plan was divided into nine elements, each of which was considered and written sequentially from the least to the most controversial. These elements included Marine Environment, Coastal Land Environment, Appearance and Design, Coastal Development, Energy, Transportation, Public Access to the Coast, Recreation, and Government Organization and Powers.[65]

The drafting and adoption of the plan occasioned a five-stage process. First, in consultation with advocacy groups and others with expertise, the state commission staff prepared an initial draft that included a technical report and a summary written in nontechnical language. These items were packaged and sent to the regional commissions and interest groups. Second, these recipients sent the materials to local government officials, representatives of affected businesses, and civic organizations, soliciting comments. Regional staff revised the elements accordingly, sent the draft plan to regional commissioners, and issued a press announcement about a forthcoming public hearing. Taking input from the hearing, the regional commissions reworked the draft plan and sent it back to the state commission. Third, based on the amended document, the state staff incorporated the proposed changes into another draft of each plan element and sent the resulting document to the state and regional commissioners, interested citizens, and the press. The state panel then held public hearings, the results of which led to the drafting of policies and recommendations. Fourth, the state commission adopted the revised package, including maps, of the nine elements into the so-called Preliminary Coastal Plan. Next, public meetings were held on the preliminary plan in dozens of coastal communities. The state and regional commissions then jointly conducted formal public hearings, thereby bringing to a close citizen involvement in the planning process. Fifth, the state commission adopted the Coastal Plan in the fall of 1975, forwarding it to the governor and Sacramento lawmakers. Twenty-five thousand copies of the 432-page foundational document, which included 206 recommendations, were printed for the public.[66]

Naturally, Douglas was monitoring and helping to guide the preparation of the Coastal Plan through all of the stages just described. He christened the resulting document "the Constitution of the Coast," calling it the "quintessential coastal planning document anywhere."[67] This characterization of the Plan was not universal. Generally, critics charged that the document was too environmentally focused at the expense of economic growth, including job creation. A number of economists stressed this criticism.[68]

A brief look at a somewhat broader assault on the Plan will illuminate the depth and breadth of the hostility that the document elicited from some critics. University of Southern California law professor Robert C. Ellickson, for example, saw no merit in the coastal regulatory framework and, in a *Southern California Law Review* article, urged the legislature to reject the Plan.[69] Describing the Plan as "extraordinarily complex," Ellickson confined himself to critiquing only "selected" aspects of it. According to him: the maps (comprising a third of the Plan) were inadequate; the Plan lacked specificity; the authors of the document failed to grasp economic theory; and the instrument was "chock-full of inefficient policies" that were unmindful of the capacity of "private markets to allocate resources."[70]

While granting the good intentions of the Plan's authors, Ellickson's article was severely one-sided, and its designation as a "commentary," seems a mislabeling. Still, the piece is notable in at least two ways. First, it anticipated several of the major criticisms leveled by builders and real estate interests at the state coastal agency during ensuing decades. Chief among these criticisms was the charge that the Plan betrayed "a definite antigrowth bias."[71] In this case Ellickson mistakenly conflated *regulated* growth, which the Plan clearly permitted, with antigrowth—a grossly inaccurate characterization. Another of these criticisms was that enactment of the Plan would mainly benefit "California's economic and intellectual elites," because restrictions on coastal housing development would push real estate prices far beyond the reach of most mainstream families, and that the Plan's design guidelines showed "contempt for middle-American tastes."[72] This ad hominem argument, common in media attack-ads, seems out of place in a law review article. Second, Ellickson's critique presaged California's ever-growing debate over the use of alternative energies, toward which its author exhibited a profound closed-mindedness. In being dismissive of solar and wind energies,[73] he again showed an unmistakable partiality, one that ran throughout the entire article, rendering it a one-sided legal brief and paean to free market economics rather than a balanced, scholarly analysis of the Coastal Plan.

Whether the Plan was as good as Douglas thought it to be or as bad as Ellickson claimed, it assuredly was visionary. Supporters of the Plan expected it to become the essence of a permanent coastal act. With that expectation in mind, state commission chair Melvin Lane submitted it on time to the Sacramento legislators. In doing so he posed two future scenarios: "One ... is a return to the wasteful, piecemeal, sprawling kind of development that has already overrun many once-open parts of the coast, and to overdevelopment in some coastal cities that has congested ... streets and walled off coastal vistas from all but those [who] live on the immediate oceanfront. Another ... is to protect the unique qualities of the coast, both in cities and rural areas, and to guide coastal conservation and development accordingly." Having clarified the choice before them, Lane said in closing, "Now the future of the California coast is in your hands."[74]

ANOTHER LANDMARK LAW

By 1976—the year of the showdown on coastal conservation legislation—citizen groups intent on passage of a permanent law had become seasoned participants in Sacramento politics. Specifically, they knew the ways in which key committees, like the Senate Natural Resources Committee, could make or break a bill by simply stalling or even preventing a vote in the upper chamber. Civic and environmental groups knew that, to achieve success, they had to stay involved in the campaign for a lasting coastal protection measure. This meant working with Douglas and many others to keep supporters unified on strategy and message, negotiating compromises with opponents, and helping shepherd a coastal bill through the legislature. The way forward would not be smooth and easy. Nor would it be without eleventh-hour political surprises and suspense.

Drawing from their experience in the Proposition 20 campaign, advocates of coastal conservation took several critical steps in the mid-1970s to increase the likelihood of legislative success in 1976. Shortly after passage of Proposition 20, coastal advocates correctly anticipated an upcoming vacancy on the senate's Natural Resources and Wildlife Committee, a body that had earlier obstructed passage of the coastal initiative. When the vacancy occurred, senate president pro tem James R. Mills filled the empty committee seat with a senator supportive of a coastal bill. To further ensure their cause against a reprise of the earlier legislative defeats, environmentalists during the 1974 elections canvassed districts up and down the state on behalf of candidates for the Sacramento legislature who indicated their support for a coastal protection law. Smartly, that same year they also campaigned for assembly candidates who, if elected, would support Leo McCarthy for the speakership of that chamber. McCarthy, who received that leadership post, was known to favor the establishment of a BCDC-like commission to manage California's coast. In 1975, coastal protection advocates persuaded McCarthy to appoint Assemblyman Charles Warren (a Democrat from Los Angeles) as chair of the Natural Resources, Land Use, and Energy Committee, one of the two committees in that chamber charged with vetting a proposed coastal bill.[75]

With this groundwork nearly complete, coastal advocates in the legislature had to decide what to do with the Coastal Plan. Cognizant of the political capital required to secure formal adoption of the Plan in early 1976, they instead decided to use selected provisions of the document without attribution as a source for crafting a permanent coastal law. Though Douglas and others saw the Plan as "the Constitution of the Coast," the document's role in the unfolding lawmaking drama was seldom publicly referenced.

In the sphere of citizen action, coastal conservation groups and civic organizations mobilized for the struggle ahead. They formed a steering committee composed of representatives from the Coastal Alliance, the Planning and Conservation League, the Sierra Club, the League of Women Voters, PACE (People, Access, Coastal Environment), and other groups. Working together, the steering committee compiled a list of thirteen "indispensable" provisions that should be incorporated into a proposed coastal bill. Such provisions would constitute the essence of the kind of law they envisioned. These readily understandable core features presented a stark contrast to the 206 highly technical recommendations listed in the complex Coastal Plan.[76] Nearly all of these core provisions were incorporated into the coastal measure being drafted.

Between December 1975 and February 1976 the bulk of the bill that became the California Coastal Act was written. As with many such team drafting efforts, the record is not clear on who wrote which portions of the measure. According to numerous sources, Douglas had a large hand in craft-ing the statute, but others were also instrumental in its preparation as well. So why draw attention to his role? The answer is because he alone of the bill's authors went on to become the long-serving head of the commission made permanent by the terms of the measure. As such, Douglas was superbly if not uniquely informed about the intent and content of the legal instrument that would guide California coastal management ever afterward.

Not surprisingly, passage of this legal instrument to manage California's coast involved twists and turns and parliamentary skills of a high order. A brief narration of how passage came about is entirely fitting, as most likely few who were not closely involved in the matter know the adroit political maneuvering that took place.

At the outset, two coastal bills were considered in 1976. The first of these (Senate Bill 1579), sponsored by Senator Anthony Beilenson (a Democrat from Beverly Hills), was killed in the Senate Finance Committee by a one-vote margin on June 11, 1976.[77] With only ten weeks remaining in the session, legislators for a coastal regulation bill quickly turned to a back-up vehicle—a bill by Senator Jerry Smith (a Democrat from Santa Clara County), which originally had only aimed to save trees in danger of being removed along scenic highways. With Smith's assent, this measure (SB 1277) was rewritten into a second coastal bill. Smith's bill afforded the major advantage that it had cleared senate committees and could not be watered down by further amendment in that chamber. In the rewriting process, much of which took place during the legislature's July recess, some thirty-five pages from the first bill were deleted, the commission's permit area was restricted to one thou-sand yards inland generally, and a provision allowing state commissioners to appeal regional permit decisions to the state panel was added.

Aided by Governor Jerry Brown's support for a strong law,[78] Assemblyman Charles Warren, chair of the Natural Resources, Land Use, and Energy Committee, scheduled informational hearings on SB 1277 to be held in Southern California, where opposition to coastal regulation was strongest. The goal of the hearings was to bring together opponents and supporters of the bill in hopes of working out compromises so the measure could move forward. As a consultant to that committee, Douglas was heavily involved with these proceedings.

One of those gatherings, held at Loyola University in Los Angeles, was especially important. Here's Douglas's version of what transpired:

[In July, Chairman Warren told me] we're going to have a hearing on this bill, and I want the Coastal Zone boundary mapped. And I want . . . those maps . . . put on the wall around the room where we're going to have the hearing. . . . I [Douglas] said, "Why are we doing that, Charlie? We've got multiple zones here." "Don't argue with me, just do it." I said, "Why?" And he said, "You'll see." So . . . we put the maps up, had the hearing and all these lawyers and big property owners; and they were all looking at the map, and they were all looking at their property. And at the end of the day, we ended up changing the lines in a whole bunch of places because of the politics of the people in the room. And we walked away from the hearing, and I turned to Charlie and I said, "Nobody really paid any attention to the policies. That's the essence of the act. They were all focused on the map and the lines." He said, "See?" That's how we got the strong policies in the Coastal Act: because he diverted everybody's attention to the lines on the map. So that's how we got this jagged political Coastal Zone boundary. It doesn't make a lot of sense, but the trade-off was the strongest land use policies in the country. It was worth it. It was smart. I learned a big lesson.[79]

When the legislature reconvened in August, both Warren's committee and the Ways and Means Committee approved SB 1277, sending it to the assembly floor, where Sieroty and Speaker McCarthy warded off a handful of unfriendly amendments. On a largely partisan vote, the bill passed forty-five to twenty-eight. Only two Republicans voted for it; eight Democrats voted against it.[80] While important hurdles had been cleared in the lower house, the legislative clock was ticking.

Like the proverbial sword of Damocles, time threatened to be the bold measure's executioner. On August 13, with only twelve legislative days in the session remaining, the bill went to the senate. A canvass of that chamber showed proponents of the bill that they were three votes short of the twenty-one ayes needed among the forty senate members. Smith observed, "The only people who could deliver those [votes] were unions."[81] With help from Preble Stolz in the governor's office, Smith met with John Henning, leader of the California AFL-CIO. With a week to go before the session ended, Melvin Lane and Bodovitz joined Smith in these talks with Henning. Several days went by with no discernible progress. Unsure of the outcome, Smith felt he had to bring his bill to a vote on August 23. It fell three votes short of passage.

The sword of expired time had fallen, but not completely. Because eight legislators had not voted, senate rules allowed Smith to "call" on the vote. In effect, advocates of the bill could and did delay announcing the outcome of the first vote and had the rest of that day to round up the three needed votes.

FIGURE 8. A pensive Peter Douglas, who was probably strategizing a next step regarding the terms and implementation of the California Coastal Act of 1976. Photo courtesy of the California Coastal Commission.

Meanwhile, a staffer in the governor's office warned one nonvoting senator that if Smith's bill failed, a strong initiative like Proposition 20 would likely appear in the future.[82] An hour before the deadline, Smith received a phone call, after which he rushed to the governor's office. More negotiations there led to an impasse. A dejected Smith concluded, "We just don't have the votes."[83] Thirty minutes later Smith received a phone call in the senate chamber, after which he dashed to the entrance, where he met Governor Brown, Henning, Bodovitz, several senators with strong labor connections, and television cameramen. Brown handed Smith a list of concessions from both sides, and told him that now the AFL-CIO and the building trades supported the coastal bill. Smith immediately called up the bill for a final vote. Along with the three new "ayes" from previously nonvoting senators, four others joined them. With scarcely a moment to spare, the coastal bill passed twenty-five to fourteen.[84]

At the bill-signing ceremony on September 29, 1976, Brown feigned amazement at the outcome. He credited mostly the labor leaders and their cadre of senate supporters for the result. A good number of those present, however, were well aware of how the governor's influence at virtually the last minute had made possible the victory being celebrated.[85] Appropriately, among the celebrants were Sonoma County Supervisor William Kortum, former Coastal Alliance executive director Janet Adams, Assemblyman Alan Sieroty, activist Ellen Stern Harris, and other prominent veterans of the long but successful campaign for the prize—a strong coastal law.

The 144-page California Coastal Act of 1976, which has been amended multiple times, comprises ten chapters beginning with "Findings and Declarations and General Provisions" and ending with "Severability."[86] The statute affirms California's commitment to public access to the coast and to "protecting and conserving coastal resources, including wetlands, sensitive plants, animals and habitats, agriculture, and scenic rural landscapes."[87] Most importantly, the act made the commission permanent. Jurisdictionally, the commission's authority extended minimally three miles seaward from the mean high tide line (including all offshore islands); inland it extended variously from several blocks (up to one thousand yards) in cities and to five miles in a few less populated areas. Within this geographical reach, the measure restricted building to existing developed areas but, under specified conditions, made allowances for commercial fishing, boating, energy plants, and visitor-serving facilities. Unlike Proposition 20, the Coastal Act transferred permitting authority, with certain powers reserved for the state, to local governments. That is, once such governments drafted and gained the commission's certification of Local Coastal Programs (LCPs), these polities would be empowered within their jurisdictions to issue permits for new development. Where local and state interests clashed, "the State interest trumps and must be protected," Douglas held.[88] This was a cardinal principle, essential to equipping the commission with the power to implement statewide policies among coastal cities vigilantly protective of local "home rule" within their geographic boundaries. LCPs also reflected and helped the commission remain cognizant of the varying topographies and demographics along the state's seaboard. While the commission's authority was formidable, the Coastal Act safeguarded property rights, underscoring the fact that that regulatory body "was not above the law and needed to be mindful of private rights as it promotes its public mission."[89] When faced with scientific uncertainty, the Coastal Act, like Proposition 20, invoked the precautionary principle. "When in doubt, deny," was how Douglas characterized the application of that standard.[90] Also, as in the case of Proposition 20, the commission's regulatory decisions were subject to judicial review, one of the necessary checks on that agency's authority.

Douglas acknowledged that the Coastal Act would need improvement. He lamented the fact that the measure did not embrace watersheds, which affect ocean pollution and the sand-sustainability of many beaches. "The Coastal Plan [of 1975] called for including all watersheds," he recollected. But instead of science-based geomorphologic factors shaping the Coastal Zone boundary, which defines the commission's jurisdiction, political considerations were often the determining ones.[91] Nor did the Coastal Act provide for guaranteed funding. The agency's reliance on the general fund rendered it vulnerable to hostile budget cuts by administrations of both political parties. As a result, the commission's ability to carry out its statutory mandates would later prove problematic.[92]

In any case, the permanent statutory foundation for coastal protection was in place. The next step involved setting up the bureaucratic apparatus needed to implement the landmark law. Douglas would be closely involved with that task, taking on an ever more visible role while learning the art of coastal management.

DOUGLAS'S COASTAL MANAGEMENT APPRENTICESHIP

With the Coastal Act in place by the fall of 1976, Douglas went on to serve as the statewide commission's legislative representative in Sacramento. By then he had a firm grasp of how decision making occurred, both at the committee level and on the floors of the assembly and senate. Alan Sieroty's protégé had come a long way since arriving in Sacramento broke and inexperienced in political lawyering some five years earlier. Whatever exhilaration Douglas and other environmentalists might have felt with passage of the Coastal Act and its early implementation could not have lasted long in the face of mounting business and political opposition to governmental regulation in general and coastal management in particular.

Douglas's new position marked his transition from aide and consultant to recognized political broker working on behalf of an agency he had helped establish. He now had a new boss, Joseph E. Bodovitz, the first executive director of both the temporary and then the permanent coastal commission. Making sure the commission had the legislative support it needed in budgeting, staffing, and related matters kept him busy during what remained of 1976.

In January of the following year, as the new commission got up and running, Douglas was promoted to deputy director, a position he would hold until 1985. This meant an important shift in his focus and duties, from those of legislative liaison to those of administrator. As the coastal commission underwent a change in leadership at the top, from Bodovitz to Michael L. Fischer in March 1978,[93] Douglas, who was then transferred to the San Francisco office, continued handling duties and responsibilities that both included and went beyond those expected of the deputy director. These entailed overseeing the commission's legislative program, representing the agency before both houses of the Sacramento lawmaking body, and managing the commission's relationships with other state agencies and its public participation functions.[94] Douglas's involvement with setting up a planning retreat for senior staff fell within the scope of his heavy workload. His agenda for the all-day retreat for April 3, 1981, provides a glimpse into the deputy director's penchant for injecting a tincture of wry humor into an otherwise demanding day of planning. An excerpt from the agenda reads as follows:[95]

Proposed Agenda for Retreat

9:00–10:30 What should our goals be? (What do we hope to see accomplished 20 years from now?) Should we have short-term goals and long-term goals? If so, what should they be?

10:30–12:00 What should our objectives be? (Travis will provide an erudite discussion of the differences between goals and objectives. Generally, objectives should be defined as the means for achieving our goals.)

12:00–1:00 Lunch (Bring your own and be prepared to explain why the Byzantine Empire survived for 800 years without ever having established any goal or objectives.)

In addition to undertaking considerable and diverse management tasks, Douglas served the commission in another capacity too, one that is perhaps less apparent than others but equally important: he was the agency's repository of its short institutional memory. With Bodovitz gone and Fischer new to his post, Douglas embodied what little continuity existed as the reins of commission leadership changed hands.

Of greatest importance, deputy director Douglas would be instrumental in helping the commission survive the draconian budget and staff cuts (discussed in chapter 5) that loomed in the near future, the declining morale of commission staffers,[96] and public disenchantment with the commission. For good reason, he feared that if the Coastal Act's provisions requiring developers of large properties to assure affordable housing were not removed—with the help of the commission yet—then conservative legislators in Sacramento would force the weakening or even the entire deletion of other provisions in that law.[97] Indeed, commission opponents succeeded in securing amendments to the Coastal Act that removed any mandate that builders provide middle- and low-income housing in large subdivisions.[98] Worse still, the public's regard for the commission declined. What had started as an idealistic movement to preserve the coast had morphed, in many people's eyes, into a faceless bureaucracy buried in paperwork and minutiae. UC Irvine professor Judy Rosener, a former commissioner and an expert on the agency, opined in 1978 that "after three or four years, any agency begins to lose its momentum."[99] A Field Poll conducted in September 1980 found that only half the people sampled (down from 55 percent in a poll taken five years earlier) had even heard of the Coastal Commission, and a majority of those aware of the agency rated its performance "fair" or "poor."[100]

Governor Brown became unhappy with the agency, and growing dissatisfaction with the commission registered in the state legislature. When the commission took legal action against musician Linda Ronstadt, Brown's then-girlfriend, and her Malibu neighbors for building an unpermitted seawall, the governor fumed. In the aftermath of the Malibu-Agoura fire that destroyed several waterfront homes, some commission staffers announced that victims of the blaze might have to assure public beach access in order to obtain permits to rebuild their homes. With the 1978 gubernatorial election fast approaching, Jerry Brown blasted the commissioners as "bureaucratic thugs."[101] Such a public slap down, characteristic of Brown's capricious support for the commission, further discredited the besieged, young agency. From the governor's office to the statehouse, anger stalked the commission. Michael Fischer recalled, "People were fighting mad.... [S]tate legislators found it impossible to go to a cocktail party anywhere in the state and not find somebody who was pissed off at the Coastal Commission."[102] In 1981, more than sixty bills were introduced in the assembly and senate relating to the Coastal Commission; some aimed at significantly watering down the Coastal Act, and at least one provided for the abolition of the regulatory agency.[103]

Other miscellaneous woes added to the agency's travails. The six regional coastal commissions were terminated in July 1981, leaving the state commission with full authority and responsibility for reviewing Local Coastal Programs. Often understaffed, the state commission found that this added to the workload without endearing it to local officials. Nearly continuous

Republican opposition to the commission would have been even greater had it not been for Melvin Lane, whose stature within that party had given the agency some cover.[104] By the early 1980s, however, that highly regarded former commission chair supported the Alliance of Coastal Management, a property owners group that rebuked the panel for its unfriendly relations with local governments.[105] At the same time, Ellen Stern Harris, widely heralded as the "mother" of Proposition 20, decried the agency's failures to stand up to developers and to assure public access to beaches.[106]

In the face of these onslaughts, Douglas steeled his resolve and sharpened his resourcefulness, readying himself for a battle to protect the agency's very existence. According to Fischer, "Peter . . . said, 'Look I'm going to take this precious flower of the coastal commission and I'm going to carry it through this [Governor George] Deukmejian dark period, and it's going to be like a desert crossing. It's going to be a terrible time for us, but when we're through on the other side of the desert, we'll have this commission with its law intact to be able to blossom again." Fischer gave his deputy director "extraordinarily high marks" for handling this rescue mission.[107]

While Douglas battled to save the commission, Dr. Carlotta H. Mellon, Governor Brown's appointments secretary, assisted Fischer in securing two highly talented female appointees for the commission—Naomi Schwartz and Dr. Judy B. Rosener—in order to add some gender balance to the panel.[108] Schwartz later chaired the commission. In addition to being an expert on how administrative commissions function, Rosener was a prominent academic authority on the role of women in the workforce. "Women ask different questions than men and were pro-environment," she maintained. At Coastal Commission meetings held up and down the state's shoreline, Rosener and Schwartz shared a room together. "People [mistakenly] thought we were lesbians," chuckled Rosener.[109]

For seven years, during which stalwart commission chair Naomi Schwartz resigned, in part owing to the hostility of recently elected Governor Deukmejian toward the agency,[110] Douglas served as Fischer's understudy. This apprenticeship in coastal management, especially during a time of mounting business and local-government opposition to the commission, would one day pay big dividends for both the agency and its signal role in protecting California's shore, because it equipped Douglas for the even more demanding leadership role awaiting him.

High Tide

THE EXECUTIVE DIRECTOR YEARS

JUST BEFORE STEPPING DOWN as executive director of the Coastal Commission in July 1985, Michael Fischer appointed Peter Douglas as the acting chief of that agency. "You can't do that [make that appointment]," some commissioners charged. "Yes, I can; I just did," retorted Fischer.[1] The transfer of leadership, as this incident shows, was not without drama even though Fischer merely appointed Douglas to an interim position. Only the commissioners themselves, per the Coastal Act, could fill the vacant post on a lasting basis. Before Peter Douglas applied for the permanent position, the then commission chair Melvin Nutter warned him that the job was "permanently situated between the dog and the fire hydrant."[2] Undeterred, Douglas stayed in the running, with the result that the commissioners, by a split eight-to-four vote,[3] chose him as the agency's new head. Time would show that their choice was momentous.

Douglas ascended to such a responsible position at the worst time. Republican governor George Deukmejian (in office 1983–1991), a proponent of deregulation of business who believed the Coastal Commission should not exist, was well into his first term in office. Ronald Reagan, who saw government as the cause of America's problems, occupied the White House. Throughout the nation the political pendulum had swung to the right. This meant that the Coastal Commission's new executive director would have to adapt to stringent budgets, directives to close regional offices, staff downsizing, and mounting pressures from developers and their allies who wanted to build along California's shore. In such inauspicious circumstances, Douglas began what would be a tumultuous and historic twenty-six-year tenure as the state's titular coastal manager.

The term *bureaucrat,* often hurled derisively at the agency's new leader by opponents, was far off the mark. In many ways Douglas did not look, dress, or speak like a government administrator, nor did he ever fit the stereotype of a wonkish functionary. One former coastal commissioner, Susan McCabe, rightly saw Douglas as the "antibureaucrat" and, more than anything, as an "activist."[4] Assuredly, Douglas was a different kind of official, a highly resourceful and charismatic maverick on a mission to save California's coast from overdevelopment and for public access.

His visage was not that of a high-ranking civil servant. In dress, he donned a suit and standard necktie only when the occasion demanded it; otherwise he was known for his signature bolo ties, hiking pants, and Birkenstock sandals. Powerfully built and sporting a well-trimmed beard, this near six-footer was the picture of an outdoorsman. His slightly wrinkled and at times halfway untucked shirts contributed to the look of a busy man preoccupied with action over fashion and appearance.[5] He drove up and down the state in his vegetable-oil-powered Mercedes Benz, and he was known for occasionally interrupting drives along the coast "to stand in front of bulldozers operating without a permit."[6]

As in these externalities, in his persona he was very much the iconoclast and, in his politics, decidedly liberal. A freethinking intellectual and self-described child of 1960s California, he worked until the end of his life "at maintaining and maturing my idealism and commitment to service on behalf of people and Nature."[7] Both his writings and speeches on occasion evoked a mystical bond with nature, expressed in language at once poetic and compelling. Though Jewish, he did not practice that religion but was drawn instead to the more eclectic and unorthodox views of mythologist Joseph Campbell, who urged taking the heroes' journey to serve humankind and, in so doing, experiencing a life of "bliss."[8] Douglas's unorthodox description of himself as a "radical pagan heretic" was indeed apt.[9] His sacred sites were in nature: a cabin on the Smith River, coastal haunts, and desert solitudes. Susan Jordan, a prominent coastal activist and close friend of Douglas, saw him as "philosophical, devoted to protection of the planet, spiritual, and very brave."[10] According to his politically liberal view,[11] government had a strong role to play in securing basic human rights—especially when these were in conflict with individual property rights—and in safeguarding the natural environment. Douglas's weapon of choice in protecting the shore was the

FIGURE 9. Iconic photo of Peter Douglas capturing his resoluteness and love of wilderness. Photo courtesy of the California Coastal Commission.

Coastal Act, of which his knowledge seemed unmatched, said Flossie Horgan, former executive director of the Bolsa Chica Land Trust.[12]

At the same time that Douglas was an idealist and agent of social change, he was also a political pragmatist who had little use for ideologues and starry-eyed utopians. By the time he stepped up to the executive directorship of the commission, he had experienced firsthand how Sacramento worked and become highly adept as a political strategist. He knew when and how far to compromise in fighting for the shore, which, for him, meant always staying within the bounds of the Coastal Act. And, as will be shown, he nearly always obtained the critical seven-vote majority necessary for the twelve-member commission to get things done. His sense of high purpose was fortified by uncommon courage and leavened by his dry wit. Apropos of this, a sign in his San Francisco office read: "Be Bold. Eschew Pusillanimity!"[13] Also he had a cartoon on his wall of a crane trying to eat a frog; while the frog's head was perilously in the crane's mouth, the frog's front legs were squeezed tightly around the bird's neck making the swallowing of the amphibian impossible.[14] The caption read, "Never ever give up!" Former coastal commissioner Steve Blank characterized Douglas as a shrewd, bare-knuckled "Machiavellian political operator."[15] Nearly always facing a barrage of criticism from developers and their allies, Douglas invariably fought back boldly and effectively without being shrill. "He liked the fight; he loved argument and questioning things," said his younger son, Vanja Douglas.[16] Still, sometimes the commission staff urged their boss to "tone it down." Said Douglas, "My answer always was 'Why? Somebody's got to speak truth to power.'"[17] Generally, even his opponents and those commissioners who might have disagreed with him on various issues respected him for his abilities and commitment to the coast.[18]

At least one former coastal commissioner, attorney Esther C. Sanchez, told this writer that "Peter was stubborn [but] not in a bad way." Her view was that he "would not compromise the coast [because] once it's gone, it's gone." In battling developers, Douglas would "not go down without a fight," she asserted.[19] Former commission chair Rusty Areias and many others agreed, though Areias was not alone in criticizing Douglas for engaging in too many fights, some of which resulted in retaliatory budget cuts for the agency.[20]

Related to this last point, onetime commission chair Gary Giacomini faulted Douglas, whom he greatly admired, for not prioritizing issues that came before that agency. As executive director, Douglas seemed to devote nearly the same amount of time and energy to dealing with a permit for a single house in the Coastal Zone as to a large housing subdivision. "Many staffers and commissioners felt Peter should better pick his battles" given the always limited resources of time and money.[21]

The fact that Douglas was perceived as stubborn and a fighter, however, should not obscure another side of his complex personality: namely, that he could be amicable in dealing with developers and adept and constructive in reaching agreements with local government officials. A former officer with a major Orange County land development company recalled meeting with a tired Douglas in the latter's Sacramento office after normal work hours: "He seemed worn by his workload but was nevertheless courteous and a respectful listener to whatever I said."[22] Robert H. Burnham, former Newport Beach city attorney, related to this writer that on those occasions where the Coastal Commission staff refused to budge on matters, a meeting with Douglas, whom he characterized as "very bright," nearly always resulted in the executive director "cutting the proverbial Gordian Knot" in a way that was reasonable and consistent with the Coastal Act.[23] While describing Douglas as "brilliant," coastal commissioner Wendy Mitchell stressed that he was a "good negotiator . . . [who] knew how to make deals."[24]

Another feature of Douglas's leadership style, which some saw as a flaw, was his alleged authority problem—that is, his supposed unwillingness to view the commissioners en masse as his boss. Former commissioner McCabe said that while Douglas gave due regard to commissioners, he showed, for lack of a better word, little *deference* toward them. To her and some others, such as former Coastal Commission chair Steve Kinsey, he communicated no clear sense of to whom he was answerable in the state government bureaucracy.[25] Douglas's immediate predecessor in office, Michael L. Fischer, opined, "Peter didn't see his job as serving the Commission, he saw his job as serving the people of the State, whether the Commission agreed with him or not."[26] Former commissioner and panel chair Mary K. Shallenberger agreed.[27] Of course, Douglas knew that, since the commission had the power of appointment and dismissal of executive directors, he served at the pleasure of the commissioners.[28] He just did not *act* like he knew that. Though he was respectful and certainly did not go out of his way to alienate commissioners, it simply was not in him to genuflect, figuratively speaking, before anyone.

One way this deference/authority issue played out was in the matter of staff independence. As former commission chair Sara Wan notes, Douglas generally did not allow commissioners to intervene in the work of staff; for example, they were not to instruct personnel on what positions to take on issues and could not decide for staffers which issues should be investigated. Accordingly, to assure the independence of staff findings, Douglas discouraged communication between commissioners and staffers. Thus, to Wan, it was not a matter of Douglas refusing to recognize commissioners' authority over him but rather his insistence (like that of his predecessors) on the need for staff independence in the preparation of reports and recommendations. To her, Douglas's stand on staff independence did not mean "that he didn't know who his bosses were. He was being a good supervisor and making certain his staff could do their jobs without undue pressure."[29]

To the above profile of Douglas must be added integrity and frugality in his life and behavior. His sons and others attested to his practice of principled living—that is, being fair, hardworking, honest, compassionate, open, and consistent in one's own conduct and dealings with others.[30] A former city manager of Laguna Beach, Kenneth Frank, related an incident illustrative of this.[31] After the hotly contested permitting and building of the five-star Montage resort along that city's coast, the resort's officials arranged for the Coastal Commission to meet there on occasion. Douglas and the commissioners took advantage of the offer for meeting space. However, when presented with the option of a special, greatly reduced, *lodging* rate for government personnel, Douglas, speaking for himself and the commissioners, politely declined, staying instead at a nearby budget motel from where they could easily walk to the Montage meeting room. Douglas not only preached against materialism and what he regarded as luxury but, as this incident suggests, also lived the principles he espoused, as attested to by Frank, a Republican and defender of local prerogative over regulation.

In short, Douglas was a complex, brilliant, independent-minded, likeable (even charismatic), gutsy helmsman of a powerful state agency he helped create who seemed to fit no mold or stereotype. As a principled human being and coastal manager who could not be bought or controlled, he would steer the commission ably through the many political storms that lay ahead.

BUILDING AND MENTORING A STAFF

"My proudest accomplishment," wrote Douglas when looking back over his long career in coastal management, "is putting together such an excellent staff." He both recruited and screened job applicants, some of whom were activists. Douglas then mentored and empowered the ones he employed. Those not "team players" he eventually counseled out, along with those with "negative attitudes who were not cut out for this work."[32]

Naturally, building and training an expert staff took place within a political-financial context. Personnel had to be paid and salaries had to fall within the agency's modest budget for staff and operations. When Douglas became executive director of the Coastal Commission, Governor George Deukmejian had already cut the agency's staff by 40 percent and slashed the commission's budget (most of which went to staff salaries) by more than a third.[33] The cuts also forced the discontinuance of the agency's publication, *Coastal News*. In the budget year 1985–1986, total commission funds amounted to $7,047,000.[34] Douglas's own salary of $70,000 a year during the Deukmejian era reflected the austerity budget within which the commission had to work;[35] a good many staffers earned about half of that. Highly capable professionals applying for the competitive Coastal Commission jobs obviously were motivated by something other than a desire to get rich.

A good number of the 125 or so staff members were lawyers and public policy specialists; some were scientists.[36] Former coastal commissioner Shirley Dettloff commended the professionalism and commitment of the entire staff, saying she was especially impressed by the reliability of the scientific reports of Dr. John Dixon, the commission's lead ecologist.[37] Many, like him, had graduate and professional degrees. Among the materials Douglas distributed to them was a 145-page, stapled, paperback copy of *California Coastal Act of 1976*. Staffers highlighted, underlined, and did whatever else was necessary to master this foundational document. Familiarity with its contents was a basic requirement for staff.[38]

Douglas knew what is axiomatic among the most effective teachers: that the learning process is optimized by the building of a relationship between mentor and mentee. His responsibility was to build that relationship. To him, that meant being fair, listening to others, and remembering that "communication is a two-way endeavor, with listening more important than talking." Over the years, Douglas learned he had to "leave [his] ego at the door," and that teaching could not take place in a "command-and-control kind of way."[39] Though he evidently did not see himself as commanding and controlling, Gary Giacomini, an avowed friend and supporter of Douglas, said the executive director was "the Duke of Earl, who ran the commission with an iron hand," overseeing virtually every detail in staff reports.[40] Likewise, and using the same language, Rusty Areias affirmed that Douglas controlled staff "with an iron hand."[41] Others who worked closely with the executive director dispute this view.[42] Whether or not he micromanaged them, the chief clearly trained staff "to believe they should be independent" of commissioners and lobbyists.[43] Douglas's job, as he saw it, was to inspire staffers, helping them always to be clear about the agency's mission—namely, "to protect the coast for future generations, and to maximize opportunities for the public to use and enjoy the coast."[44] As Douglas's mentoring skills grew, so did his relationships with staffers. "They were a family, not just a bureaucracy," noted a former coastal program analyst for the commission.[45] Former commissioner Susan McCabe affirmed that he "gave his staff a sense of cause"; he referred to them, she said, as "coastal warriors."[46]

In a characteristic moment of self-reflection, Douglas acknowledged that when he had ascended to the executive directorship he had had little of the patience required for mentoring and carrying out his other responsibilities.[47] Drawing perhaps on his undergraduate work in psychology and on the precious mentoring provided him in Germany by retired high school teacher Henri Lohrengel (see chapter 1), Douglas gradually learned patience.

As a result of Douglas's own growth as a leader and manager, the Coastal Commission staff functioned at the high level necessary to carry its workload of cases. This seems to have been true even during the most trying years, when governors and legislators unfriendly to the work of the agency cut budgets, thereby forcing staff reductions, the closure of the Eureka office, and use of outmoded computers and other dated equipment. Through even the leanest times, Douglas and the staff somehow carried out the agency's mission. For example, in 1987 Governor Deukmejian ordered Douglas to close the commission offices in Santa Barbara and Santa Cruz. The recently installed executive director refused, contending that those closures would have prevented the agency and its staff from serving those critical regions, and that the governor lacked authority over an independent commission. "The offices remained open and[,] even though he tried to starve us out, we hung in there," declared Douglas.[48]

COASTAL BATTLES WAGED, WON, AND LOST

The fact that few, if any, California public agencies have been sued as frequently as the Coastal Commission attests to the centrality of high-stakes clashes over treasured real estate in the history of that regulatory body. For example, Pacific Legal Foundation attorney Ronald A. Zumbrun estimated that he had sued the commission about thirty times.[49] Controversy, often bitter and protracted, characterized every stage of the commission's development and operations from the 1970s through the first several years of the twenty-first century. With striking regularity, Peter Douglas's name popped up in the media coverage of these coastal battles that took place both in and out of courtrooms, largely over development and public access. Like an admiral tasked with defending his government's vulnerable coast, he strategized and deployed his usually outgunned forces with uncanny skill, winning far more conflicts than he lost.

Each battle waged by the commission during Douglas's tenure is both a story in itself and a part of the larger narrative of that agency's fight to save California's shore from unrestrained development and to ensure open beaches. Some of the clashes have been of such complexity and duration that entire volumes could and should be written about them. Such accounts, however meritorious, would likely be too narrowly focused to provide a comprehensive view of Douglas's and the commission's management of coastal matters. Hence, the following attempt to provide broad, abbreviated coverage of twelve discrete, representative episodes that in both their singularity and coherence furnish grist for a history of commission battles on Douglas's watch. The episodes are arranged in rough chronological order based on when (the year is indicated in parentheses) each first came before the Coastal Commission.

Episode 1: Nollan v. California Coastal Commission *(1982)*

In the 1987 case of *Nollan v. California Coastal Commission,* the U.S. Supreme Court demarcated the commission's power to secure concessions from private property owners seeking coastal building permits for projects that demonstrably impeded or degraded a public interest.[50] The tribunal's ruling set a legal standard for determining when a state's regulatory power could be invoked to protect a public interest without violating the property protections of the Fifth and Fourteenth Amendments to the U.S. Constitution.

A synopsis of the facts is in order. In 1982, James and Marilyn Nollan, a married couple, sought and received a coastal development permit to replace their rundown bungalow on the Ventura coast with a larger, three-bedroom house. The permit, however, was conditioned on the Nollans' agreement to grant a lateral access easement across the front of their property to facilitate pedestrian transit to the public beaches just north and south of the private beach in front of their home. The Nollans claimed that such conditioning amounted to a taking without just compensation.[51]

A series of litigations followed. The Nollans (acting through James Nollan) challenged this condition in the Ventura County Superior Court, which remanded the case to the commission for a further hearing on evidence. As a consequence of the hearing, the commission upheld the condition, reasoning that by blocking public views of the beach, the new and larger house would impose a psychological barrier to shoreline access. Contending that an easement could not be conditioned unless the commission could prove that the replacement home blocked beach access, the Nollans took their case to the Court of Appeal, which upheld the commission. On further appeal, the Nollans' case came before the U.S. Supreme Court, which in a landmark five-to-four decision in 1987 ruled in favor of the plaintiff.[52]

What made this ruling historic? First, the Supreme Court set a standard for legitimizing conditioned permitting of development. The court majority reasoned that there had to be an "essential nexus" or close connection between a commission-imposed condition and the public interest to be served. In the Nollan case, declared the tribunal, that connection was too loose: that is, the blockage of the public's view of the ocean from the street behind the Nollan's property had little, if anything, to do with impeding public beach access. Thus, requiring an easement in front of the Nollan house did nothing to correct for any loss of public view. Absent an "essential nexus" the commission could not condition the issuance of coastal development permits without justly compensating property owners for meeting the required condition.[53] The court ruled that without just compensation, the imposition of such an easement would be a taking of property in violation of the Fifth and Fourteenth Amendments' guarantee against such expropriations. Conditioning a permit under such circumstances would constitute an "out-and-out plan of extortion," averred Justice Antonin Scalia, speaking for the court majority. Second, the profound impact of this decision is clearly seen in its subsequent application to the issuance of building permits nationwide. Douglas foresaw this several months before the Supreme Court ruled in the case. If the Nollans prevailed, he warned, "this case will likely have major ramifications for every state and local government in the country."[54]

In California, coastal property owners and their defenders understandably heralded the Nollan decision as a victory for them and a defeat for the Coastal Commission. The *Los Angeles Times* noted, "Developers scored a big victory last June [1987], when the high court ruled [in the Nollan case] that the California Coastal Commission could not force a land owner to allow the public to cross his property in exchange for getting a building permit."[55] The *San Francisco Chronicle* captioned an article on the Nollan case: "Beach Access Law—Property Rights Wins a Ruling in Top U.S. Court."[56] The formidable Pacific Legal Foundation, which handled the Nollan lawsuit against the Coastal Commission, counted the court verdict among the foundation's "Top Ten Victories" for homeowners and property-rights advocates.[57]

This case had been working its way through the court system when Douglas assumed his duties as executive director of the commission. Politically savvy, he saw that in the Reagan era of the 1980s the commission would be dealing with courts that had swung to the right in favor of developers and property owners, and away from defending the broader public interest. Looking back on the Nollan decision from the 1990s, Douglas lamented its effect on the work of the Coastal Commission. "The Nollan decision, for the first time, established a bright line and direct nexus between project impacts and permit conditions that cannot feasibly be met.... The fact is, most public agencies do not have the fiscal or human resources needed to make the kind of showing the Nollan court [decision] now requires.... Since Nollan, the Coastal Commission and local coastal governments no longer seek offers to dedicate public access or public trail easements in 9.9 cases out of 10 that previously would have included such provisions."[58]

Douglas perceptively saw this swing to the right against land use regulations as more than a temporary shift in the political winds. To him, the Nollan case and others that same year marked a turning point,[59] akin to a sea change, in how the courts, at all levels, began raising nearly insurmountable legal barriers to governmental land use regulation.

Episode 2: Malibu and Beach Access (1983)

Santa Barbara, Malibu, Laguna Beach, and La Jolla: these scenic, recreational Southland beaches are known internationally and are especially popular among surfers, skimboarders, swimmers, volleyball enthusiasts, and others. Assuring public access to these storied beaches has, at times, been a thorny and protracted problem since at least the mid-twentieth century. Of these locales, Malibu has doubtlessly been the most controversial and garnered the most media attention nationwide. Though the building of hillside homes in Malibu has pitted wealthy, property-owning local celebrities against the Coastal Commission, the focus here will be on beach access. This is because that issue involves a much larger public and goes to the heart of the commission's mandate, emblazoned in Proposition 20 and the Coastal Act, to provide citizens with a shore they can visit.

Malibu (especially Paradise Cove) began to attract increasing public attention after the release of the Hollywood coming-of-age surfing movie, *Gidget,* in 1959. At the same time, a number of highly paid actors and screen executives purchased or built large beach houses in what rapidly became an enclave of celebrity exclusivity. Against this backdrop of rising numbers of beachgoers and escalating home prices in the 1950s and 1960s, the problem of public beach access in Malibu festered, becoming more and more intractable. As noted (chapter 4), when coastal protection activist Ellen Stern Harris drove through Malibu with her children in the late 1960s her kids complained about not being able to see the beach because of built structures. A nearly unbroken wall of homes and other developments on the ocean side of Pacific Coast Highway blocked sea views from that thoroughfare. To keep out the most determined beachgoers, homeowners put up signs warning "No Trespassing" and "Private Property," while deploying private security guards to discourage, if not prevent, public access to the shore. By law, that shore belonged to the public seaward from the mean high-tide line. But this meant little when walking routes to the public area were barred by signs and impassable gates, which was often the case.

Perhaps the most illustrative example of a homeowner's unwillingness to allow public use of Malibu's surf and sand in front of his house was that involving Hollywood music mogul, billionaire, and philanthropist David Geffen. His adversarial interactions with the Coastal Commission regarding the remodeling of his Malibu mansion at scenic Carbon Beach can be traced back to 1983; the matter was not resolved until 2005. In the former year, Geffen entered an agreement with the commission by which he signed an "offer to dedicate" (OTD) an easement "to the People of California or the [Coastal] Commission's designee" that would give the public vertical (perpendicular to the ocean) and lateral access to the shore.[60] If not activated or implemented, the OTD would expire within twenty-one years. He, in turn, received a conditioned permit to build his imposing Cape Cod-style compound.[61] In 1991 and 2000 the commission issued two additional development permits for the same Malibu property, which were likewise conditioned on Geffen signing two more easement OTDs. Again, Geffen signed those documents.

For the next nineteen years, during which Geffen's house was remodeled on four contiguous beachfront lots and owner-occupied, the commission refrained from pursuing public access to the beach in front of his home, located in the 22100 block of Pacific Coast Highway. This was because neither Geffen nor any public agency agreed to maintain and pay the liability insurance required to activate the easement. During that nearly two-decade interim, Geffen blocked public access to the nine-foot-wide contested easement by installing locked gates at both ends of the transit corridor. In 2002 the easement OTDs were slated to expire. The Coastal Commission decided early that year to push for public beach access at ten exclusive Malibu enclaves, beginning with Geffen's property.[62] On January 16, Steve Hoye, director of Access for All, a nonprofit entity in Malibu that battled for opening beaches in the city and maintained points of public access, accepted Geffen's OTDs and entered an agreement with the Coastal Commission and the California Coastal Conservancy to manage both the vertical and lateral easements granted by Geffen. Accordingly, Access for All developed a Public Access Easement Management Plan to operate the prospective walkway from Pacific Coast Highway to the beach from dawn to dusk. Meanwhile, Geffen attempted to void his OTDs by filing and hoping to win a lawsuit against the defendants: the Coastal Commission, the State Coastal Conservancy, and Access for All.[63] His lawyers contended that public access constituted an unlawful taking under the Fourteenth Amendment, that the state had not conducted an environmental review of the proposed public pathway, and that Access for All lacked the financial resources to manage a public right-of-way across his property.[64] A legal battle lasting nearly three years ensued, pitting Geffen, joined by the City of Malibu for a time, against the parties just listed above.

The court feud became more complicated when in late April 2002 Geffen's next-door neighbors on the west side, John M. and Mary Ann K. Heidt, attempted to join the lawsuit in an effort to void the easement, which would have allegedly compromised their privacy. Their home, they said, was situated less than twenty feet from the public easement in question. The Heidts complained that they had never received notice that the commission had accepted Geffen's OTDs, nor a copy of Access for All's plan for managing the easement in question. On June 30, 2003, the trial court ruled that the Heidts would not be permitted to intervene because the issues they raised were "far different [from Geffen's] and will greatly enlarge the issue that must be resolved in this case." To protect their interests, said the court, the Heidts would need to file a separate action.[65] On November 6, the Heidts appealed the trial court's ruling, arguing that they had a "direct and immediate interest" in the ongoing litigation. The Court of Appeal on April 25, 2005, upheld the trial court's ruling denying the couple the right to be a party to Geffen's lawsuit against the defendants.

With the Heidts ineligible to participate in the litigation under way, Geffen, through his attorneys, continued his pitched court battle against the defendants in an all-out effort to nullify the OTDs of 1983, 1991, and 2000. Geffen's attorneys submitted six petitions and complaints to the trial court in the years 2002–2005. The defendants invariably demurred, with the result that the plaintiff made little headway in his effort to annul the OTDs.

Finally, in mid-April 2005 Geffen capitulated, for unspecified reasons, by dropping his lawsuit against the defendants, agreeing to reimburse the state three hundred thousand dollars for legal costs, and giving Mr. Hoye a gate key, thereby allowing public use of the easement. A thirty-five-thousand-dollar grant from the Coastal Conservancy funded Access for All's management of the pedestrian right-of-way. On Memorial Day, May 30, happy beachgoers began traversing their new walkway to surf and sand, quickly and wryly nicknamed by locals "the Hooray for Hollywood Moguls path."[66] Clearly, the Coastal Commission had won a major victory for beach access in one of the Golden State's toniest shorefront communities.

While Geffen and his spokesman, Steven Amerikaner, refused to comment on the out-of-court settlement, some beachgoers expressed jubilation. Jayna Mims, a young mother living nearby on the inland side of Pacific Coast Highway, used the recently opened beach access route alongside Geffen's estate accompanied by her eight-month-old son, Ryder. She praised environmentalists and government officials for holding the media titan to his promise made decades earlier to provide a public pathway to the beach. "Thank you, guys. Now I can get to the beach," she exulted, as Ryder gleefully dug his feet into the sand.[67]

Douglas, whom Malibu supporters of Geffen saw as too insistent on public beach access, was likewise highly pleased with the outcome. "It's huge," said the coastal agency's chief, "that a guy with his [Geffen's] resources—who brought all those to bear to fight the public's right to go to the beach—to have him back off is a strong signal to everybody out there who is holding out and resisting or trying to prevent the public from exercising their right to go to the beach. We're going to pursue these access ways as vigorously as we can."[68]

Significantly, the triumph for beach access in this episode deservedly brought credit to the commission and its intrepid leader. Still, many more Malibu battles involving megarich glitterati awaited Douglas and the agency he led.

Episode 3: Opening the Jonathan Club to Women and Minorities (1985)

In the same year that Douglas ascended to the Coastal Commission's executive directorship, 1985, he and the agency took a strong stand for nondiscriminatory membership in a bastion of white male affluence and exclusivity, Los Angeles's Jonathan Club. Founded in 1894 by Republican supporters of President William McKinley, its roster of membership-by-invitation-only included Southern California business magnate and arts patron Henry Edward Huntington. The club's website declares, "Jonathans [as members are called] Edward Dickson and Ernest Moore conceived the idea of [founding] UCLA over lunch in the fall of 1917. Never underestimate the power of lunch at the Club!"[69] In short, this organization provided a gathering place for the city's corporate and government elite where business was transacted in an elegant, sequestered setting.

The club owned and operated a facility on the beach in Santa Monica. For years the City of Santa Monica had chided the club for allegedly not admitting Jews, women, and nonwhites as members. In the 1980s the club set out to expand its footprint on, and exclusive use of, a publicly owned beach in Santa Monica. The effort landed it in the crosshairs of Douglas and the commission, eventuating in a U.S. Supreme Court decision spotlighting and linking the issues of public beach access and social justice.[70]

The ostensibly unrelated issues of the club's expansion and membership policy arose in 1984, when, in response to Jonathan Club plans for extending its Santa Monica facility onto state-owned beach, the California State Lands Commission agreed to a lease. Next, the club would need a building permit from the Coastal Commission. That's when the episode, owing to the raising of social justice issues, took a dramatic turn into uncharted legal territory.[71]

In January 1985, Santa Monica's Planning Commission grudgingly approved a permit allowing the Jonathan Club to expand its site footprint. The club's remodel called for, among other things, a new exercise room, lockers, an elevator, paddle tennis courts, a children's pool, a pro shop, and an outdoor bar—in all a 13,664-square-foot-expansion at its beachfront property.[72] Simultaneously, that planning group voted to send a letter to the Coastal Commission stating that the club's membership policy may affect the public's beach access at the site.

Since public beach access is protected in the Coastal Act, Douglas put his mind to work on how to condition a Coastal Development Permit so that permission for a private organization's expansion plans would require a nondiscriminatory membership policy. In other words, he needed to formulate a compelling answer to the question: Could the Coastal Act be invoked to end discrimination in a private club? Douglas came up with the theory that the U.S. Constitution's Equal Protection Clause (in the Fourteenth Amendment) could be used to leverage the Coastal Act's definition of "public access" so as to force a change in the club's membership policy.[73] With the state attorney general's office highly skeptical about the likelihood of this theory prevailing in court, Coastal Commission staffer Nancy Cave reluctantly began the process of issuing a permit *unrelated* to the Jonathan Club's membership policy.

Douglas, nevertheless convinced that his theory would work, but realizing that he needed a way to test it without putting the credibility of the staff at risk, hatched a veiled, behind-the-scenes strategy to deploy his idea. Unknown to Cave and other staffers, he spoke confidentially to a few key coastal commissioners, telling them about his theory and urging *them* to press the discrimination issue regarding the Jonathan Club's expansion proposal. That way the staff would not be risking defeat, because it would seem that the commissioners were raising the controversial discrimination issue. This back-channel maneuver worked. Accordingly, on July 25, 1985, the day of the commission's permit hearing, only one person from the general public testified, saying, "I am David Lehrer[,] the Western States Counsel of the Anti-Defamation League of the B'nai B'rith. I'm testifying on behalf of the Asian Pacific American Legal Center, the Community Relations Council of the Jewish Federation Council of Greater Los Angeles, [and] the Los Angeles Chapter of the National Association for the Advancement of Colored People. . . . When the corporate and the political elite meet for lunch or dinner at a downtown club, and there is a long standing policy to exclude most visible minorities—women and Jews—from membership in that institution, a message is sent out to the community at large, that minorities and women are somehow not fit, not equal to those who are making decisions of moment. It is an anachronism which is ripe for change. It is particularly appropriate that the Coastal Commission consider the issue of social club discrimination as it deliberates on the application of the Jonathan Club."[74] Lehrer urged the commission to condition a permit on the club's ending of its discriminatory membership policy. Only then would that institution be allowed to expand onto state property.

When Commissioner Marshall Grossman questioned the club's attorney, Robert Philobosian, at the hearing as to whether his client organization discriminated against, blacks, women, or other minorities, the latter responded, "The issue is simply not before this body, and the issue is not within the purview of the Coastal Commission." Philobosian did not deny that the club discriminated. Grossman then displayed a 1981 article appearing in *Los Angeles Magazine,* which featured interviews with Jonathan Club members. One such member was quoted as saying, "Too much is made about this thing with Jews. A few of them are in now. And what about the thing with Blacks? God, if you think about it, everything is working in the Black's *[sic]* favor. One day the Clubs will probably have to take them. Some cockamamie law will probably mandate it."[75]

Except for the few commissioners Douglas had earlier advised, the other panelists were taken by surprise to find that permitting was being discussed in conjunction with an allegedly discriminatory and patently secret membership policy of a private club. Could the Coastal Act be used in this manner to compel a nondiscriminatory membership policy? asked commissioners. This time Deputy Attorney General Anthony Summers responded "Yes," marking a virtual reversal of his office's previous stance. Douglas expected this would occur, which perhaps explains why some of his colleagues have held that he could "see around corners"—that is, anticipate with a high degree of accuracy how complex matters would play out in both the political and the legal arenas.

Commissioner Grossman, who, at the behest of Douglas did so much to raise the issue of discrimination at the hearing, delivered in trenchant language what some witnesses described as the pivotal argument: "Many of you are not members of minority groups, and you don't know the feeling of walking by an institution and knowing it is really a symbol, a vestige of racism, of social discrimination. While racism and social discrimination is [sic] not the same as genocide, they are the seeds of genocide. It is in clubs like this, which are lily-white, all male bastions, free of the impure except for a chosen few, where prejudice is passed on from generation to generation. The kids grow up being served by blacks, being served and babysat by Hispanics, having their food cooked by Asians, but yet knowing that these people may not join as members, as they inherit memberships of their parents. The Jonathan Club can discriminate if it wants, but not at my expense. It cannot take public, sandy beach and public parking lots and convert them to its own use at my expense and discriminate against my kids. Public access means access for everybody."[76] In retrospect, Douglas said Grossman's testimony swayed the commissioners, who then voted nine to three to condition the club's permit so that discrimination could not be used in admitting members.[77]

Not surprisingly, the club mounted a vigorous legal challenge to the commission's decision. In October 1985, a trial court ruled that the commission *did* have the authority to impose the nondiscriminatory membership condition because the Coastal Act required maximum beach access to the public. Shocked, the club next took its case to the Court of Appeal, whose three judges upheld the lower tribunal's verdict. "They [the Jonathans] were furious," said Douglas,[78] and took the matter to the California Supreme Court. For reasons not entirely understood,[79] that tribunal refused to hear the case, letting the earlier verdicts against the club stand. As determined as ever, the club placed its case before the U.S. Supreme Court. Finally, on October 11, 1988, the nation's highest judicial body decided to let the verdicts of the lower courts prevail.[80] This meant that the Coastal Commission had succeeded in boldly applying the Coastal Act to compel a private organization leasing and using state-owned beach to admit members on a nondiscriminatory basis.

In the aftermath of these court decisions, the admission policy of the Jonathan Club (and San Francisco's Olympic Club, another bastion of exclusionary white male privilege) did in fact change owing to Douglas's and the commission's efforts. Gender, ethnicity, and religion could no longer serve as barriers to membership. Some years later Douglas and Coastal Commission personnel had a meeting at the Jonathan Club; among those in the audience were blacks and Latinos. The club's president, an Asian Jew, expressed gratitude for the changes that had occurred: "I wouldn't be a member of this club if it hadn't been for the Coastal Commission."[81]

Doubtlessly, a number of factors led to this outcome. Arguably the most pivotal of these was Douglas's bold and creative leadership. This was evidenced in his fresh interpretation of the Coastal Act and the finesse with which he quietly choreographed the opening scenes of the commission-hearing drama that unfolded in mid-1985. Up to that point in this episode, his interpretation of the Coastal Act had met with resistance only from the state attorney general's office. Not dissuaded by that initial resistance, as shown, he risked defeat and forged ahead. And won.

Episode 4: A Shameful Attempt to Fire Douglas (1991)

Common sense suggests that the head of a governmental agency tasked with regulating coastal development and assuring public access to the shore would be watched closely by builders and their political allies. This is particularly the case if the agency headed by that person is perceived as being too independent and beyond the control of moneyed interests. Such was the situation in 1991, when opponents of the Coastal Commission sought to fire Peter Douglas. Of the various attempts to remove him from office, this was the first, the murkiest, and arguably the most egregious.[82]

Coastal commissioners David Malcolm and Mark L. Nathanson, prodeveloper appointees of the Democratic assembly Speaker, Willie Brown, launched the effort. According to Douglas, Malcolm suggested to other commissioners that he had secret personal information on the executive director that was so damning it compelled his removal. According to reporter David Rolland, Douglas would not say what the accusation against him was, only that it was "a horrendous, outrageous charge" that "would have been, if true, a firing offense."[83]

Douglas later claimed that Malcolm and Nathanson had been after him for years, trying to get him to conform his staff recommendations to the desires of his two accusers. He had responded by telling the two commissioners that he would be happy to ask their fellow panelists if he should request that staff base their reports and recommendations on the opinions of particular commissioners. The two accusers backed away from that challenge but nonetheless hired an investigator to dig up dirt on Douglas. According to the latter, the investigator came up with nothing. Undaunted, Malcolm told several commissioners that he knew the accusations were true and that documents filed with the Marin County government would prove it.

Coastal commissioner and attorney Gary Giacomini, a strong Douglas supporter, perused the Marin County documents alluded to by Malcolm and Nathanson and found that those papers said "nothing about Douglas."[84] At the next commission meeting, Giacomini went up to Malcolm in the lobby and "took him apart," said Douglas. "They almost got into fisticuffs. People were just aghast because [Giacomini] was loud.... He just totally intimidated Malcolm—basically just beat him up verbally."[85]

As gratifying as that may have been for Douglas, he suffered under the stress of having his character attacked. "I can't do my work," Douglas told reporters shortly before the meeting about to be held at the Huntington Beach Civic Center on July 19. "The distraction and energy that have gone elsewhere in the last couple of weeks just has [sic] been incredibly draining for everybody."[86]

At that meeting commissioners took a vote on whether to reappoint or fire Douglas. Nathanson was absent. Malcolm was in the building but sent his alternate, Wes Pratt of San Diego, to vote on the regular commissioner's behalf. Interestingly, Pratt offered a motion to *reappoint* Douglas, and the motion carried unanimously, ten to zero. The vote of confidence ended what Douglas called "painful" weeks of "anxiety and distress."[87]

If vague and unsubstantiated "information" was not at the root of Malcolm and Nathanson's effort to remove Douglas, what else may have driven the two commissioners? A *Los Angeles Times* inquiry into the matter offers a major clue: reportedly Malcolm and Nathanson were greatly displeased that Douglas had earlier opposed "legislation that would permit the Walt Disney Co. to fill up to 250 acres of Long Beach shoreline for a proposed $3-billion theme resort and amusement park."[88]

So a highly plausible alternative explanation exists for the unspecified and unsubstantiated accusation against Douglas. The fact that Commissioner Giacomini's investigation was carried out by a pro-Douglas person arguably could render moot the finding of innocence. Beyond debate, however, are the verifiable facts in Douglas's defense that his accusers did not even vote on his job tenure and, more importantly, were not credible persons as shown by later developments. In 2003 Malcolm was convicted of illegal dealings while a member of the San Diego Port Commission. In the early 1990s Nathanson pled guilty to charges of racketeering, tax fraud, and bribery; he was convicted and sentenced to four years and nine months in prison and fined $200,000. Essentially, he had been taking bribes—allegedly extorting $250,000 from permit-seekers—in exchange for favorable Coastal Commission votes on various building projects.[89] Finally, the fact that the panel voted solidly in favor of retaining their chief shows their confidence in him and skepticism about the unsupported charges. Given all of this evidence, Douglas's exoneration and reappointment by the commission seem eminently reasonable and just.

This disreputable episode shows that the high-stakes disputes before the commission occasionally brought into play clashes between powerful developer interests and a formidable regulatory agency led by someone who could not be bought, intimidated, or controlled. In Douglas, the state of California had such an official, and the coastal commissioners and others who knew him recognized it.

Episode 5: The Marine Forests Lawsuit (1993)

Within a few years of fending off the personal attacks of David Malcolm and Mark Nathanson, Douglas and the commission became embroiled in a set of legal actions against the agency in which the stakes were even higher. These legal actions culminated in the pivotal 2005 California Supreme Court case of *Marine Forests Society v. California Coastal Commission.* The commission's constitutionality and, hence, the validity of its rulings since the 1970s were at issue. Two previous lower court decisions regarding this case had gone against the commission, whose efficacy was on the line in a trial reaching the state's highest tribunal.

The facts of the Marine Forests case are straightforward.[90] In 1988, Marine Forests Society, a nonprofit research corporation headquartered in Newport Beach, California, erected without the requisite commission permits a so-called reef on the ocean floor some three hundred yards seaward of the Balboa Peninsula. The stated purpose of the experimental artificial reef was to replace lost marine habitat. This underwater structure consisted of approximately fifteen hundred car tires, two thousand plastic milk containers, PVC pipe, nylon cordage, and concrete blocks. In 1993 the commission first learned about the project when the founding director of Marine Forests Society, Rudolph Streichenberger, sought to expand it.[91] Later that same year commission staff determined that the artificial reef was unpermitted development under the California Coastal Act and directed Marine Forests to submit an after-the-fact application for a permit. Two years later Marine Forests submitted an application for such a permit, which the commission denied in April 1997. Citing a *Los Angeles Times* article, executive director Douglas noted that marine biologists and a spokesperson for the California Department of Fish and Game considered this reef project "totally unscientific" and held that rubber tires made ineffective artificial reefs. In October 1999, after multiple attempts to resolve the dispute amicably, according to Douglas, the commission issued a "Notice of Intent to Commence Cease and Desist Order Proceedings" to get the underwater structure removed.[92]

In response to the notice, Marine Forests hired Pacific Legal Foundation attorney Ronald A. Zumbrun to ask the court to enjoin the commission from taking enforcement action against the corporation. By 2001, what had originated as a discrete coastal environmental issue in Orange County had suddenly morphed into a full-blown constitutional battle over the legitimacy of the commission itself and its prior rulings. On behalf of the plaintiff (Marine Forests), Zumbrun argued before the trial court that the commission had no authority to issue cease-and-desist orders, because such orders require exercising a judicial power, which, he contended, the commission did not possess since—in his opinion—it was exclusively a legislative agency. Moreover, Zumbrun reasoned, the commission lacked authority to issue, deny, or condition permits, because doing so involved exercising executive power. Both the commission's issuance of cease-and-desist orders and its permitting functions, Zumbrun held, violated the California Constitution's provision regarding the separation of powers.[93]

The case hinged on Zumbrun being able to demonstrate before the court that the commission, created by the state legislature, operated solely as an agency of that lawmaking body. In making that case, Zumbrun noted that eight of the commission's twelve voting members were appointed by the Speaker of the assembly and the Senate Rules Committee, and these appointees could be removed by the legislature. This argument, relying on the appointive structure of the commission, prevailed. The trial court decided in favor of the plaintiff, granting Marine Forests an injunction against the commission's cease-and-desist order. Thereby, the commission was prevented from issuing or denying permits and promulgating cease-and-desist orders. In 2002 the commission took its case to the 3rd District Court of Appeal, which upheld the trial court's verdict.

In response to the appellate court's decision, senate president pro tem John Burton persuaded Governor Gray Davis to call the state legislature into an immediate session in 2003 to amend the Coastal Act in order to fortify it against separation-of-powers challenges.[94] The amendments stipulated that the commissioners appointed by the Speaker of the assembly and the Senate Rules Committee now had four-year terms in office and could no longer be removed at the pleasure of the legislative appointing authority. In effect, the changes in the law rendered the commission more independent of the state legislature than previously had been the case.

With the Coastal Act so amended, the commission then brought its case before the California Supreme Court. The tribunal decided that, just as the lower courts had rendered verdicts based on the Coastal Act as it was worded at the times of the earlier trials, similarly the high court's ruling in Marine Forests would be based on the provisions of that amended law as it was written in 2005, at the time that case came up for adjudication before the state Supreme Court. In the words of Chief Justice Ronald George: "Our determination of the validity of the judgment granting injunctive relief necessarily rests upon our assessment [of the Coastal Act] as it presently exits."[95] Also, the high court held that the separation of powers clause in the state constitution, as opposed to the counterpart clause in the U.S. Constitution, would govern its judgment.

Thus, focusing on the separation of powers clause in the state constitution, the court concluded that rather than impermeable boundaries separating executive, legislative, and judicial functions, "the substantial interrelatedness of the three branches' action is apparent and commonplace."[96] The then current appointing structure of the commission was found not to intrude illegally into the proper functions of the three branches of state government. No judgment was made regarding the constitutionality of the commission's roughly one hundred thousand vulnerable prior rulings on permits and other matters. Hence, there was no finding that past and pending commission decisions were or would be invalid. The injunction that the Court of Appeal had granted was, in effect, voided. Marine Forests then appealed the verdict to the U.S. Supreme Court, which declined to hear the case.[97] Consequently, the California Supreme Court's decision was final. With a host of major issues pending before the commission, including offshore oil drilling and the siting of liquefied natural gas terminals and desalination plants along the coast, the state Supreme Court's finding was especially timely and would influence coastal policy for decades afterward.[98] In short, the commission had been saved by a unanimous verdict of the state's highest court.

Predictably, the responses of the contending parties were quite different. James Burling, an attorney with the Pacific Legal Foundation, was gravely disappointed: "I thought we would have some members of the court going our way."[99] Zumbrun complained, "[Marine Forests] should have been dealt with under the old law, not the new law." He said he was "just shocked by some of the analyses" in the opinion. The commission chair, Margaret Caldwell, praised the court's verdict "for removing the cloud of uncertainty over the commission's decisions and statutes." When asked how he felt about the outcome, Peter Douglas responded, "Relieved, greatly relieved. . . . [With] all of the threats facing the coast, one simply cannot underestimate the enormity of this decision."[100]

The significance of this episode is that it revealed the very legitimacy of the Coastal Commission could not be taken for granted at times, especially given the Pacific Legal Foundation's mission and courtroom clout. While trying to carry out its mandate, the Coastal Commission would seemingly forever be fending off attacks from businesses that could reliably count on the services of the Pacific Legal Foundation, a nonprofit, public interest law firm committed to property rights litigation. Occasionally, as in this instance, the commission would have to call in support from the governor's office and Sacramento legislators.

Episode 6: Bolsa Chica Wetland (1995) and Another Attempt to Fire Douglas (1996)

While the stakes in Marine Forests were higher, in Huntington Beach a longer-lasting and far more contentious legal battle loomed over the building of houses on the periphery of the Bolsa Chica Wetland, one of Southern California's last relatively undeveloped coastal estuaries. To Douglas, the battle ended in a major defeat for the commission,[101] instanced another major attempt to dismiss him, and resulted in a major victory for the Coastal Act. A dispute associated with such a mix of disparate outcomes requires some explaining.

The tortuous, ongoing Bolsa Chica controversy spanned more than three decades, going back to the mid-1970s, when developers sought to build a marina on the wetland.[102] By the early 1980s the development plan additionally called for fifty-seven hundred residential units, thirteen hundred boat slips, a road bisecting the wetland, and a 150-room hotel. Signal Landmark Holdings, the developer, in return for the prospect of receiving the requisite permits, offered to provide the public with 950 acres of "high quality" marshland.[103] In 1989 the marina plan was shelved, and the building of residential units on the Bolsa Chica lowlands and an adjacent upland mesa became the central focus of stakeholders in the area's future. The major players in this protracted, complex dispute were the wetland preservationist groups Amigos de Bolsa Chica and the Bolsa Chica Land Trust, Huntington Beach city councilpersons, a succession of developers whose businesses were spinoffs or affiliates of Signal Landmark, the Wildlife Conservation Board, Surfrider Foundation, Sierra Club, the Shoshone-Gabrieliño Nation, the Juaneño Band of Mission Indians (Acjachemen Nation), and the California Coastal Commission.

In December 1995, Douglas and his staff had issued a report that analyzed, and recommended denial of, the proposal of Koll Real Estate Group—a Signal spinoff—to build nine hundred homes on the lowlands, on the grounds that such development did not conform to the Coastal Act. Koll also planned to build twenty-four hundred homes on an adjoining upland mesa. For mitigation, Koll offered to restore a separate part of the degraded salt marsh.[104] This had not been acceptable to Douglas and his staff, and they recommended against approval. Nevertheless, in January 1996 the commission approved, by an eight-to-three vote, the entire thirty-three-hundred-home Koll project.[105] The commission's executive director was greatly displeased by this decision. Douglas did not believe the commission could prevent *all* home construction on the lowlands, since, in his opinion, the courts would strike down such a prohibition as an unconstitutional "taking" that would result in the imposition of financial damages on the meagerly funded regulatory agency. Thus preservationist groups would have to accept some development there, but not the excessive number of homes panelists had approved.[106] The commission's 1996 approval touched off a legal firestorm that came to a head three years later.

While the tempestuous Bolsa Chica imbroglio dragged on, Douglas's Republican enemies sought to fire him. In May 1996, during Pete Wilson's governorship, the bipartisan commission for the first time had a Republican majority, consisting of eight of the agency's twelve voting members. The GOP takeover of the state assembly, whose Speaker—Kurt Pringle—had the power to appoint four of the commission's members, made possible the agency's new Republican majority.[107] Developers, who had long bridled under the Coastal Act's regulations and Douglas's leadership, finally had a commission friendly to their interests. (It must be noted that Democrats, too, were occasionally solicitous of developer interests and, as noted, tried on at least one occasion—in 1991—to unseat Douglas.) Before their appointments to the commission, at least two of Pringle's new appointees—Arnold Steinberg and Patricia Randa—had battled the agency for years in efforts to obtain permits for construction on their respective family properties in the Santa Monica Mountains.[108] Both Steinberg and Randa believed the commission, particularly under Douglas's executive directorship, had been insufficiently protective of private property rights. Not for the first time, nor likely the last, Douglas's job was on the line.

In the wake of the commission's approval of the Koll project in Bolsa Chica, the new Republican-dominated agency, encouraged by the state resources secretary, Douglas Wheeler,[109] sought Peter Douglas's removal in July 1996. GOP pollster Arnold Steinberg, newly appointed to the commission, said he wanted to "reform" that agency. "It is reasonable to ask whether a new executive director would be better able to do that."[110] Attorney Joseph Gughemetti, a litigator who battled the Coastal Commission many times on behalf of property owners, complained that the agency's staff "was very environmentally oriented. It's a nightmare." Douglas should go, he urged, and be replaced by someone more probusiness.[111] Accordingly, commission Republicans, led by chair Louis Calcagno, called for a special closed-door meeting on July 12 in Huntington Beach "to clear the air" about Douglas's continued employment and take steps, if deemed necessary, to seek his replacement. Calcagno told this writer in 2016 that he "did not want to fire Douglas," as he doubted commissioners would have had the votes to succeed, and that if they did sack Douglas it would hurt Republican prospects in future elections.[112] Wheeler mentioned that his former deputy, Carol Whiteside, was a replacement candidate for Douglas's job.[113]

Did Douglas's actions really warrant losing his job? When asked in 2016 by the author whether Douglas *deserved* to be fired in 1996, Calcagno declined to answer the question directly. What the Republican commissioner tasked with firing Douglas said long after the event may help readers make up their own minds about what Calcagno thought of this matter in hindsight: "He [Douglas] was probably the right man for the right time. . . . During his tenure he did uphold the Coastal Act to the highest standards possible. . . . He had a major good impact on the coast of California." Asked whether public enjoyment of the coast would have been significantly affected by Douglas's removal, Calcagno replied, "Beach access would be less." Recalling the Bolsa Chica controversy, Calcagno remarked, "Peter Douglas was trying to do his job. He allowed the fewest number of homes built, which was a good outcome." Then,

FIGURE 10. Louis Calcagno in his Moss Landing home, 2016. Calcagno expressed his gratitude for the role played by Peter Douglas and the Coastal Commission in nixing a housing development that would have wiped out the beauty of a nearby hillside visible through Calcagno's living room window. Photo by the author.

looking out the large window in the living room of his Moss Landing home, Calcagno appreciatively pointed to the lush green hill sloping down to Elkhorn Slough, which abuts his property, and expressed gratitude to the Douglas-led Coastal Commission for "preserving this whole area."[114]

The plan to fire Douglas, orchestrated by developer-friendly, high-ranking Republican officials and implemented by their subalterns on the commission, galvanized into action the executive director's many supporters throughout the state. Douglas knew the public was with him, and he planned his defense accordingly. In an interview, he warned that his removal would destroy the commission's independence and undermine the effectiveness of the Coastal Act to save California's shore. He faxed commissioners a letter requesting that the meeting about his future be held in public in accordance with his right under state law. Former state legislators Alan Sieroty and John Dunlap met with Governor Wilson, urging him to help Douglas keep his position.[115] Newspapers throughout the state editorialized in favor of him retaining his job, and messages from 250 Democratic and Republican elected officials across the state urged the commission to keep Douglas in office.[116] For example, Republican state assemblymen Brooks Firestone (Santa Barbara) and Bruce McPherson (Santa Cruz) jointly stated, "We agree that without the stewardship of Mr. Douglas, the people of California will lose the tremendous institutional memory and experience he brings to the commission." Similarly, U.S. Senator Barbara Boxer supported Douglas retaining his job.[117]

Hundreds of angry protesters attended the Huntington Beach July hearing in support of Douglas, who "rose at the front of the hall and, Moses-like, raised his arms for quiet. The crowd instantly hushed, allowing the meeting to proceed."[118] Pringle's appointees, who were inclined to fire Douglas, backed down, and Calcagno did not call for a vote on the agency chief's dismissal. This was despite strong pressure via a profanity-laced directive from one of Governor Wilson's staffers ordering Calcagno to topple Douglas.[119] Consequently, the besieged administrator remained at his post. "I am personally humbled and awed by the tremendous support for my leadership," he told the attendees. They responded by giving the executive director a standing ovation.[120]

How could this have happened? "He has a cult-like following," complained Steinberg after having gone off the commission himself. "His boosters feel anyone besides Peter would be a threat to the environment. But I think he's been there too long."[121] Former coastal commissioner Ellen Stern Harris noted that Douglas, who had just received "excellent marks" in an official performance review and had just been awarded a raise, had been saved by what she called "People Power"—that is, the high regard that vocal activists had for him.[122] One reason, among many, that these vocal activists had this high regard was that they knew the agency's chief and his staff had gone on record opposing the extensive Koll real estate development project proposed for the nearby Bolsa Chica Wetland.

Douglas and his adviser throughout this firing ordeal, commission chief counsel Ralph Faust, accounted for the failed dismissal in a way that did not contradict other views but at the same time stressed the incompetence of those orchestrating the attempted coup. Said Faust, "My impression was that they were simply inept. Peter characterized them as 'the gang that couldn't shoot straight.' They did not coordinate their actions well, did not appear to have a clear strategy, and seemed to shy away from the media spotlight that Peter had helped create with his insistence on a public hearing."[123] Whether one of these somewhat overlapping explanations or a combination of them best explains the outcome reached, this signal triumph had to have been one of the salient and most gratifying moments in Douglas's long career.

FIGURE 11. The Bolsa Chica Wetland and its meandering waterways. Photo courtesy of Jane Lazarz of the Bolsa Chica Land Trust.

While the beleaguered executive director had survived in office, the Bolsa Chica issue made its way into the court system in the late 1990s, fueling even more conflict and leading to a watershed legal decision.[124] Dismayed by the commission's 1996 approval of Koll's bid to build up to thirty-three hundred homes on the Bolsa Chica lowlands and upland mesa, lawyers Paul C. Horgan, Deborah A. Cook, and Philip A. Seymour—jointly representing the Bolsa Chica Land Trust, Sierra Club, Surfrider Foundation, Shoshone-Gabrieliño Nation, and Huntington Beach Tomorrow—won a Court of Appeal decision that protected the wetland, a nearby pond, and a eucalyptus grove on the upland mesa. This 1999 ruling set a legal precedent: in accordance with the court's interpretation of the California Coastal Act, developers' housing projects could not disturb environmentally sensitive habitat areas.[125]

Though this decision marked a major defeat for the Coastal Commission, which had approved the development over the objections of Douglas and staff, it bolstered the clout of the Coastal Act. The defeat resulted from political overreach: the commissioners had approved a project without any of the necessary legal findings required by the Coastal Act. Consequently, the litigation and the court's ruling actually enhanced the law by underscoring and enforcing its prohibition on development in environmentally sensitive habitat areas. Afterward, and later, near the end of his life, Peter Douglas privately expressed approval of the commission's defeat because ultimately the Coastal Act was strengthened.[126] For coastal stewards like him, therein lies the significance of the Bolsa Chica episode.

There was another positive outcome of this episode as well. In the aftermath of this historic court decision, a major wetland restoration project at the site was well under way in 2006. This has resulted in one of the largest and most successful efforts in that regard in California. "Seventy percent of the Bolsa Chica mesa has been preserved as upland habitat to complement the adjacent 1,200-acre restored Bolsa Chica Lowland ecosystem," reported Coastal Commission executive director Dr. Charles Lester in 2015.[127] Though the Bolsa Chica Land Trust and other citizens' groups must be accorded a large share of the credit for this triumph in marshland preservation, perhaps the most credit should go to the Coastal Act itself. Looking back on the struggle, Flossie Horgan of the Bolsa Chica Land Trust aptly declared, "But for the Coastal Act, Bolsa Chica would be absolutely paved over and the wetlands would be gone," replaced by thousands of houses.[128] The multitudes of students from elementary grades through college who visit the Bolsa Chica Wetland annually to learn about marsh ecology and habitat restoration are among the many beneficiaries of the hard-fought campaign to save this rare coastal resource from the bulldozer.

Episode 7: Hearst Ranch and Highway 1 (1998)

"This is the crown jewel of California's undeveloped coast. What we do in this case [regarding Hearst Ranch] is going to make a lasting mark on a place beloved to many, many people," said Peter Douglas.[129] "It's probably the coastal issue of the 90's," he noted a few days later with reference to developers' plans to transform parts of Hearst Ranch into a golf resort.[130] The world-famed Hearst Castle in San Simeon is situated on a gentle, verdant slope overlooking the Pacific, surrounded by some eighty thousand acres of rolling pristine grassland, studded here and there with outcroppings and clusters of oak trees. La Cuesta Encantada (the Enchanted Hill), Hearst called the promontory on which his castle was situated. This bucolic site and environs is home to reputedly the largest cattle ranch on California's coast. In 1957 the Hearst family donated San Simeon land and the castle to the state, which the following year Sacramento officials minted as a new state park and historic monument. The Hearst Corporation, operated by descendants of newspaper titan William Randolph Hearst, proposed in the early 1990s building a large commercial complex on a remaining tract of their property.

This complex was to include several hotels (one of which would be a 650-room behemoth), a golfing venue featuring twenty-seven holes, a dude ranch, hundreds of new homes, a shopping mall with restaurants, and housing for employees of these concessions. Proponents of the project supported a widening of two-lane, scenic Highway 1 to accommodate the planned development.[131] In effect, Hearst-connected developers planned to site and build a small city on land that had been pastoral since the days of Spanish haciendas. To allow this the San Luis Obispo County Board of Supervisors would have to alter the county's Local Coastal Program to permit the relaxation of provisions related to environmental protection and the preservation of agricultural holdings in the face of proposed development. The stage was set for a high-profile clash between advocates of private property rights on the one hand, and defenders of the public interest along the coast on the other hand.

At the Coastal Commission hearing in January 1998 a coalition of environmentalists, ranchers, and other local residents vied with spokespersons for the building industry, organized labor, and other business groups favoring Hearst Ranch and less stringent regulations in the county's Local Coastal Program. Neither commission chair Rusty Areias nor executive director Douglas subscribed to such a stark, dichotomous view of the Hearst Ranch issue as might be suggested by the contending sides. Both officials, to varying degrees, could abide development *and* conservation. According to a journal article on the Hearst Ranch dispute, Areias told the packed meeting that while the coast must be protected, so also must property rights. "We are here today to find out if that delicate, elusive balance can be maintained." In that same article, Douglas was quoted as saying, "The Coastal Act is not anti-development. It is for appropriate development appropriately sited."[132] The emotion-packed hearing on this issue would show just how difficult it was to balance development with conservation, especially along California's picturesque central coast.

Dramas unfolded both outside and inside the meeting hall at the Embassy Suites in San Luis Obispo, where the commission hearing was held. More than a thousand people, virtually all opposed to the development and carrying signs to that effect, lined the commissioners' bus route to the meeting venue in rain, while about two hundred members of this group sat inside. There, two members of the Hearst family testified against green-lighting the project.

Patricia Bell Hearst, former wife of George Hearst (chairman of the board of the Hearst Corporation) recalled "a decade of summers at San Simeon, eating and sleeping in the old ranch house . . . galloping through towering majestic trees." Sobbing and then regaining her composure, she pleaded, "In my heart, I pray that today you will vote for our state, our country and for the world's most majestic coast." A representative of the Sierra Club read a letter from family member William R. Hearst II: "The soul of humanity needs . . . quiet . . . contact with the balance and beauty of the natural world. San Simeon's peaceful beaches and unspoiled loveliness have long served my family in this way. . . . The clank, whir, flash, buzz and blink of commercial complexes would easily obscure, if not obliterate it." On the other hand, Philip Battaglia, a lawyer representing the Hearst Corporation, urged commissioners to disregard the views of these two "dissidents," reminding the panel that eight Hearst family members were on the corporation board and all of them favored the development.[133] Battaglia argued that the staff report was "seriously flawed and contain[ed] numerous factual errors." For example, he said the report was off by nearly two-thirds in gauging the amount of water that could be depleted from streams without endangering wildlife.[134]

In accordance with the staff's recommendation, the commission rejected the proposed changes in the Local Coastal Program by a vote of nine to three, thereby nixing the project. The staff had found that the county's plan was "not consistent with the development, agriculture, recreation, visual resource, environmentally sensitive habitat, public access, hazards, and archeological policies found in chapter three of the Coastal Act."[135] "There are about 140 separate issues in the plan that the county needs to adjust to live within its means, in terms of available water, and to protect sensitive resources," asserted one Coastal Commission staffer.[136] At the same time, demonstrating reasonableness and flexibility, the staff recommended moving the project forward *if* the proposed hotel were limited to 375 rooms instead of 650, the golf course was dropped, and all the development concentrated at the base of San Simeon Point. Commission members praised the staff report for being a model of clarity in analysis and writing. On hearing the vote outcome, hundreds of people in the packed hearing chamber gave the commissioners a standing ovation.

"This action," said Susan Jordan of the League for Coastal Protection, "sends a clear, strong message to the county supervisors and the Hearst Corporation: Go back, rethink this and come back with something that meets the protections of the Coastal Act."[137] Eventually, the corporation scaled back considerably its development plans; evidently, some of the rethinking Jordan called for had taken place.

At any rate, in 2005 the denouement of the contentious Hearst Ranch issue was reached and was not much to Douglas's liking. Negotiations between the state, two environmental groups,[138] and Hearst representatives resulted in the state paying the corporation $95 million ($80 million in cash, $15 million in tax credits) in return for a thirteen-mile stretch of San Simeon beach that would be opened to the public, a ban on development on nearly all the rest of the ranch, the right of the corporation to build a hundred-room inn, twenty-seven homes, and fifteen employee housing units. Also, the corporation could use up to thirty-six hundred ranch acres for orchards, vineyards, and row crops. "We were very disappointed that the deal was made because we thought it was a raw deal for the public," lamented Douglas. Not only was the monetary cost high, but no enforcement mechanisms were in place to assure that ranchland development remained within the parameters of the agreement. "We just have to be vigilant now over the next many years to make sure the deal that the public was promised is in fact delivered," he stated. Moreover, he pointed out that use restrictions did not greatly improve public access to the coast.[139] He was right about this. Progress on that matter would take time. That said, without his leadership and willingness to stand up to the Hearst Corporation, the San Simeon stretch of the California coast today would look far more like a high-end commercial playground than the wild, idyllic shore of wonder that it remains.

Episode 8: Crystal Cove (c. late 1990s)

"It would have been a colossal giveaway of a public resource," exclaimed Peter Douglas. He was referring to the possibility of the state acceding to a developer's plan in the 1990s to convert forty-six vintage 1920s and 1930s cottages, located at Crystal Cove on the Orange Coast between Corona Del Mar and Laguna Beach, into a luxury vacation venue. Added amenities listed in the plan included three swimming pools, a hundred-seat restaurant, and valet parking. Lodging rates would run between $375 and $700 per night. If the developer and his corporate officers intended to go forward with their plan, Douglas told them, "they'd have to go through me, and I was going to fight this thing to the end because it [the beach and historic cottages] needed to be open to the public. It was the crown jewel on the [developed] coast."[140] Earlier, in 1979, "cove-ites," as former residents called themselves, had seen to it that their "crown jewel" gained listing on the venerable National Register of Historic Places.

The path to the Coastal Commission's involvement in Crystal Cove is, as in many other cases, a compelling story of how citizen activism/vision and Douglas's grit were joined to produce a remarkable outcome for the public—and, this time, to save a historic seaside vacation site, as well. Moreover, the story is in some ways an unlikely one that culminates in a twist of irony.

In the early twentieth century the relatively isolated, picturesque Orange Coast began to have more and more visitors. Like the movie industry of which it was a part, Crystal Cove—so named by residents in 1927—began to draw attention with the rise of Hollywood during and after World War I; additionally, plein air artists, also of that era, helped immortalize the area with their seascapes so coveted by collectors and museums. Actors and film production crews frequented the surf and sand there for the making of both silent and talking ocean-themed movies such as *The Sea Wolf* (1920) and *Treasure Island* (1934). The shore and its hinterland had been owned by the Irvine Company, some of whose employees summered there along with other beachgoers, who built cottages and simpler shelters out of materials at hand, often consisting of the flotsam and jetsam that storm tides washed onto the sand. The still largely unsettled strand backed against low sandstone cliffs and dotted with rustic cottages attracted prominent painters like William Wendt and Edgar Payne, among others. Their seascapes put the area on the art map of California.

By the 1950s, Crystal Cove had become the embodiment of Southern California beach culture. Volleyball, surfing, swimming, horseback riding, and luaus had come to define this summer mecca for several generations of cove-ites (one of whom—Laura Davick—would later be instrumental in the effort to preserve the history and marine ecology of her childhood playground). Before long, weekend visitors and year-round residents became common sights. Meanwhile, in the 1960s and 1970s, Orange County beach-front real estate values began their steep ascent. To assure continued public use of Crystal Cove, amid escalating coastal property values and closures of access ways to beaches, the state purchased the land in 1979, turning the area into a state park.

Even so, developers eyed this stretch of the Orange shore for the siting of a luxury resort. A 1982 Crystal Cove State Park general plan called for affordable reuse of the cottages by the public, preservation of the historic district within the park, and the siting and building of public campgrounds for day use. Unfortunately, state budgetary constraints made carrying out the plan impossible. Ever-ready private developers in 1997 secured a sixty-year lease from the cash-strapped state government to go forward with a project to convert the cottages into a $35-million luxury resort in a state park.

To derail the developers' envisioned project and save this coastal gem from the bulldozer, citizens' groups formed. Laguna Beach lawyer and Sierra Club activist Jeannette Merrilees founded and headed Save Crystal Cove, a coalition of environmental organizations that included the Sierra Club and Village Laguna. Merrilees launched the movement to both stop the high-end resort and vacate the residents at Crystal Cove in order to render the site more public-serving.[141] Drawing on her legal expertise, she discovered that the contract between the State Parks Department and the developer could be terminated without penalty if the parties agreed to it. More to the point, that contract should have been invalidated, Merrilees contended, because the 1997 concessionaire agreement failed the legal requirement of being consistent with the general plan for the state park, and the resort developer, Michael Freed (with the firm of Crystal Cove Preservation Partners), had failed to obtain the necessary permits.[142] Merrilees's legal research was essential because it pointed the way toward ending the contract. Had that compact remained operative, plans for the luxury resort most likely would have gone forward in lieu of cottage restoration and the other state park features mentioned below.

Davick, similarly, played a signal role in stopping the resort and especially in shaping plans for Crystal Cove's future. She organized the Alliance to Save Crystal Cove in 1999, which evolved into the Crystal Cove Alliance. The Alliance generated plans for the historic district, a marine research/education facility, hiking trails, and more. Davick met with preservationist and philanthropist Joan Irvine Smith and representatives of environmental groups to build support for the Alliance's plans and raise money for cottage restoration. She was highly effective in these efforts, becoming the public face of an impressively reconfigured Crystal Cove. Moreover, Davick became the point person in taking the Alliance's plans to Coastal Commission chief Peter Douglas.

In the late 1990s and the first several years of the twenty-first century, Douglas inserted himself in the behind-the-scenes interactions between the Alliance and developers. As shown, he exerted his considerable sway on behalf of the effort to nix the luxury resort project.

The turning point for all parties involved in the Crystal Cove dispute came in early 2001. At a clamorous, pivotal, January 18 meeting organized by Merrilees at Lincoln Elementary School in Corona del Mar (located in

Newport Beach) with state parks chief Rusty Areias and developer Michael Freed, some six hundred attendees—including the author and his wife—voiced their unwavering opposition to the luxury resort project.[143] When Merrilees publicly challenged Michael Freed to exercise his option to terminate the contract if after three years he still had none of the needed approvals, the audience gave her a standing ovation.[144]

Shortly afterward, the California Coastal Conservancy, a sister organization of the Coastal Commission, provided $2 million to buy out the concession contract of the developers. Later that same year the state parks staff met with stakeholder groups and the public to devise a conceptual blueprint or model for the development of the Crystal Cove Historic District per the unrealized 1982 general plan.

Crystal Cove Alliance's plan was ambitious, public oriented, and attractive. In 2003, phase 1 of a three-part Crystal Cove Historic District Preservation and Public Use Plan was launched. State parks bond revenues provided seed money for the endeavor, and Peter Douglas saw to it that $5 million in Coastal Commission mitigation funds went toward restoration of the first twenty-two historic cottages. The completion of all three phases would culminate not only in the preservation of the cottages and the historic district but also in the establishment of a trails system and educational/research facilities that would be used by students taking field trips to the site from area schools.

Looking back on the highly successful struggle, Douglas offered these thoughts: "There is no question, if I look at the California coast and all the places where activists made a difference, Crystal Cove . . . stands right at the top of the list. People like Laura Davick, Susan Jordan, and some others . . . just got in the way of the bulldozers and said, 'We're not going to let you come through here; this is the people's asset.' And now, when you see what they've done to restore that historic treasure, it's just amazing."[145] (For unclear reasons, Douglas mistakenly neglected to mention Merrilees's role. Since she did the heavy intellectual lifting on legal matters, Merrilees was as instrumental as anyone in stopping the resort.) Amazing to be sure, it was also somewhat ironic, because the forty-six cottages, situated so close to the shoreline, seemingly exemplified the very development that the Coastal Act of 1976 aimed to prevent. Conceivably, today's Coastal Commission might disallow the construction and siting of such structures.

Still, the outcome of the Crystal Cove episode marked a big win for coastal ecology, youth-targeted marine science education, cultural preservation, and the public's use and enjoyment of a premium beach setting. The efforts of coastal activists, with help from Douglas, made it happen.

Episode 9: Offshore Oil Drilling under
President George W. Bush (2004)

Compared to the Crystal Cove battle, the struggle of coastal towns and environmentalists to curb oil drilling off California's coast has been much more complex and of longer duration. The state has a long history of dealing with this matter, as "the world's first offshore oil well was drilled in 1896, in waters off Summerland in Santa Barbara County."[146] Since then, offshore drilling along California's coast has been ongoing and, in part, accounts for the fact that in 1969—when the Santa Barbara drilling rig blowout occurred—the Golden State ranked third in the nation, behind Texas and Louisiana, in oil production.[147] During the presidency of Ronald W. Reagan in the 1980s, the executive branch of the federal government tried mightily to rein in the Coastal Commission's authority to require major mitigation concessions from oil companies seeking agency permits to drill in waters along the Outer Continental Shelf (submerged lands lying seaward of the state's three-nautical-mile limit).[148] Then, during the presidency of George W. Bush, the offshore drilling issue in California shifted somewhat from mitigation to disagreement over the spatial reach of the commission's regulatory power. Accordingly, between 2004 and 2009, Peter Douglas and the Coastal Commission paid particular attention to the matter of deep-sea oil drilling beyond the state's three-nautical-mile zone.

Ever since the catastrophic 1969 Santa Barbara oil spill (see chapter 3), drilling for that energy source off California's coast has remained a controversial issue in the Golden State. Douglas and the Coastal Commission played a key role, but assuredly not the only role, in the decision-making process regarding offshore drilling. That decision-making process is complicated by the fact that the commission has claimed some contested authority over pumping operations in federal waters—that is, beyond the three-nautical-mile state limit.

In the wake of the 1969 Santa Barbara blowout, the California State Lands Commission declared a moratorium later that year on the issuance of drilling leases within the three-nautical-mile offshore limit. According to one estimate at that time, the state would lose some $29 million in revenue over the next three years as a result of the moratorium.[149] To codify the suspension, in 1994 the Sacramento legislature passed the California Coastal Sanctuary Act, which prohibited, except in defined instances, the state's issuance of new leases for the extraction of oil and gas in designated offshore waters within the three-nautical-mile boundary. Similarly, Congress in 1984 had imposed a moratorium on new leasing sites in federal waters beyond California's statutory limit, renewing the suspension annually until it was lifted in 2008, under President Bush. The State of California Natural Resources Agency affirmed that under both the state and federal moratoriums, "development on existing... leases [was] not affected and may still occur within offshore areas leased prior to the moratorium taking effect."[150] Consequently, within both state and federal maritime zones, oil companies with existing leases have continued their pumping operations, resulting in more than 1 billion barrels of oil issuing from the state zone alone since the 1969 Santa Barbara disaster.[151] Accordingly, some twenty-two offshore rigs owned by Exxon-Mobil, Plains Exploration and Production Company, Aera Energy, Venoco Energy, and Pacific Operators Offshore have been pumping oil in both state and federal waters off California's shore.[152]

When Golden State gasoline prices rocketed to $4.50 a gallon in July 2008, many Americans, including 51 percent of Californians polled by the nonpartisan Public Policy Institute, urged the sale of more offshore leases to increase the supply and lower the pump price of gas.[153] "Drill, baby, drill!" became the Republican Party's mantra. Accordingly, four days before President Bush left office in 2009 his administration announced a new plan to open large offshore areas to drilling along the coasts of California, Alaska, the Gulf of Mexico, Florida, and Atlantic states between 2010 and 2015. For California, the targeted drilling areas included waters between Shelter Cove in Humboldt County and Point Arena in Mendocino County; along the Santa Barbara and Ventura coasts from Vandenberg Air Force Base to near Oxnard; and in Orange and San Diego Counties from Laguna Beach to La Jolla. Environmentalists and fishing groups spoke out, stressing the risk the Bush plan posed for the Golden State's $90-billion-a-year coastal tourism economy and the anticipated harm to "sensitive kelp forests, otters, whales, fish and sea turtles off California's world-famous beaches."[154]

Most authorities agreed there was little chance that new leases would be sold to open up wells within the established three-nautical-mile zone. Republican governor Arnold Schwarzenegger, Democratic senators Barbara Boxer and Diane Feinstein, and House Speaker Nancy Pelosi, among others, publicly opposed new lease sales in federal offshore waters.[155] On the other hand, in that same year Vice President Dick Cheney called for more drilling in federal marine zones; Senator John McCain (Arizona), and Representatives

John E. Peterson (Pennsylvania), Jeff Denham (California), Tom McClintock (California), and Jim Costa (California) agreed.

Even with the lifting of the federal moratorium, the question remained: Could the California Coastal Commission block expanded oil production in waters beyond the state's three-nautical-mile limit? Oil companies believed the answer was no. Apropos of this belief, four years earlier, in 2004, Frank E. Holmes, manager of Western States Petroleum Association, had declared that the California Coastal Commission's authority did not extend outside the three-nautical-mile area.[156]

Douglas and the commission disagreed strongly with Holmes, contending in 2004 and afterward that that agency could oppose new drilling in federal waters if such activity did not comply with state standards.[157] In this case, Douglas was referring to California's standards regarding the discharge of toxic metals and other substances associated with pumping oil and known to be hazardous to ocean health. When asked in early 2009 if the commission would take legal action to stop such drilling in federal waters, he responded that the chance of the agency filing a lawsuit to block new drilling proposals was "as likely as the sun coming up tomorrow."[158] "This is a turf issue, and an attempt by oil companies trying to get around protecting water quality at a higher level," Douglas had noted five years earlier.[159] His view had not seemed to change. To spokespersons for the oil companies, the commission's assertion of some authority beyond the statutory state limit was a clear case of regulatory overreach; to those identified with protecting the coast, this was an instance of California officialdom vigilantly safeguarding the ocean environment in accordance with the Coastal Act.

This episode revealed how Douglas argued vigorously for the most expansive interpretation of the Coastal Act, especially when battling corporate giants like oil companies. The sign on his desk, "Be Bold, Eschew Pusillanimity," comes to mind here. Whatever else his critics said of him, seldom if ever was he charged with lacking boldness in thought or courage in acting. But as the dispute over offshore oil drilling showed, what was boldness and courage to Douglas and many environmentalists was denounced as overreach by oil companies.

Episode 10: BHP Billiton's Proposed Offshore Liquid Natural Gas Terminal (2007)

When it came to offshore enterprises deemed hazardous to marine life and habitat, the Douglas-led commission was leery not only of oil production but also of operations involving liquid natural gas (LNG). A major permitting battle, focused on that vaporous fuel, erupted in California in 2007.

Industry efforts to site offshore LNG terminals (facilities that regasify, store, import, and/or export LNG) have met with effective opposition from California state government agencies and segments of the public, which included not only environmentalists but others as well. Opponents have mainly been concerned about safety and greenhouse gas (GHG) emissions tied to climate change. Thus, the Golden State's passage of Assembly Bill 32, the California Global Warming Solutions Act, in 2006—requiring a reduction of GHG emissions to 1990 levels by 2020[160]—played an important role in the Coastal Commission's handling of the LNG issue.

In lay terms, LNG is natural gas (predominantly methane, a fossil fuel) used as an energy source much like oil or coal, though its use results in fewer carbon emissions than those two energy sources. Some motor vehicles, homes, and businesses are powered by LNG. To safely transport potentially flammable LNG to areas not reached by gas pipelines, it is cooled to minus 259 degrees Fahrenheit, becoming a clear, colorless, odorless liquid.[161] In this form, when imported the fuel is shipped via oceangoing tankers that carry it to offshore terminals, where the fuel is unloaded and converted back to gas, or regasified. These offshore terminals are often floating on the ocean surface. Next, the gas is conveyed, often by submerged pipelines, to receiving facilities on land, from where it is distributed to power providers.

In 2007, Australian mining and energy giant BHP Billiton, purportedly the world's largest corporation of its kind, sought permits from the relevant government agencies to build a large LNG floating terminal in federal waters about fourteen miles seaward of Ventura County. The LNG would originate in one of the company's Australian gas fields and be shipped across the Pacific to the proposed floating regasification and storage terminal. Submarine pipelines, according to Billiton, would transport the gas from that terminal to the mainland via a subsea "pipeline system known as the 'Cabrillo Port' project." The proposed eight-hundred-thousand-dollar terminal would be about 971 feet (three football fields) long by 213 feet wide, and it would tower some 266 feet (equivalent to a fourteen-story building) above the ocean surface. Once the regasified fuel reached the coast via two subsea pipelines, it would be routed underground about fourteen miles to an existing Southern California Gas Company pipeline distribution system.[162]

On April 9 the State Lands Commission deliberated on the company's request for a lease to install the underwater pipelines, expressing concern about the firm's flawed environmental impact report.[163] More than seven hundred people, nearly all opponents of the Billiton project, had gathered in the Lands Commission hearing room, while hundreds more spilled into a courtyard where they could listen to the proceedings. Susan Jordan, the highly effective head of the California Coastal Protection Network, had coordinated the opposition effort.[164] After hearing testimony, the commission denied the lease request by a two-to-one vote on environmental grounds that only marginally included global warming. Lieutenant Governor John Garamendi and State Controller John Chiang, both Democrats, voted against the project; Anne Cheehan, a Republican appointed by Governor Schwarzenegger, voted for it.[165] Doubtlessly disappointed, Billiton president Renee Klimczak still believed her company's proposal would have worked, saying, "We believe California needs natural gas. We'd like to be part of California's energy future." Kathi Hann, the firm's environmental consultant, responded to the turndown matter-of-factly: "If California doesn't want it [LNG], we're still going to find someone to purchase it."[166]

Next, the Coastal Commission took up the permit matter, as Billiton needed permits from multiple agencies to go forward with its plans. Though the proposed LNG terminal would be located beyond the state's three-nautical-mile limit, federal law gave the commission authority to regulate such development when adverse environmental impacts could be shown to endanger marine creatures and habitats within California's waters. In preparation for the commission's handling of the permit request, and amid growing state government concerns about climate change, the company, cognizant of the state's regulatory authority, offered to power its tankers on LNG, rather than diesel fuel, when entering California's waters.[167] This overture seemed to have little, if any, effect on the agency's decision making.

The commission's staff report, issued in February 2007, recommended denial of the permit request for several major reasons. Most importantly, the project would "result in numerous substantial impacts to coastal resources." Billiton's proposed mitigation measures were deemed to be consistent with the California Coastal Management Program but failed to fully address "impacts to air quality, including its expected greenhouse gas emissions." Annually, several million tons of carbon dioxide, a major GHG, would be released into the atmosphere by the Billiton operation when emissions from the entire supply chain and users were factored into what was being proposed. Other key staff objections included the escape of air pollutants injurious to public health, the project's adverse impacts on sea-level rise, ocean warming, and risks to marine mammals, fish eggs, and planktonic organisms.[168]

At the April 12 Coastal Commission meeting, where the Billiton LNG permit request was unanimously (twelve to zero) voted down, Peter Douglas had this to say: "We feel we have the responsibility to make this recommendation to you [commissioners], not only for consistency with the Coastal Act, but for the planet." Douglas's phrase "for the planet" reflected the broader global environmental context in which he approached so many of the thorny issues that came before him and the commission. That broader context, noted Susan Jordan, included "the whole change in attitude about global climate change."[169] By invoking the state government's new mandate under AB 32 to reduce GHGs, the Coastal Commission for the first time utilized its authority to factor climate change into its decision making.[170] Governor Schwarzenegger, who had been an advocate of AB 32, supported the Coastal Commission's decision.[171] The agency's handling of this issue was closely watched, as contemporaneously the state was reviewing at least four other proposed LNG plants, none of which subsequently passed permitting scrutiny. At the time of this writing, in part owing to Douglas and the commission, no LNG terminals exist in California's offshore waters.

Episode 11: Permitting the Poseidon Desalination Plant in Carlsbad (2007)

Just as industrial development and climate change were linked in the Coastal Commission's handling of a proposed LNG project in 2007, the same was true for the agency's decision regarding the siting of a desalination facility later that same year. On the matter of desalination, as compared to LNG, Douglas and his staff took a position that was less categorical, more nuanced, and which left more room for negotiation with the permit-seeking corporation.

The controversial matter of the commission issuing a Coastal Development Permit to Connecticut-based Poseidon Resources to build a seawater desalination plant on the shore of Carlsbad's Agua Hedionda Lagoon unfolded against a backdrop of happenings.[172] These included a growing governmental and public concern about supplying affordable drinking water to San Diego County's expanding inland population, and global warming. Desalination plants are powered by fossil fuel energies—largely coal and oil—that emit GHGs, a factor that did not go unnoticed by the Coastal Commission in dealing with the Carlsbad project. With these developments in mind, in November 2007 the commission deliberated on Poseidon's application for a permit to construct and operate a desalination plant in Carlsbad, a beach city located in San Diego County. This episode is particularly illuminating because it affords an example (as in the Bolsa Chica imbroglio) of commissioners not being in sync with the staff report, and Peter Douglas nonetheless working to optimize the staff's input on whatever conditions would shape the panel's decisions about the project.

The regulatory process, particularly obtaining the requisite permits, was a lengthy and litigious one for this project. In 1998, in response to San Diego County's inland housing and population growth, Poseidon Resources proposed its building of a desalination plant in Carlsbad. In 2003 the company began applying for permits; three years later it applied to the Coastal Commission for a Coastal Development Permit (CDP), which, contrary to the staff's recommendation, it received in 2007.[173] The proposed plant would employ reverse-osmosis membranes to bring seawater to potable standards. Construction of the first phase of the $900-million facility, designed to produce 50 million gallons of high-quality drinking water per day for three hundred thousand area residents, began in November 2009. In all, opponents mounted fourteen legal challenges, including at least two attempts to revoke the CDP and nine lawsuits, all of which Poseidon's desalination project survived.[174] The plant, reputedly the largest of its kind in the Western Hemisphere, was scheduled to go online in 2012 but did not begin serving the people and businesses of San Diego County until December 2015.

The eighty-eight-page commission staff report released on November 2, 2007, argued for denial of a CDP for Poseidon's Carlsbad project as initially proposed. With that report in mind, meeting on November 15, commissioners agreed by a nine-to-three vote to permit the project if Poseidon agreed to some twenty conditions. Some discussion of the main conditions is in order.

At the top of the staff's list was a concern that the proposal "would cause significant adverse impacts to marine life and water quality in Agua Hedionda and in near-shore ocean waters."[175] The plant's anticipated intake of 304 million gallons of estuarine water daily would negatively impact the productivity of an estimated thirty-seven acres of the lagoon. Large quantities of fish, fish eggs, larvae, and plankton would be killed in the processing of seawater.[176] Use of "subsurface intake," which would draw in seawater from the ocean floor or farther offshore, would diminish the harm done to marine life in the lagoon, contended the staff report. Poseidon's senior vice president, Peter MacLaggan, countered that the technology required to do that would even more seriously endanger aquatic life and, with an estimated price tag of $650 million, would be cost-prohibitive.[177] Staff members maintained that the plant's anticipated discharge of water with a higher saline content than the estuary's receiving waters would inflict further losses on marine resources. All of these ecological impacts had to be fully mitigated, but before that could happen reliable figures were needed. Said Peter Douglas, "The figures they [Poseidon] gave us, we don't have any confidence in those. We haven't seen the study that underlies those numbers."[178] In the absence of the credible data that staff needed from Poseidon, Douglas speculated that the permit applicant would have to mitigate at a level comparable to Southern California Edison's spending of $86 million to restore San Dieguito Lagoon earlier as an offset for building the San Onofre nuclear power facility. Like Edison, said Douglas, Poseidon would have to pay heftily in terms of mitigation. To comply with the permit conditions, Poseidon prepared and submitted to the commission its Marine Life Mitigation Plan proposing a sixty-six-acre wetland restoration site in South San Diego County's Otay Bay Flood Plain. In February 2011, the agency approved the mitigation plan.

Global warming also figured prominently into the staff's objection to permitting the Carlsbad project as proposed and into the commission's conditioning of a CDP. Given California's lead nationally in addressing climate change in AB 32, this is not surprising. Poseidon had claimed that the Carlsbad desalination plant would emit no GHGs and, in its operation, would be carbon-neutral. A Poseidon plan explaining how that would be the case—which was of special interest since GHG-emitting sources would be generating the electricity to power the plant—was absent. Commission staff aimed to rectify that omission. In a May 22, 2008, staff document titled "Recommended Revised Findings," the commission's policy analysts specified the following as a tenth special condition: "Poseidon [will] develop an Energy Minimization and Greenhouse Gas Reduction Plan for Commission Review and approval."[179] The applicant drafted such a plan and the commission approved it in August of that year.

Throughout the decade-and-a-half struggle, Douglas and commission staff could count on support from civic sector groups, while Poseidon's backers included local governments and water districts. Surfrider Foundation led a coalition of at least thirty-one environmental and good-government organizations that went on record in fall 2007 as opposing the Carlsbad project.[180] Advocates of the plant included the City of Carlsbad, Valley Center

Municipal Water District, Sweetwater Authority, Santa Fe Irrigation District, City of Oceanside, and other water agencies.

From the inception to the outcome of the Carlsbad permitting episode, Douglas deftly steered developments in the direction of maximizing staff input to wring as many environmentally beneficial concessions from Poseidon as possible. The Coastal Commission chief acknowledged publicly that he and staff saw a need for desalination plants in thirsty and sometimes parched California: "We clearly see that desalination is part of California's water future. The real questions are how it's done, where it's done, by whom it is done and under what conditions."[181] When Poseidon complained about the years invested in securing permits and the commission's conditioned approval of a CDP, Douglas smartly seized the opportunity to sound an alarm about the perennial problems of the agency's underfunding and understaffing. "We want to move forward as fast as we can but it's going to be more difficult with our staffing cuts and the cuts coming up," he declared in a public hearing.[182] Douglas's measured and strategically prudent position on Poseidon's permitting did not deflect criticism of him from proponents of the Carlsbad project, who lambasted his "intrusion" and "arrogance," which, they said, slowed the regulatory process; moreover, some environmentalists rebuked the commission, but not Douglas, for surrendering on the issue.[183]

Significantly, this episode underscored the fact that climate change would figure into the Coastal Commission's permitting of power plants, and that Douglas was not unalterably opposed to siting such facilities along the state's shore. That said, he calibrated with skill the mitigation measures that would be required to secure a permit. This instance also shows that, early on, the scientifically literate executive director was aware of the dangers that climate change posed to the coast. Lastly, the watchdog agency, under Douglas's vigilant and adroit leadership, deployed the Coastal Act effectively to safeguard the public interest and marine life in San Diego's tidal waters.

*Episode 12: The State Route 241 Toll Road
and Trestles Beach (2008)*

Far more dramatic than the Carlsbad desalination controversy, the battle over the Foothill Transportation Corridor South, State Route 241 Toll Road (Foothill South) extension in Orange and San Diego Counties, sparked emotion-laden Coastal Commission hearings that drew media coverage. Proposed construction through a state park, jobs in a down economy, and a threat to an iconic surf break all assured a high level of public engagement with this toll road project undertaken by the Transportation Corridor Agency (TCA).[184] Construction estimates ranged from $875 million to $1.3 billion.

The Foothill South project purportedly aimed at relieving traffic congestion mainly in south Orange County, whose freeways and major highways seemed to fill to vehicular capacity nearly as fast as they were built. In terms of TCA planning, Foothill South constituted the last segment of SR 241, a state-owned, Southern California toll road that parallels much of Interstate 5 in Orange County. By the early twenty-first century, the remaining segment of the Foothill South project consisted of a proposed sixteen-mile, six-lane extension from Oso Parkway in Rancho Santa Margarita to Interstate 5 at Basilone Road just south of San Clemente. This route would cut through both the San Mateo Campground (a California state park that stood to lose 60 percent of its land to the project) and the Donna O'Neill Land Conservancy (a twelve-hundred-acre preserve), affect endangered species habitats and cultural sites, and open up one of Southern California's last pristine coastal canyons to new development. Also, it threatened ocean-water quality and the surf break at Trestles Beach, one of Southern California's premier wave-riding venues that has been integral to the history of the sport in the Golden State.[185] In short, the proposed toll-road route guaranteed a high-profile clash between the Save San Onofre Coalition of environmentalists and surfers opposing the project,[186] on the one hand, and TCA authorities and city and county officials, largely supporting the toll road, on the other hand. As the battle lines were drawn, the TCA set about the lengthy process of applying for the mandatory permits and trying to meet the environmental requirements of state and federal wildlife agencies, the U.S. Environmental Protection Agency, and the U.S. Army Corps of Engineers—all of which were critical for funding and for Coastal Commission approval.

Amid the permitting process, the Foothill South project was taken up at a packed Coastal Commission meeting on February 6, 2008, at the Del Mar Fairgrounds in San Diego County. Surfrider campaign manager Stefanie Sekich-Quinn and environmental director Chad Nelsen, as well as other grassroots organizers, oversaw the distribution of T-shirts and signs and arranged the use of buses to encourage a large turnout.[187] Some thirty-five hundred people attended, and about twenty-five hundred of those submitted requests to speak during the public comment period. Peter Douglas's remarks evoked thunderous cheers from the audience when he stated, "This is the most significant project to come before this commission since the San Onofre

FIGURE 12. People of all ages displaying "Save Trestles" signs in Del Mar, California, 2008. Photo courtesy of Daniel Soderberg.

nuclear power plant in 1974. It is most significant because of the large area of environmentally sensitive habitat, wetlands, and other public resources it will destroy. . . . Since the passage of the California Coastal Act in 1976, I know of no other coastal development project so demonstrably inconsistent with the law that has come this far in the regulatory review process." Sounding more like a seer than a bureaucrat, he closed by saying poignantly that the project "raises fundamental questions about what kind of environmental and social future we want for our coastal communities, our families, our children, and theirs."[188] Commissioner Sara Wan, among others, criticized the TCA for not presenting accurate information about how the project would endanger the Pacific pocket mouse and other wildlife. The commission voted eight to two to reject the toll road extension. A key reason for the rejection was that commissioners, after conducting a consistency review, could not certify that the project was compatible "with multiple Coastal Act policies."[189]

Later in 2008, other hearings were held by various public agencies to consider the advisability of permitting the 241 Toll Road and the Transportation Corridor Agency's request for a $1.1 billion loan, which the *OC Weekly* newspaper characterized as a "bailout."[190] Susan Jordan, director of the California Coastal Protection Network, led strategy meetings and testified against the project;[191] public opinion remained strongly opposed to the toll road's extension;[192] and the federal government weighed in against it as well.[193] Douglas and others saw all these developments as salutary for California's coast and the commission he led.

This episode is particularly telling in that it demonstrated Douglas's strong connections to environmental activists, in this instance surfers. A former surfer himself, he understood the reverence wave riders had for their favorite breaks. Little wonder that the Surfrider Foundation could be counted among Douglas's and the commission's most vocal and reliable supporters.

In an interview on public radio the day after the commission turned down the toll road extension permit, Douglas spoke a little more broadly about the matter. To KCRW's Warren Olney, host of *Which Way, LA?* Douglas said the TCA did not truly explore other options because "they make money off of toll roads. Public transit is what needs to happen. Widening more roads, [adding] more lanes, is not the long-term answer" to traffic congestion.[194] So while Douglas rightly focused in the hearing on ways the proposed toll road extension violated the Coastal Act, he also had in mind long-term considerations that centered on the need for mass rail transit.

The same ability to take a clear, bold stand that was evident in the way Douglas dealt with the State Route 241 Toll Road episode was perceivably resident in his handling of nearly all of the twelve issues just examined, and it carried over into the waning years of his tenure with the Coastal Commission. It also characterized his thinking and actions in the last months of his life, by which time the high tide of his executive directorship had ebbed.

Ebb Tide

THE RECEDING YEARS

HAVING WAGED MANY BUREAUCRATIC battles on behalf of California's coastline and survived at least several political attempts to remove him from office, Peter Douglas finally faced a foe that could not be outwitted or out-fought: terminal throat and lung cancer. This rendezvous with impending death edged him toward retirement and launched Douglas into his deepest metaphysical musings and on road trips up and down the state to visit again the people and places that had meant the most to him.

He seemingly did all of this with the same fearlessness, strong will, and optimism that had characterized nearly his entire Coastal Commission career. What was different about the lion in winter, however, was the gentle-ness, the measured acceptance of what lay ahead for him, and a lessening of combativeness toward external foes that settled over him. In large part the warrior-administrator had evolved into the coastal sage.

DECLINING HEALTH, A LAST CONFERENCE, AND RETIREMENT

A former smoker, Douglas was diagnosed with advanced stage 4 throat can-cer in May 2004.[1] For the next six years he underwent medical treatment, at the end of which doctors told him he was free of the scourge. Whatever relief this message may have given him was short-lived. About one month after his cancer-free diagnosis, further tests showed he had developed lung cancer. The prognosis was not good.

Nothing so concentrates a person's thinking as news like that. The time and energy remaining him had to be prioritized and rationed to allow him to live as fully in every moment as his declining health would allow.

One of Douglas's last full moments in the public spotlight occurred in Sacramento on June 23, 2011, at a daylong conference on the California Coastal Commission, sponsored by the *Capitol Weekly,* a Sacramento organ of reportage on governmental affairs. Both supporters and opponents of the commission delivered prepared remarks.[2] This was Douglas's swan song of sorts, and he made the most of the occasion to trumpet the commission's work. The warrior/sage described his tenure with the commission as "a labor of love" and proceeded from that point to warn about a possible five-foot coastal sea-rise by 2100, explain the benefits of the precautionary principle,[3] caution against the seaboard becoming the preserve of "people of wealth," and urge the legislature giving the agency power to fine. Local governments were "parochial" and "not strong enough to protect the coast." He ended by saying, "We're not going away," to hearty applause. The commission and its many staunch supporters, assuredly, were not "going away," but its ailing leader knew that he would be, as his time was running out.

Unable to keep up with the challenging pace and duties of his office, Douglas went on medical leave from the Coastal Commission in August 2011 and in November retired. Throughout that time he struggled off and on with breathing, occasionally needing oxygen, and with the side effects of chemotherapy and radiation treatments. Coastal commissioner Steve Kinsey told this writer that Douglas's health challenges were quite evident to him and other panelists in the first half of 2011.[4] Increasingly, Douglas turned to Eastern medicine, taking turkey-tail and reishi mushroom extracts and drinking essiac tea. His goal was "maintaining a good quality of life as best i can."[5]

TRIPS AND TIME WITH FAMILY AND FRIENDS

As his health permitted, he drove his Ford Escape hybrid to his cabin on the Smith River, just south of the Oregon border, and to his other favorite haunts throughout the state. From his apartment in Larkspur, he visited with family and friends in the Bay Area, afterward driving north or south as his inclinations led him. Reportedly, he went on a whale-watching trip off Orange County.[6]

October found Douglas in the Anza-Borrego Desert area, near the home of his sister, Christiane. He loved and frequently visited this part of the state, where for years he had annually camped and hiked alone to meditate and "recalibrate" his values. Such natural places he called his "churches." He had to see and experience them while he still could. "You see," he told his blog readers at the end of that month, "I am living in the Now of each day—not tomorrow nor yesterday, but fully immersed in each moment."[7]

At the Smith River, close friends visited him and saw to his needs. There he exchanged emails, read, and wrote blogs "telling how we 'Saved the Coast'"—starting with the campaign for Proposition 20—while resting by the fireplace, which devoted commission staffers had stocked amply with wood. Robert H. Burnham, who had known Douglas since their law school days together, recalled that in several email communications from Douglas, "he was so open and thoughtful regarding his cancer . . . and how he planned to deal with it."[8] "The bottom line for me," Douglas wrote to friends, colleagues, and well-wishers, "is that I am not treading water till i die—i am paddling onward with love and gratitude in my heart."[9] This was vintage Douglas: he seldom if ever waited for things to happen; instead, in his final days he lived intentionally, boldly making things happen by shaping as much as possible the world around him.

His sickness probably made him especially conscious and critical of what he saw as America's inequitable health-care system, and his road trips to the Anza-Borrego area heightened his concern about the future of California's deserts. Driving the back roads of Del Norte County, perhaps the poorest in the state, Douglas saw and decried "the lack of health care." "It saddened me to see how we as a society treat our least fortunate! A friend who lives locally told of her monthly Blue Cross health payment ($680.) with a $4000. Deductible!!!. She basically only has catastrophic insurance. . . . It was a stark reminder [of] . . . how regressive our society is."[10] In another blog, he voiced "dismay over the direction [that] the environmental Bigs [corporations] are taking to compromise principle and substance" by introducing "industrial solar in fragile places."[11] At the time of that writing, to Douglas's chagrin, San Diego Gas & Electric was experimenting with the large-scale installation of solar panels in the desert community of Borrego Springs.

FINAL REFLECTIONS

Unlike his targeted and specific views about health care and industrial solar use in fragile ecosystems, most of Douglas's musings during the last year or so of his life were of a broader, more philosophical nature. Whether Douglas's final reflections differed much from his earlier thinking is hard to say. Most likely the seeds of those mature thoughts had been planted in his youth by his maternal grandmother, Alice Ehlers, whom he adored. She, as noted in the first chapter of this book, exposed her young grandson to Dr. Albert Schweitzer's "reverence for life" ethic. Others close to him in his early adulthood nurtured those seeds, as he himself did by his reading of Viktor Frankl's *Man's Search for Meaning* and the writings of Barry Lopez and Joseph Campbell, among others.[12] All of these earlier influences were seasoned by Douglas's experiences with Coastal Commission work and brought to fruition by the daunting health challenges of terminal cancer.

Through his writings in 2010–2011, especially blogs and emails, posterity has been given some idea of his final thoughts about the earth, the California coast and citizen activism, what property owners owed the community, purposeful living and public service, and the meaning of death and dying. However separate or disconnected these thoughts may seem, they were all laced together into a core of values that both animated and defined Douglas. On such vital and profound matters that shaped his life's work, he of all people did not need someone (like this writer) to speak for him or paraphrase his conclusions; his own words expressed them best:

The Earth, the Cosmos, and Nature

We are not merely *on* the Earth but *of* the Earth—indeed, of the cosmos. Being in Nature is the pathway to the sacred.... It is where words will not go and where the soothing sense of oneness with the universe and the infinite is all.[13]

I am a believer in Gaia [the idea, named after the ancient Greek earth goddess, that the planet is a living organism] ... and began thinking of the Universe the same way. There is an awareness everywhere though perhaps not a consciousness.[14]

Mother Earth is being used, abused, and severely wounded everywhere. On a global scale we live in a time of environmental catastrophe: accelerating habitat loss, widespread species extinctions, species invasions, pollution and devastating climate change. The greatest threat to our living home, Gaia, stems from ignorance, apathy and greed.... Mindless greed is perhaps the central driver of environmental destruction.[15]

When I pass on, I ask you not [to] weep for me but for Gaia who is surely more sorely wound[ed] than I. If you would honor my life, I can think of no better way than that you find some way to defend the well-being of our Mother Earth.[16]

The Coast and Citizen Activism

People . . . know the coast as the geographic soul of California.[17]

You can't take our relationship with the [California] coast for granted, because it took a lot of sweat, blood and tears to preserve it so we have what we have today. These things didn't just happen. The coast is what it is because a lot of people worked really hard and sacrificed to protect it. And if we want it to be there for our children, we have to keep fighting to protect it. In that way, the coast is never saved, it's always being saved.[18]

Long-term coastal protection requires constant vigilance and an army of intrepid and indefatigable environmental warriors. [The hope] lies in public activism and education.[19]

Property Rights versus Community Rights along the Seaboard

But the reality is that the coast belongs to everybody. When you buy coastal property, you have a special responsibility. That means the use of your property has more oversight because it's necessary to protect the long-term best interest of future generations of Californians.[20]

Purposeful Living and Public Service

When the Reaper knocks, foremost among many thoughts triggered in one's head is whether you have lived a purposeful, meaningful life. . . . [A]lready in [my] university days I settled on public service as a vocational path. . . . I can think of no more ethical, noble and ennobling way of living a meaningful, purposeful life than answering the call of service for the benefit of life. . . . When inevitably despair and resignation gnaw at my will to continue, I think of the children and unborn life and know capitulation is not an option. . . . [P]ublic service was once viewed in our culture as a noble calling and valued as such. Sadly, that is no longer the case. . . . I attribute this relatively recent regressive shift in collective thinking to the self-centered, self-righteous, opportunistic, harshly conservative ideology promoted by myopic politicians, self-appointed babbling apostles of anger and greed, and governance dynamics of the contemporary corporate kakistocracy that rules America.[21]

Money has never been a motivator for me because of my past. To me, the most rewarding, lucrative job one can do is that which fulfills one's moral, philosophical sense of value. And I'm driven by that, not the money. . . . I can pay the bills. I knew what I needed and it wasn't much.[22]

Death and Dying

From my perspective of the Universe, there is no beginning or end, no birth or death—only a continuity of essential being that nourishes a ubiquitous life force in perpetuity and all its manifestations. Everything, animate and not, is interconnected so when one life force (e.g. my own) transitions into another it enters the realm of interbeing. I intuit this looking out my [Smith River] cabin window across a dynamic river gorge cut deep into the steep mountain side covered in evergreen old-growth forest [that] I consider my wise and wizened elder of many thousand years. It permeates fine fingers of morning fog drifting westward soon to be dissipated by the rising sun suspended low on the eastern horizon this time of year. I feel it in the gentle breeze that gives voice to my deep-throated chimes. The continuity and vitality of life forces permeating the interbeing of everything in Nature around me is palpable and brings me profound inner tranquility and harmony. This perspective is a refuge, a temple of comfort I embrace with gratitude and grace. It empowers me to accept my passing into the other realm with non-fear in my soul.[23]

THE AQUARIUM OF THE BAY / PIER 39 CELEBRATION

On the evening of September 30, 2011, some four hundred of Peter Douglas's family and friends assembled at San Francisco's Aquarium of the Bay / Pier 39 at the Embarcadero to honor Douglas's leadership role in fighting to save California's shore. Tributes, stories, and a song celebrating the man and his work carried into the night. From his wheelchair, an ailing, appreciative Douglas seemed to be enjoying immensely the outpouring of admiration and love.

A proclamation that had been passed that same day by the California legislature was read. The document compared Douglas's accomplishments to those of John Muir, Rachel Carson, and Ansel Adams. Adapting Woody Guthrie's folk anthem "This Land Is Your Land," fifty commission staffers sporting bolo ties like those worn by their chief, and accompanied by guitars,

A Celebration of the Coastal Career of Peter Douglas

Peter Douglas spent 41 years working as a dedicated public servant for the State of California and 26 of those years as the Coastal Commission's Executive Director. Peter Douglas' leadership and vision secured the protection of the coastline of California for all to appreciate and enjoy. His legacy provides a framework to remind us all that the "coast is never saved; it's always being saved".

September 30, 2011 • San Francisco • Aquarium of the Bay • Pier 39

FIGURE 13. "Celebration" announcement, 2011. The memorable event drew many of the leading coastal conservationists in California. Photo of author's copy.

sang, "This Sand Is Your Sand." As the crowded roomful of celebrants looked on, the singers belted out the chorus:

> This sand is your sand, this sand is my sand
> From the first big ridgetop, to the Channel Islands
> From the redwood forest, to the Mexican border
> This coast was made for you and me.

A thin, rallying, teary-eyed Douglas smiled tellingly.[24]

The last week of Douglas's life was spent at Christiane's home in the desert community of La Quinta, California. A steady stream of family, commission colleagues, and coastal activists came by to pay their respects and extend their love to the fallen leader they so admired. From his sickbed he gave special time to some of those who had come. Touching her arm, he said to Susan Jordan, his longtime friend and the founder and executive director of the California Coastal Protection Network, "Susan, you have to stop desalination"—that is, "see that it is the last resort." Wistfully recalling that moment, Jordan said, "I promised him I would. . . . His brain to the end was sharp."[25] So went just one of the mutual, sacramental benedictions that some who were present can still scarcely talk about. His sister said Peter was "very touched" by the visits, that they "gave him closure to things that had been important to him," and that "he was so much at peace with himself."[26]

There, in the watchful embrace of family and a few close friends, Peter Douglas drew his last breath on the evening of April 1, 2012.

SEVEN

———

Footprints in Sand

PETER DOUGLAS'S LEGACY

BIG NEWS TRAVELS FAST and far in our time. Naturally, given Peter Douglas's prominence in coastal management, a fount of memorial statements soon gushed from newspapers and other organs of opinion, mainly from within California but also from as far away as the Atlantic seaboard. The year of his death, 2012, also marked the fortieth anniversary of the passage of Proposition 20, coauthored by Douglas. To the California Coastal Commission, a celebration of that foundational law seemed in order and was held in San Francisco on the evening of December 12. As one would expect, Douglas's role as a principal drafter of that initiative was highlighted at the packed commemorative event and reception afterward, attended by this author.

Both Douglas's passing and the anniversary celebration afford an opportunity to glimpse the condition of California's coast in that year. Such a snapshot would be a way of gauging the legacy of Douglas's thirty-four years of service in various capacities with the commission, and of assessing, in a preliminary way, his place in the Golden State's and the nation's environmental histories. A preliminary assessment of the condition of the coast, and of Douglas's legacy, such as this must be informed by a few arresting facts regarding the diminishing financial and personnel resources at his disposal: adjusting for inflation, the Coastal Commission's funding declined by 26 percent, from $22.1 million in 1980 to $16.3 million in 2010, with full-time staff decreasing from 212 in 1980 to 125 in 2010.[1]

MEMORIAL STATEMENTS

Mindful of the always-limited resources at Douglas's disposal as the head of a major regulatory agency, a survey of what others said about his leadership of the commission is revealing. His death elicited a raft of such assessments.

The thrust of the numerous obituaries appearing in the press should occasion little surprise among readers who have come this far in the narrative. Public officials, especially at the level of state government, and environmental activists lionized Douglas. Property rights advocates, usually after expressing condolences, either conveyed somewhat grudging recognition of the decedent, or communicated their relief that they no longer would have to contend with him. Few obituaries were neutral. Just as in his life, so in his death, Douglas was a polarizing public figure, engendering strong reactions from those watchful of coastal affairs.

Among the larger city dailies, the *Los Angeles Times* described him as "a seminal figure in conservation" who "helped write the 1976 Coastal Act, a landmark law that became a model for other states and countries."[2] The *New York Times,* America's and perhaps the world's paper of record, titled its lengthy obituary "Peter Douglas, Sentry of California's Coast, Dies at 69." After a laudatory description of Douglas's role in coauthoring Proposition 20 and the Coastal Act of 1976, a recitation of the Coastal Commission's achievements during his executive directorship followed: helping to create "thousands of acres of parklands and public trails," securing "more than 1,300 easements for paths to the shore through private property," stopping the heirs of William Randolph Hearst from building "a 650-room resort and golf course" in San Simeon, and more.[3] In a column captioned "Notable Deaths," the *Washington Post* declared that Douglas "spent a career fighting to rein in development along one of the world's most alluring coastlines."[4] The *San Francisco Chronicle's* obituary was headlined "Peter Douglas Dies, Crusaded for State's Coasts."[5] "Peter Douglas, Champion of the California Coast, Dies at 69," announced the *San Jose Mercury News.* The deceased luminary "did more than any other Californian to preserve the state's coastline and ensure that its beaches were open to the public."[6] "Friends and colleagues remembered Douglas as a champion for preserving California's coastline," stated the obituary in the *Sacramento Bee.*[7] Said the *San Diego Union-Tribune,* "Under his guidance, the quasi-judicial commission transformed into one of the nation's most powerful land-use authorities, tackling issues from coastal construction to public beach access to offshore oil drilling."[8]

The coverage of Douglas's retirement and death in some of the smaller coastal newspapers is also telling, particularly because the fiercest battles involving the Coastal Commission were often waged on their turf. Malibu, as suggested, was ground zero in that regard. Announcing the executive director's impending retirement from the commission, the *Malibu Times* stated, "The strong-willed Douglas sparred frequently with Malibu in his 26 years as executive director of the commission.... [He had] earned a national reputation as one of the nation's most influential environmental regulators." Mention was made of Douglas being the first recipient of the national Julius A. Stratton "Champion of the Coast" award for his leadership in coastal management at Coastal Zone '95, an international symposium on shoreline governance.[9] The *Carmel Pine Cone* noted that Douglas's announced retirement ended "a career which made him a revered figure for environmentalists, and at the same time a bête noire for many property owners and local government officials, who said he routinely trampled on property rights and even the Constitution."[10] As these two examples suggest, when newspapers in small coastal towns did publish articles on Douglas, such pieces, seemingly, were often less laudatory and more likely to remind readers of how local citizens and builders suffered at the hands of the commission and its chief.

Self-avowed environmentalists, particularly those involved in ocean ecology, expressed the most praise for Douglas's work. Dr. Chad Nelsen, then environmental director for Surfrider Foundation and now its national CEO, wrote, "It is with great sadness that we report the passing of a legendary advocate of coastal protection in California and beyond. Peter Douglas will remain an icon of coastal protection.... During his lengthy and successful career Peter was a true champion of coastal protection and beach access who led the Commission with integrity and compassion. He inspired many to join him in becoming active to protect what we love about the coast, myself included. Peter was a personal hero to me and many, many others. I am not alone in saying that he inspired my career choice and my dedication to protecting California's amazing coast for the benefit of all of us.... Peter, your spirit will live on in those fighting to protect our oceans, waves and beaches and will be honored by all who enjoy them."[11] From Dr. Serge Dedina, a surfer and executive director of the environmental group WildCoast: "Every time you spend time at a public beach in California, remember to thank Peter Douglas for conserving our coastline!!"[12] Said Annie Notthoff, California advocacy director for the Natural Resources Defense Council, a national organization: "California set the standard for protecting the coast, and that has expanded to almost every other coastal state in the country. So if you look out to sea anywhere in the country, California and Peter Douglas have had a major impact."[13] Documentary filmmaker Janet Bridgers called

Douglas "the Thomas Jefferson of the coast," while others compared him in stature to John Muir.[14] Former Coastal Commission chair Sara Wan told this writer that, although Douglas was stubborn and she differed with him many times, she believed his intent was to protect "the integrity of the commission. . . . His keeping the [commission] strong and independent has made all the difference."[15] Similarly, former coastal commissioner Toni Iseman averred, "No other person could have achieved what he [Douglas] did. . . . He was strong, brilliant, personable, fearless, [and] stubborn. . . . He picked fights with the big boys [oilmen, developers, and wealthy landowners]. . . . He could see problems before others. He was afraid of no one."[16] According to former coastal commissioner Shirley Dettloff, "He believed in the coast of California and had a great love for every mile of it. His work was of great economic value [through tourism] to the state" because he made sure the coast was not overbuilt and beaches remained "open to all."[17] "He deserves a medal of valor," concluded attorney Paul C. Horgan, who with two colleagues sued the Coastal Commission and won a precedent-setting case involving the Bolsa Chica Wetland in 1999.[18] Dr. Charles F. Lester, Douglas's successor as executive director of the commission, declared, "Peter was a giant in the world of coastal protection. . . . [His] undying dedicated service played an essential role in the building of California's coastal protection program, which is a model of success for communities around the world."[19] National Oceanic and Atmospheric Administration director Margaret Davidson stated in June 2012: "Peter [Douglas] was a legend in California's coastal history and his legacy today is a model for others [to] follow."[20] Former Assemblyman Fred Keeley of Santa Cruz called Douglas one of the hundred most important Californians in state history.[21]

Other memorial statements, mainly but not exclusively from opponents of the commission or its deceased leader, ranged from grudging recognition of Douglas's integrity and talents to expressions of hope that property rights would now, with a new executive director, be given what his critics deemed as due regard in the agency's decisions. While most of his opponents remained unsparing in their criticisms of Douglas, some of his most implacable foes acknowledged his competency, sincerity, and effectiveness as a coastal manager and communicator. Pacific Legal Foundation cofounder and attorney Ronald Zumbrun, for example, remarked about Douglas's formidable skills and leadership of the commission: "Peter has been such a dominant person and so effective in his maneuvering and political instincts, I doubt anyone can match that."[22] Lloyd Billingsley, another staunch critic of Douglas and the Coastal Commission, acknowledged that Douglas's role in cowriting Proposition 20 and the subsequent Coastal Act, as well as his serving as deputy director of the commission, and then executive director of that panel were "feat[s] . . . practically unrivalled." In terms of influence, "Douglas outdid" all other officials in California government.[23] More negatively, attorney Paul Beard, another lawyer with the Pacific Legal Foundation, complained, "It is kind of frustrating from our perspective the kind of praise he's getting. The idea that this guy's some kind of hero is foreign to us and the thousands of property owners that happen to live in the coastal zone. . . . One would hope in this change in leadership, we replace a zealot with someone who's a little more pragmatic."[24] Coastal commissioner Wendy Mitchell, who had been appointed by Governor Arnold Schwarzenegger, called Douglas a "demagogue" and "cultish." Yet she added, "I have tremendous respect for him. He was a master of issues. . . . Peter Douglas will always be synonymous with the coast."[25] Doubtlessly, if Douglas had been less charismatic and more accommodating to the wishes of property owners, developers, local governing bodies, and antiregulation interests, criticism of him and the commission likely would have been more muted. When such criticism was directed at him during his tenure as the commission's executive director, Douglas seemed to wear it as a badge of honor.

THE CONDITION OF THE COAST, CIRCA 2012

While the opinions just surveyed are illuminating, they are also pretty subjective. To more objectively gauge the effectiveness of Douglas and the agency he headed, a cursory look at the condition of the coast around 2012 should prove helpful. Given the mandates of the Coastal Act, attention here is focused on two matters of overriding importance: public access to beaches and the extent of development in the Coastal Zone.

Public Beach Access

The big picture regarding public beach access is heartening. This is due in large part to section 30211 of the California Coastal Act (1976) and its enforcement by government agencies and the courts. That provision reads in part: "Development shall not interfere with the public's right of access to the sea . . . including the use of the dry and rocky coastal beaches to the first line of terrestrial vegetation." This provision of the law, largely Douglas's handi-work, outlived him to serve as an instrument of beach access justice.

What evidence is there that this provision of the famed Coastal Act and its enforcement have worked well? According to the Coastal Commission's authoritative *California Coastal Access Guide* (2014) the number of public coastal access ways increased from 721 in 1981 to 1,150 by 2014. That is a 63 percent increase! The commission, under Douglas's leadership during nearly that entire period, obviously did its job well—too well for some people—in that regard. When the agency does its job that effectively in assuring coastal access, some wealthy property owners intent on maintaining the exclusivity of beaches in front of their homes almost invariably complain loudly about commission "overreach" and "disregard" for property rights. Seldom did these critics attack the Coastal Act itself (though, as shown, the Marine Forests case was a major exception); instead, they pilloried the commission and especially its controversial chief.[26]

Thanks largely to the commission and its enforcement of the coastal law, more coastal access ways have recently been opened, and in other instances outcomes are pending. In Malibu (as shown in chapter 5), billionaire land-owners fought long and hard against the Coastal Commission to block the public's use of premier beaches close to their respective properties. The battles lasted years and involved Douglas near the end of his lengthy career with the commission, and he did not live long enough to witness and savor all of the victories for which he had fought. Such was the case when, in 2015, a long-contested public access route to Carbon Beach, Malibu, was opened up and made wheelchair-accessible.[27] Up the coast at Martins Beach, near Half Moon Bay, another billionaire permitted temporary public access to the coast in an ongoing battle begun by Douglas and the commission in 2008.[28] The ultimate disposition of the matter has yet to be decided in the courts.

Another measure of public access is the availability of short-term lodging in beach areas. For example, with strong support from Peter Douglas the Coastal Commission directed $5 million in mitigation monies toward the restoration of historic Crystal Cove cottages in South Orange County. Those quaint beachfront accommodations rent for approximately $35 a night per bed in a dorm lodge; the most expensive cottage sleeps up to ten people for $245 a night.[29] These are family-friendly, bargain fees in a picturesque seaside area known for its extremely expensive real estate.

Finally, public access—especially to what many regard as the most scenic areas along the state's littoral—has been enhanced by the slow but steady extension of the California Coastal Trail, a work-in-progress according to one Coastal Commission staffer (see map 4 in chapter 4). Eventually, it will allow hikers and others not using motorized transport to traverse most of the state's coastline. As shown (chapter 4), the trail was an outgrowth of the passage of Proposition 20 and was envisioned in the Coastal Plan. The trail is about 50 percent complete today, thanks to the joint efforts of the Coastal Commission, Coastal Conservancy, State Parks Department, and Coastwalk California (a citizens' volunteer organization).[30]

For sure, the Coastal Commission was not solely responsible for these achievements facilitating people's use of the shore, but its role was substantial and arguably paramount. By any reckoning, California's beaches were considerably more accessible to the public when Douglas retired from the commission compared to when he started working for that governmental entity that he had helped create.

Coastal Development

Was California's coast more developed in 2012 than when Douglas began his service with and leadership of the commission? Yes. There were several more power plants and the Carlsbad desalination facility (see chapter 5). More homes dotted shoreline areas, especially in Southern California. The Los Angeles–Long Beach port terminals, America's largest and busiest, have undergone significant expansion to accommodate an ever-increasing trans-pacific trade. Much of the rural Coastal Zone, on the other hand, "looks as it did in 1972." Mendocino County, Big Sur in Monterey County, and the Gaviota coast in Santa Barbara County "are largely unchanged from their rural character forty years ago," affirmed Dr. Charles Lester in 2013.[31]

Significantly, in most instances of development the Coastal Commission secured mitigation funds from developers whose projects demonstrably harmed the environment. A highly publicized instance of this occurred early in the twenty-first century when the twin ports of Los Angeles and Long Beach expanded their shipping complex, which resulted in a loss of valuable marine habitat. In exchange for approving the needed permits, the commission arranged for the joint port authorities to pay about $79 million in mitigation money, which went toward restoration of the degraded Bolsa Chica Wetland in Huntington Beach.[32] So, though harbor development went forward in one place, wetland restoration began in another—thanks largely to Douglas's leadership. The benefits from this kind of offsetting are relatively easy to show: for a certain quantity of habitat loss a specified number of dollars was paid and used for protecting coastal resources. The public benefits of Douglas's and the commission's role in managing coastal development can in many instances be quantified and, consequently, shown to be virtually unarguable.

As unarguable as these offsetting benefits may be, some skeptics might need further assurance that the state's coastal economy has not suffered unduly as a result of regulated development. Per the National Ocean Economics Program's report to the State of California (2005): "California has the largest Ocean Economy in the United States, ranking number one for both employment and gross state product." Moreover, California's ocean economy, listed at $45.7 billion in that report, accounted for 86 percent of the state's total economy.[33] Going back to 1990, these figures and others show a pattern of increase and the state's sustained dominance in coastal/oceanic economic activity.[34] The conclusion, then, is patently evident: in coastal California, regulated development and record-setting levels of economic activity have gone hand-in-hand during Douglas's tenure with the Coastal Commission.

As great as the above-mentioned benefits have been, some people, including this writer, contend that the greatest benefits to the coast most likely have been the unquantifiable ones. Douglas, as always, said it earliest, most often, and best: "Many of the most significant accomplishments in my specific area of work, coastal management, are things one can NOT see—the wetlands not filled, the public access not lost, the water pollution that does not occur, scenic vistas not spoiled, the subdivisions not approved, the offshore oil drilling that is not happening. Our work is not obviously self-promoting[;] and the better we do it, the less likely people will think there is a problem that needs fixing." Judy B. Rosener, a former coastal commissioner and UC Irvine professor, concurred.[35] This insight is profound. Though it flies in the face of our common inclination to measure and quantify outcomes, nevertheless it corresponds with what our eyes tell us when we visit the coastlines of Florida and other Gulf and Atlantic seaboard states, where high-rise structures (Florida), oil-drilling platforms (Texas, Louisiana, Alabama), power plants (New York, New Jersey), and other industrial facilities abound. Perhaps that is one reason why a visiting delegation from the World Bank told Douglas in 2011 that California has the world's most protected coast. Members of that delegation expressed surprise that the Coastal Commission had not been captured by the business interests it regulates.[36]

Thus on Douglas's watch as executive director, public access to the beach was greatly increased and development was controlled and mitigated so as to restore and enhance coastal resources. All of this was accomplished in a state with a nation-sized economy, powerful corporate interests, and celebrity property-rights advocates—many of whom battled the Coastal Commission relentlessly in courtrooms. Under such circumstances, coupled at times with crippling budget cuts for the commission staff, the fact that so much of the state's storied coast has remained relatively unspoiled, scenic, and open to the people is nothing short of amazing. Figuratively speaking, the biblical trope of an undersized and courageous David versus a gargantuan Goliath may come readily to mind for some.

COASTAL SAGE

To say Peter Douglas's career in coastal management was impressive would be an understatement; his leadership of what some experts recognize as America's, if not the world's, most powerful land use agency was a tour de force.[37] As shown, even some of his most indefatigable opponents with the Pacific Legal Foundation have granted as much.

That Douglas was an environmental leader for his time seems incontestable. Beyond that, some hold that Douglas's place in California's and the nation's environmental history should rank with that of John Muir, David Brower, Rachel Carson, and others in that pantheon of revered historical figures. In that regard, several points come to mind. Unlike them, and although he was a fluid writer, Douglas did not leave behind seminal book-length publications—like Carson's blockbuster, *Silent Spring*—on environmental issues of great moment. Instead of writing books, Douglas coauthored foundational state laws and federal regulations.[38] Nor was he a principal launcher of a movement like Muir (conservation) or Brower or Carson (ecology/environmentalism). The movement to preserve the coast from overdevelopment and for public access was already under way (chapter 3) when Douglas signed on to it. Instead, he was a major founder and later manager of a powerful state regulatory body, the California Coastal Commission. Whereas Muir, Brower, and Carson pushed and lobbied government to act on environmental matters, Douglas was an agent of government and worked entirely within its mandates—mandates that he was instrumental in crafting—to save the coast. With these distinctions in mind and Douglas's short-term environmental repute assured, more time and a wider perspective are needed to tell where his standing in the annals of environmental history will come to rest. Clearly, in his favor, Douglas's influence—like that of other environmental giants—extended across the country and to other parts of the world. His wise counsel on coastal management was sought by the governments of Japan, Turkey, Israel, and Vietnam; moreover, he served on a China–United States panel on integrated coastal management.[39]

While Douglas's influence extended spatially far beyond the borders of California, there is every reason to believe his environmental imprint will extend temporally, too, at least into the near future. In this regard, the work of three surfer–coastal activists comes immediately to mind. Dr. Chad Nelsen, CEO of Surfrider Foundation, is just one of the many talented young stewards of the coast mentored by Douglas. Dr. Serge Dedina, currently mayor of the city of Imperial Beach (San Diego County) and executive director of WildCoast, a marine conservationist organization active in California and Baja California, is another highly able early career leader who feels he owes a debt of gratitude to Douglas.[40] High-profile environmental attorney Mark Massara, former director of the Sierra Club's California Coastal Program, described Peter as a "legal mentor and father figure" for him.[41] In short, a generation of younger coastal preservationists who have been inspired by their hero have already moved into positions of leadership in environmental organizations and local government and are fighting hard to save the coast. For them, Douglas not only exemplified the courage of leadership but equally, if not more importantly, helped provide the tools needed to succeed: namely, the California Coastal Act and Local Coastal Programs that bind local governing bodies to policies aimed at assuring public beach access and closely regulated development.

Finally, as much as Peter Douglas was a high-ranking administrator in California and a notable warrior-bureaucrat, near the end of his career if not sooner he took on the mantle of a wise elder statesman who saw coastal management and citizen-activism as intertwined components of an earth-centered stewardship. Shortly after his death, when particularly troublesome issues would be deliberated at often-packed Coastal Commission meetings, one could hear from someone testifying in public comment: "What would Peter do?" If ever there was an oracular voice on such occasions, assuredly it was—and will continue to be in the foreseeable future—that of California's and America's coastal sage.

A Selected Time Line

CALIFORNIA COASTAL CONSERVATION
AND PETER DOUGLAS

1961 Kay Kerr, Sylvia McLaughlin, and Esther Gulick formed Save the Bay to protect San Francisco Bay from overdevelopment and pollution.

Peter Douglas entered UC Berkeley as a freshman.

1962 Public opposition blocked siting of a nuclear reactor at Bodega Head on California's North Coast.

Douglas transferred to UCLA, and graduated three years later with a bachelor's degree in psychology.

1964 Governor Edmund G. "Pat" Brown convened a conference of scientists and policy makers in Los Angeles on "California and the World Ocean."

1965 The McAteer-Petris Act established the temporary San Francisco Bay Conservation and Development Commission, which became a prototype for the California Coastal Commission years later.

1966 Douglas entered UCLA School of Law.

1968 In response to the Sea Ranch developer closing off public access to ten miles of beach along the Sonoma coast, William Kortum and others formed Californians Organized to Acquire Access to State Tidelands for the purpose of assuring open beaches statewide.

Los Angeles–area civic activists Ellen Stern Harris and Dr. Richard H. Ball conceived the idea of a statewide coastal regulatory agency.

1969 The blowout of a Union Oil offshore rig near Santa Barbara became "the environmental shot heard around the world"; eight hundred square miles of ocean along thirty-five miles of virtually pristine coast was blackened by oil, killing thousands of birds and numerous dolphins and seals, galvanizing coastal environmentalists to take political action.

Get Oil Out, a citizens group organized by Bud Bottoms, circulated petitions, garnering a hundred thousand signatures of people demanding a ban on offshore oil drilling.

The California State Lands Commission declared a moratorium on issuance of new leases for oil drilling within the three-nautical-mile offshore limit.

An amendment to the McAteer-Petris Act made the Bay Conservation and Development Commission a permanent state agency.

Douglas graduated from the UCLA School of Law, passed the California Bar Examination, and traveled overseas.

1970   The California Environmental Quality Act passed, requiring lead public agencies to prepare environmental impact reports on projects likely to consequentially impact natural surroundings, including air and water quality and animal habitats.

The First Earth Day was celebrated, on April 22.

1971   A young attorney, Douglas was hired by Assemblyman Alan Sieroty (D-Beverly Hills) as a legislative aide tasked with helping to secure passage of a yet-to-be-written statewide coastal management bill.

California Coastal Alliance, a citizens coalition of more than a hundred environmental groups, formed to advocate the establishment of a statewide coastal regulatory agency and management program.

Douglas, in consultation with attorneys E. Lewis Reid and Ray McDevitt, drafted AB 1471, which became one of more than a dozen failed measures that would have established a statewide coastal commission, and traveled throughout California promoting the bill.

1972   Congress passed and President Richard M. Nixon signed the Coastal Zone Management Act, providing that if coastal states adopted comprehensive seaboard management plans protecting resources and assuring public access, then such states could regulate federal activities in coastal areas.

Douglas and Ray McDevitt drafted Proposition 20, the California Coastal Zone Conservation Act, establishing a temporary, statewide, twelve-member coastal commission (with two appointments each made by the governor, the Speaker of the assembly, and the Senate Rules Committee, and the other six selected by regional commissioners) and six regional commissions.

In campaigning for passage of Proposition 20, in which Douglas drafted proponents' answers to difficult questions, unpaid volunteers gathered 418,000 validated signatures to put the measure on the November ballot.

Senate president pro tem James Mills led a 550-mile bicycle ride from San Francisco to San Diego, with approximately a hundred riders, campaigning for passage of Proposition 20.

In the November election, voters passed Proposition 20, mustering a 55.1 percent majority.

1973   Joseph E. Bodovitz began his term as the first executive director of the statewide Coastal Commission.

Still employed by Alan Sieroty, Douglas now served as a consultant to the Assembly Natural Resources Committee and the Select Committee on Coastal Zone Resources; in these capacities Douglas began work on the California Coastal Zone Conservation Plan, which he called the "Constitution of the Coast."

Robert Moretti, assembly Speaker, approved setting up an ad hoc committee to build ties between coastal advocates and the state legislature to facilitate passage of a permanent statewide coastal act.

1975   Cowritten by Douglas, the Coastal Zone Conservation Plan was adopted by the state Coastal Commission and presented to Governor Edmund G. (Jerry) Brown.

Writing of the Coastal Act began and continued into February of the following year.

1976   Coauthored by Douglas, the permanent Coastal Act (SB 1277) passed both houses of the state legislature with timely, essential help from Governor Brown.

Douglas began new employment as the state Coastal Commission's legislative representative in Sacramento.

1977   Douglas was promoted to deputy director of the statewide Coastal Commission.

Under the aegis of the federal Coastal Zone Management Act, the National Oceanic and Atmospheric Administration approved California's coastal program, which included the Coastal Commission, the California Coastal Conservancy, and the San Francisco Bay Conservation and Development Commission.

1978   Michael L. Fischer replaced Bodovitz, becoming the second executive director of the Coastal Commission; Douglas was the repository of the commission's collective memory.

1980   A Field Poll found that only half the people sampled had heard of the Coastal Commission, and a majority of those rated its performance as "fair" or "poor."

1981   More than sixty bills introduced in the state legislature related to the Coastal Commission; some aimed at watering down its powers, and one provided for its abolition.

To Douglas's disappointment, the Coastal Act's mandate regarding affordable seaboard lodgings was weakened by amendment.

The six regional coastal commissions were terminated.

1982   Republican George Deukmejian, who wanted to abolish the Coastal Commission, was elected governor of California; under him the commission's staff was cut by 40 percent and its budget slashed by more than a third; Douglas vowed to lead the commission through the troubling Deukmejian era.

1984 Congress imposed a moratorium on new oil leasing sites in federal waters beyond California's three-nautical-mile limit, renewing it every year until it was lifted by President George W. Bush in 2008.

Surfrider Foundation, a national organization advocating healthy oceans and beaches, was founded in San Clemente, California.

1985 Peter M. Douglas replaced Fischer as executive director of the Coastal Commission; Douglas's tenure in that office would last twenty-six years.

The Coastal Commission, in accordance with Douglas's views, voted in favor of conditioning the Jonathan Club's permit for expansion onto state-owned beach property by insisting on a nondiscriminatory membership policy; women, Jews, and nonwhites thereby became eligible for club membership; the Jonathan Club challenged the decision and lost in trial court, appealing to the State Supreme Court, which refused to hear the case.

1987 Governor Deukmejian directed Douglas to close the Coastal Commission offices in Santa Barbara and Santa Cruz; Douglas refused the directive and those offices remained open.

In the case of *Nollan v. California Coastal Commission,* the U.S. Supreme Court weakened the Coastal Commission's regulatory power by requiring proof of a "nexus," or strong connection between a permitting condition and the intended public benefit to be achieved by that condition. Douglas rued the decision.

1988 The U.S. Supreme Court upheld the Coastal Commission's conditional permit regarding expansion of the footprint of Los Angeles's Jonathan Club, forcing the end of the club's discriminatory membership policy; Douglas saw this as part of the commission's and his legacy.

1991 An attempt was made by two prodevelopment Coastal Commission appointees of Willie Brown—David Malcolm and Mark Nathanson—to fire Douglas; commissioners voted unanimously, ten to zero, for Douglas to keep his job.

1994 The state legislature passed the California Coastal Sanctuary Act, prohibiting, except in defined instances, the state's issuance of new leases for extraction of oil and gas in designated waters within the three-nautical-mile zone.

1996 The Coastal Commission voted eight to three, against Douglas's advice, to allow Koll Real Estate Group to build nine hundred homes in the Bolsa Chica lowlands and twenty-four hundred homes in an adjacent upland mesa.

The Coastal Commission for the first time had a Republican majority (eight to four), during Pete Wilson's governorship, sparking a Republican-led effort to oust Douglas; newspapers and prominent Republicans and Democrats opposed the effort; the executive director's opponents on the commission backed down; a vote was not taken and Douglas kept his job.

1998   The Coastal Commission rejected changes in San Luis Obispo County's Local Coastal Program; approval of the LCP would have allowed for construction near Hearst Castle in San Simeon of a golf course, large hotel, hundreds of new homes, a shopping complex, and employee living accommodations; the widening of Highway 1 into a four-lane thoroughfare; and more. Douglas was dissatisfied with the deal later struck with the Hearst family that allowed some development.

1999   In a landmark decision in a lawsuit brought by the Bolsa Chica Land Trust against the California Coastal Commission, the Superior Court of San Diego ruled that developers' housing projects could not disturb environmentally sensitive habitat areas; Douglas later said he was glad the commission lost, because the Coastal Act's prohibition against building in environmentally sensitive habitat areas was upheld.

California Coastal Protection Network, a highly effective advocacy group for the state's seaboard environment, was founded by Susan Jordan.

The Marine Life Protection Act was passed by the Sacramento legislature for the purpose of reevaluating existing marine protected areas and designing new ones—all for the purpose of safeguarding aquatic habitats along California's coast.

California Coastkeeper Alliance, composed of twelve independent organizations, was founded to advocate protection for swimmable, fishable, and drinkable waters along the state's shore and rivers feeding into the Pacific Ocean.

2000   WildCoast was founded by Dr. Serge Dedina and headquartered in Imperial Beach, San Diego; it aimed to preserve marine habitats from overfishing and pollution, especially along the coasts of California and Baja California.

2002   Douglas and the Coastal Commission decided to push for public access to ten exclusive Malibu beach enclaves, in the face of strong opposition from wealthy homeowners and property-rights advocates.

2003   Restoration of Crystal Cove's historic cottages at Crystal Cove State Park (between Corona del Mar and Laguna Beach) began with $5 million in Coastal Commission mitigation fees secured and overseen by Douglas.

Prompted by the Marine Forests lawsuit, Governor Gray Davis called the state legislature into a special session, during which the Coastal Act was amended so as to fortify it against separation-of-powers challenges.

2004   Douglas and the Coastal Commission contended that the agency's regulatory reach extended seaward beyond the three-nautical-mile limit in instances where oil rigs in federal waters discharged pollutants into the ocean that degraded marine habitats within the three-mile zone.

2005   In the Marine Forests lawsuit, the California Supreme Court upheld, among other things, the right of the Coastal Commission to issue "cease and desist" orders and, most importantly, the constitutionality of the 1976 Coastal Act; Douglas was greatly relieved.

Having met with little success in earlier lawsuits against the Coastal Commission, Malibu celebrity-homeowner David Geffen dropped his lawsuit against the agency and allowed public access to the beach in front of his property.

2007   Amid growing concerns about climate change and against staff recommendation, the Coastal Commission issued a Coastal Development Permit to Poseidon Resources to a build a $900-million desalination plant in Carlsbad, California.

2008   Some thirty-five hundred people attended a Coastal Commission meeting at the Del Mar Fairgrounds; Douglas delivered a powerful speech condemning the Transportation Corridor Agency's State Route 241 Toll Road extension project that would have been built through a state park and nature preserve; the commission denied the building permit.

2011   In June, Douglas delivered the keynote address at a Sacramento conference on the California Coastal Commission, sponsored by *Capitol Weekly*.

In August, Douglas went on medical leave from the Coastal Commission; he traveled throughout the state visiting the people and sites that meant the most to him.

On September 30, 2011, some four hundred family members and close friends poignantly celebrated Douglas's life and his accomplishments as a coastal manager, in a gathering at San Francisco's Aquarium of the Bay / Pier 39, which Douglas attended in a wheelchair.

2012   Amid family and a few Coastal Commission colleagues, Peter Douglas succumbed to cancer on April 1 at the home of his sister, Christiane, in La Quinta, California.

APPENDIX B

A Selected List of Peter Douglas's Accomplishments and Honors

An original member of the National Oceanic and Atmospheric Administration's Science Advisory Board

Appointed by President Bill Clinton to the U.S. Panel on Ocean Exploration that authored *Discovering Earth's Final Frontier: A U.S. Strategy for Ocean Exploration* (2000)

Member of the National Academy of Sciences Committee on Science and Policy for the Coastal Ocean

Member of the H. John Heinz III Center for Science, Economics and the Environment advisory committee for the Sustainable Oceans and Waterways Program

Participated in drafting of the regulations implementing the federal Coastal Zone Management Act of 1972

A leader in the successful effort to prevent new federal offshore leasing for oil and gas development on the Outer Continental Shelf in areas lacking necessary onshore infrastructure support

As a school board member, cochaired a successful campaign in California to enact a parcel tax to support public schools

National Coast Trail Association Recognition Award (1977)

CalCoast Friend of the Coast 2000 Award

Sierra Club Distinguished Service Award (2004)

Pamela Wright Lloyd Environmental Stewardship Award (2005)

Coastal Zone Management Award from the National Oceanographic and Atmospheric Administration (2011)

Environmental Defense Center's 2006 Environmental Hero Award

Coastal Hero Award from California Lieutenant Governor John Garamendi (2009)

Source: Adapted from the California Coastal Commission website: www.coastal .ca.gov/pd-bio-comments.pdf.

NOTES

PREFACE

1. Peter Douglas, "Blog 2: Cancer and Saving the Sundown Coast—a Personal Story, Part One," June 12, 2011, http://livelovewithcancer.blogspot.com.

1. FEW SAFE HARBORS

1. Technically, baptism into the Catholic Church would not have trumped Maria's Jewish heritage in Hitler's Germany. Moreover, in accordance with orthodox Hebraic law, someone is Jewish if his or her birth mother is a Jew.

2. Typed transcript of Peter Douglas's unfinished and unpublished autobiography, a copy of which was furnished to the author by his sister, Christiane Douglas. Hereafter cited as Autobiography.

3. Peter Douglas, "Making Waves: Making a Difference," keynote speech at Surfrider Foundation's 15th Anniversary Event, August 28, 1999, San Diego, CA, www.beachapedia.org/Keynote_Speech_at_Surfrider_Foundation%27s_15_Anniversary_Event.

4. Ibid.

5. Autobiography. The initials "SS" stood for the German Schutzstaffel (literally translated as "Protective Echelon"), an elite paramilitary organization in Nazi Germany. Its members, who initially served as Adolph Hitler's personal bodyguards, were required to be of pure Aryan ancestry.

6. Ibid.

7. Douglas, "Making Waves."

8. Ibid. See also Christiane M. Douglas, *All My Children: The Life Story of Paula Elisabeth Vetter* (privately printed, 1997), 55. Hereafter cited as *All My Children*. A noncirculating copy of this revealing source, which includes family photographs, is housed in the library at the Pilgrim Place retirement community (where Paula Vetter once lived), in Claremont, CA. The VIP treatment that the party received

consisted of not having to be detained and processed at the Ellis Island immigration station. Instead, like some of the more prominent immigrants entering the United States, they were escorted to an alternative immigration office, where their entry into the country was greatly simplified and expedited.

9. Douglas, "Making Waves."

10. Ibid.

11. Douglas, Autobiography.

12. Christiane M. Douglas, sister of Peter Douglas, interview by author, December 21, 2013, in La Quinta, CA, audio recording. According to Christiane, young Peter told her he wanted to adopt the last name Douglas and suggested that she do likewise, since her last name would eventually be changed anyway when she married. See also Douglas, *All My Children,* 60.

13. Douglas, "Making Waves."

14. See Kurt and Alice R. Bergel, eds. and trans., *Albert Schweitzer and Alice Ehlers: A Friendship in Letters* (New York: University Press of America, 1991). The book's introduction provides an overview of their friendship and the numerous letters (translated into English) they exchanged. These letters, reprinted in the book's subsequent pages, furnish illuminating details on the lives and thinking of the two friends and correspondents.

15. Christiane M. Douglas, interview. Elsewhere, Peter stated: "I spent considerable alone-time with my grandmother and could not help but be influenced by her frequent mentioning of Schweitzer's environmental ethic. Those treasured Mima moments . . . planted seeds of environmentalism that went dormant in my adolescent mind to emerge in due time years later." See Peter Douglas, "Blog 2: Cancer and Saving the Sundown Coast—a Personal Story, Part One," Live Love with Cancer, June 12, 2011, http://livelovewithcancer.blogspot.com.

16. Douglas, "Making Waves."

17. "Old Nuclear Dump Off Coast Is a Relic of Era of Naivete in Toxic Disposal," *Los Angeles Times,* July 31, 1989. From the 1950s into the early 1960s the U.S. Navy regularly disposed of chemical-weapons waste in the area surrounding the southern Channel Islands. At the same time, contractors for the Atomic Energy Commission dumped some 47,800 barrels of low-level radioactive waste in the waters near the Farallon Islands (located offshore San Francisco), a major feeding habitat for great white sharks, sea lions and seals, and various seabirds. See also Robert Dawson and Gray Brechin, *Farewell Promised Land: Waking from the California Dream* (Berkeley: University of California Press, 1999), 172, 175.

18. Douglas, "Making Waves."

19. Peter Douglas, "Saving the Coast: A Job That's Never Done," speech delivered at the California Colloquium on Water, UC Berkeley, September 13, 2007, www.youtube.com/watch?v=fvFZ5cqH9KM. In this speech, Douglas mentioned his year as a UC Berkeley student in 1960–1961. In another speech, looking back on his early life in California, Douglas described himself as "an eager brainwashed disciple of the church of consumption. . . . I soon wanted to be more American than American[s]." See Peter Douglas, "Caring to Make a Difference: Environmental

Activism," speech before the Planning and Conservation League, April 14, 2007, unpublished.

20. Douglas, "Blog 2: Cancer and Saving the Sundown Coast."

21. Douglas, "Making Waves."

22. Douglas, "Caring to Make a Difference."

23. Robert H. Burnham, interview by author, August 25, 2015, at the latter's home in Laguna Beach, CA, audio recording.

24. Peter Douglas, interviewed by Jim Moriarty, CEO of Surfrider Foundation, on the occasion of presenting the former with the 2011 Wavemaker Coastal Impact Award. See digitalpodcast.com, Peter Douglas interview, at Surfrider.org. Among other things, Douglas attested to his wife's key role in facilitating his shift from political conservatism to liberalism.

25. Douglas, "Blog 2: Cancer and Saving the Sundown Coast." Douglas wrote, "Frustrated and disillusioned, even angry about the injustice, discrimination, absence of community consciousness[,] and self-righteous jingoism pervasive in America[,] we decided to leave shortly after I took the Bar exam in summer of 1969. Besides[,] what kind of regressive country was it that didn't even offer its citizens universal health care! Ironically, we took the advice of a popular jingoistic bumper sticker of the time: 'America. Love it or leave it!'"

26. Ibid.

27. Douglas, "Making Waves."

28. Douglas, "Blog 2: Cancer and Saving the Sundown Coast."

29. Ibid.

30. Ibid.

31. Ibid.

32. Ibid.

2. CALIFORNIA'S COAST

1. Peter Douglas, "Making Waves: Making a Difference," keynote speech at Surfrider Foundation's 15th Anniversary Event, August 28, 1999, San Diego, CA, www.beachapedia.org/Keynote_Speech_at_Surfrider_Foundation%27s_15_Anniversary_Event.

2. *Ophiolite* derives from the Greek word *ophis,* meaning "snake." In their appearance, ophiolites have been thought to resemble a wavy, serpentine pattern, hence the name.

3. Information about Lawson, plate tectonics, and ocean processes was communicated to this author by Dr. Gary Griggs, director of the Institute of Marine Sciences at UC Santa Cruz, in an email dated December 23, 2016.

4. Gary Griggs, *Introduction to California's Beaches and Coast* (Berkeley: University of California Press, 2010), 16.

5. John McPhee, *Assembling California* (New York: Farrar, Straus and Giroux, 1993), 9.

6. Keith Heyer Meldahl, *Rough-Hewn Land: A Geologic Journey from California to the Rocky Mountains* (Berkeley: University of California Press, 2011), 17, 28.

7. Griggs, email to author, December 23, 2016.

8. As telling as photographs of the destruction are, the reportage of writer Jack London arguably captures, even more, the scale of human suffering resulting from the catastrophe. See especially his article "Story of an Eye Witness," published in *Collier's Magazine,* May 5, 1906, reprinted online by the California Department of Parks and Recreation at parks.ca.gov.

9. See National Park Service, Point Reyes National Seashore, California, "Geologic Activity," last updated November 21, 2016, www.nps.gov/pore/naturescience /geologicactivity.htm.

10. As late as the 1750s, some European maps erroneously depicted California (extending at that time from the tip of present-day Baja California to Alaska) as an island. Though Spanish mariners had known better by the early 1600s, some of Europe's cartographers were very late in letting go of the island California myth. See, especially, Vincent Virga, *California: Mapping the Golden State through History; Rare and Unusual Maps from the Library of Congress* (Guilford, CT: Morris, 2010), 10–15.

11. Keith Heyer Meldahl, *Surf, Sand, and Stone: How Waves, Earthquakes, and Other Forces Shape the Southern California Coast* (Oakland: University of California Press, 2015), 17.

12. Ibid., 18.

13. Florian Schulz, *The Wild Edge: Freedom to Roam the Pacific Coast* (Seattle: Mountaineers Books, 2015), 36, 64. Near the end of Douglas's life, he reportedly went whale watching off the coast of Orange County; see chapter 6.

14. Elna Bakker, *An Island Called California: An Ecological Introduction to Its Natural Communities,* 2d ed. (Berkeley: University of California Press, 1984), 9.

15. For a detailed discussion of the physics of wavemaking that relates to Southern California surfing—a topic that goes far beyond the intent and scope of this book—see Meldahl, *Surf, Sand, and Stone,* 89–117.

16. Griggs, *Introduction to California's Beaches and Coast,* 27.

17. Meldahl, *Rough-Hewn Land,* 3–4.

18. Gary Griggs and Deepika Shrestha Ross, *California Coast from the Air: Images of a Changing Landscape* (Missoula, MT: Mountain Press, 2014), 3.

19. "Protecting California's Valuable Wetlands," *Coastal News* (California Coastal Commission) 4, no. 3 (April–May 1981): 4, California Coastal Commission, Executive Director Files, Personal Correspondence, R254.020, California State Archives, Sacramento. By the 1980s only about seventy thousand acres of state wetlands remained.

20. In the not too distant past, the photography of Ansel Adams (1902–1984; greatly admired by Peter Douglas) and Edward Weston (1886–1958) evoked the beauty and grandeur of the California coast, as did the paintings of impressionists Childe Hassam (1859–1935), William Ritchel (1864–1949), and the legendary William Wendt (1865–1946), and the poetry of Robert Louis Stevenson (1850–1894) and Robinson Jeffers (1887–1962), among many others.

21. Gary Griggs, *Our Ocean Backyard: Collected Essays* (CreateSpace Independent Publishing Platform, 2014), 266–267. This self-published work is a compilation of Griggs's newspaper columns, titled Our Ocean Backyard, appearing in the *Santa Cruz Sentinel* newspaper. According to Griggs, wave heights along California's Central Coast increased 1.5 feet during the period from 1980 to 2002. "Looking . . . along the southern California coast, from 1984 to 1995 there were seven storms that produced wave heights of 16 feet or greater and four storms that generated waves 20 feet or higher. Over the next 15-year interval from 1996 to 2010, there were 69 events with waves of 16 feet or greater and 10 events that resulted in wave heights of 20 feet or greater. Something is changing" (267).

22. Due to a change in the normal Pacific atmospheric pressure system, winds that usually blow in an east-to-west pattern reverse direction, moving warm equatorial water back toward South America. Earlier observers noted this phenomenon around Christmas time, calling the arrival of warm water El Niño, evocative of the birth of Jesus of Nazareth. On reaching the coasts of Ecuador and Peru, the warm waters raise tidal levels while dispersing northward and southward along the west coasts of the Americas. See Gary Griggs, Kiki Patsch, and Lauret Savoy, eds., *Living with the Changing California Coast* (Berkeley: University of California Press, 2005), 24–32.

23. Griggs, *Introduction to California's Beaches and Coast,* 29.

24. Ibid., 47, 49.

25. *Los Angeles Times,* January 19, 2015. See also NASA, "New Satellite Animation Shows 'Pineapple Express' Bringing Rains to California," February 10, 2014, www.nasa.gov/content/new-satellite-animation-shows-pineapple-express-bringing-rains-to-california/#.VL6ro1pUz9B.

26. For an informative report and apt photographs, see Megan Barnes, *San Pedro Today,* January 2012, 17–19. See also Donna Littlejohn, "San Pedro Landslide Work Continues as Excess Groundwater Is Drained," *Daily Breeze,* October 23, 2014, www.dailybreeze.com/general-news/20141023/san-pedro-landslide-work-continues-as-excess-groundwater-is-drained.

27. The literature connecting global warming and sea-level rise is extensive. See, especially, the work of two scientists, Orrin H. Pilkey and Rob Young, *The Rising Sea* (Washington, DC: Island Press, 2009), 4, 34–40.

28. Griggs, *Our Ocean Backyard,* 249.

29. California Climate Change Center, *The Impacts of Sea-Level Rise on the California Coast: Final Paper,* Sacramento: California Energy Commission, 2009, http://pacinst.org/app/uploads/2014/04/sea-level-rise.pdf.

30. National Research Council et al., *Sea-Level Rise for the Coasts of California, Oregon, and Washington: Past, Present, and Future* (Washington, DC: National Academies Press, 2012), 10, nap.edu.

31. See California Coastal Commission, *Sea Level Rise Policy Guidance,* adopted unanimously August 12, 2015, www.coastal.ca.gov/climate/slrguidance.html.

32. Allan A. Schoenherr, C. Robert Feldmeth, and Michael J. Emerson, *Natural History of the Islands of California* (Berkeley: University of California Press, 1999),

47. The fact that some of the Channel Islands contain sedimentary rocks indicates that some of these insular landmasses were not wholly volcanic in origin. California's islands are the five Farallons (located about thirty-two miles west of the Golden Gate Bridge), Año Nuevo (situated near the coast between San Francisco and Santa Cruz), and eight Channel Islands (all located just seaward of the Southern California Bight, an arc of coastline from San Diego to Santa Barbara), plus an assortment of islands and islets in San Francisco Bay and its Delta hinterland.

33. The rich human history of the Channel Islands is told well in Frederic Caire Chiles, *California's Channel Islands: A History* (Norman: University of Oklahoma Press, 2015).

34. Ibid., 33–34. According to Chiles, other accounts have Cabrillo wintering on, and dying from a fall on, Santa Catalina Island.

35. Schoenherr et al., *Natural History of the Islands of California*, 179–195.

36. Ibid., 122–124; John Ryan Fischer, *Cattle Colonialism: An Environmental History of the Conquest of California and Hawai'i* (Chapel Hill: University of North Carolina Press, 2015), 45–55.

37. Stevenson is quoted in Philip L. Fradkin and Alex L. Fradkin, *The Left Coast: California on the Edge* (Berkeley: University of California Press, 2011), 37–38.

38. Ibid., 40–41.

39. Center for Marine Sciences, Cal Poly, San Luis Obispo, "History of the Pier," n.d., www.marine.calpoly.edu/history-pier.

40. See Venice Historical Society, "On the Toss of a Coin: Our Story," n.d., www.venicehistorical.org; Thomas J. Osborne, *Pacific Eldorado: A History of Greater California* (Malden, MA: Wiley-Blackwell, 2013), 242.

41. For a useful history, see "YWCA Builds Asilomar," Asilomar State Beach and Conference Grounds, *Visitors Guide,* no. 13, visitasilomar.com.

42. Osborne, *Pacific Eldorado,* 241.

43. David M. Carlberg, *Bolsa Chica: Its History from Prehistoric Times to the Present* (Huntington Beach, CA: Amigos de Bolsa Chica, 2009), 120.

44. Banning Ranch Conservancy, "Banning Ranch Park and Preserve: A Vision for the Future," March 20, 2014, p. 10, banningranchconservancy.org.

45. Osborne, *Pacific Eldorado,* 269–270.

46. Fradkin and Fradkin, *The Left Coast,* 77–78.

47. See Demographia, "Coastal County Population: 1900–2010," n.d., www.demographia.com/db-coastalco.pdf. The statistics have been drawn from the U.S. Bureau of the Census and the National Oceanic and Atmospheric Administration.

48. Kevin Starr, *Golden Dreams: California in an Age of Abundance, 1950–1963* (New York: Oxford University Press, 2009), 12.

49. See Joshua Paddison and University of California, "1921–Present: Modern California—Migration, Technology, Cities," Calisphere, University of California, 2005, www.calisphere.universityofcalifornia.edu/calcultures/eras/era6.html.

50. Charles F. Queenan, *The Port of Los Angeles: From Wilderness to World Port* (Los Angeles: Los Angeles Harbor Department, 1983), 105–111. The containerization

and expansion of the Port of Los Angeles in the 1950s and 1960s were of epic proportions. Towering cranes appeared, five new cargo terminals were added, the 6,060-foot Vincent Thomas Bridge was erected, a twenty-four-acre Port O'Call commercial complex was built, the world's largest underwater oil pipeline was installed, and nuclear spent fuel elements and radioactive waste were handled at the harbor. All of this growth resulted in oil spills (averaging two per week) and unhealthy diesel emissions from ships, trucks, and equipment that plagued maritime workers and residents of nearby communities.

51. See Stevenson School website, "History of Stevenson," stevensonschool .org.

52. Len Hall, "Monarch Bay Booming," *Los Angeles Times,* February 27, 1997.

53. UC San Diego, "Campus Timeline," n.d., http://ucsd.edu/timeline/.

54. Tony Perry, "Backers of Desalination Hope Carlsbad Plant Will Disarm Critics," *Los Angeles Times,* June 4, 2015.

55. A useful, succinct history of the Ben Brown development at Aliso Creek is contained in the Coastal Commission Staff Report: Appeal—De Novo Hearing, December 23, 2014, Application No. A-5-LGB-14–0034, Applicant: Laguna Beach Golf and Bungalow Village, LLC, p. 22, documents.coastal.gov.

56. Coastal Conservancy, Staff Recommendation, October 2, 2014, "Aliso Creek Estuary Restoration Plan," historic photographs included, scc.ca.gov; see also Tom Osborne, "Three Amigos of Aliso Creek," Green Light column, *Laguna Beach Independent,* June 25, 2015, www.lagunabeachindy.com/green-light-18/.

57. Meg McConahey, "Sea Ranch: Coastal Legacy," *Sonoma* magazine, September 10, 2014, www.sonomamag.com/sea-ranch-coastal-legacy/#.VM_Jt1pUz9B.

58. Instead of such engagement, the architect found to his disappointment that Sea Ranchers seldom visited the shore, and that the communal mind-set he had hoped would develop among them was eclipsed by their focus on private interests. John R. Gillis, *The Human Shore: Seacoasts in History* (Chicago: University of Chicago Press, 2012), 185.

59. Connie Y. Chiang, *Shaping the Shoreline: Fisheries and Tourism on the Monterey Coast* (Seattle: University of Washington Press, 2008), 148–154.

60. Jeffrey J. Kripal, *Esalen: America and the Religion of No Religion* (Chicago: University of Chicago Press, 2007), 27.

61. See Oceanside Small Craft Harbor District, "Profiles of Special Districts in San Diego County," Service Review and Sphere of Influence Data Summary, Local Agency Formation Commission, 2007, www.sdlafco.org/Agendas/Aug2007 /Draft%20District%20Profiles%20Harbor.pdf.

62. Susan Pritchard O'Hara and Gregory Graves, *Saving California's Coast: Army Engineers at Oceanside and Humboldt Bay* (Spokane, WA: Arthur H. Clark, 1991), 183.

63. For a capsule history and telling 1964 photograph of the construction site, see *Los Angeles Times,* Photography Framework, June 16, 2012, framework.latimes. com/2012/06/16/construction-of-san-onofre-nuclear-generating-station/#/1.

64. Tom Turner's book, *David Brower: The Making of the Environmental Movement* (Oakland: University of California Press, 2015, 133–163 passim), provides thorough coverage of this issue.

65. "Throwback Thursday: Fashion Island Grew into an Upscale Outfit," *Orange County Register,* December 25, 2014.

66. Christopher Earley, "Birth of Dana Point Harbor Meant Death of Killer Wave," *Orange County Register,* August 7, 2014.

67. Iris Engstrand, *San Diego: California's Cornerstone* (San Diego: Sunbelt Publications, 2005), 194.

68. Elizabeth Blank, "Burdens on Public Access," *Sea Grant Fellows Publications,* paper no. 63, 2013, http://docs.rwu.edu/law_ma_seagrant/63.

69. Kirse Granat May, *Golden State, Golden Youth: The California Image in Popular Culture, 1955–1966* (Chapel Hill: University of North Carolina Press, 2002), 74–93.

70. Simon Winchester, *Pacific: Silicon Chips and Surfboards, Coral Reefs and Atom Bombs, Brutal Dictators, Fading Empires, and the Coming Collision of the World's Superpowers* (New York: HarperCollins, 2015), 141–144. Winchester does a good job of tracing the rise of Southern California surfing and its economic and cultural impacts on the region and nation.

71. For a commentary on the ups and downs of the Beach Boys and their lasting relevance to the genre of California-based rock music, see Jason Fine, "The Beach Boys' Last Wave," *Rolling Stone,* June 21, 2012, which focuses on the group's fifty-year reunion, www.rollingstone.com/music/news/the-beach-boys-last-wave-20120621; and Marisol Malibu, "The Beach Boys' Malibu Home," Blog Home (November 29, 2012), http://marisolmalibu.com/en/about/blog/beach-boys-malibu-beach-house/.

72. The population figures appear in Malibu Complete, "Malibu Development: 1950s–1960s," n.d., www.malibucomplete.com/mc_history_dev_1950s-60s.php.

73. Slide-show presentation by Todd Holmes, "Navigating Uncharted Territory: Mel Lane and the Formative Years of the California Coastal Commission," Bill Lane Center for the American West, Stanford University, November 18, 2015; emphasis and capitalization were in the original. See west.stanford.edu.

74. Fradkin and Fradkin, *The Left Coast,* 4.

75. See account prepared by Orange County Parks and Recreation, "History," n.d., http://ocparks.com/beaches/salt/history.

76. Carin Crawford, "Waves of Transformation" (master's thesis, Department of History, UC San Diego, 1993), www.lajollasurf.org/wavesof.html.

77. "Locked Out: Why the Key to Black's Beach Is One of the Most Coveted and Elusive Objects at UCSD," *The Guardian* (University of California, San Diego), May 30 2006, ucsdguardian.org.

78. Richard Hogan, *The Failure of Planning: Permitting Sprawl in San Diego Suburbs, 1970–1999* (Columbus: Ohio State University Press, 2003), 90–91.

1. This does not mean that coastal conservation in California in the 1960s had no historical antecedents. At least one notable earlier effort deserves mention—the founding of the Marin Conservation League in 1934. For the laudable work of Caroline Livermore with the league and other early efforts to preserve bays, beaches, and lagoons in and around Marin County, see L. Martin Griffin, *Saving the Marin-Sonoma Coast: The Battles for Audubon Canyon Ranch, Point Reyes, and California's Russian River* (Healdsburg, CA: Sweetwater Springs Press, 1998), 1–34. Also, Griffin alludes to the creation of Point Reyes National Seashore, incorporated into the National Park System in 1962, resulting from the work of Representative Clem Miller, local environmentalist Dr. Edgar Wayburn, and a "tiny band of birdwatchers" (31–32). While it deserves mention in a note, this successful effort does not compare in scope and impact with the other environmental actions and developments discussed in more detail in this chapter.

2. Tom Turner, *David Brower: The Making of the Environmental Movement* (Oakland: University of California Press, 2015), 199. While Turner's book is very good, I have come across no comprehensive historical study (excluding anthologies) of California environmentalism. Such a synthesis would provide readers with invaluable historical context and perhaps add thematic coherence, as well, to the voluminous literature already in print on such specialized topics (all within discrete time frames) as water and its distribution systems, desalination, forests, estuaries, marine ecology and sea-level rise, nuclear power plants, alternative energy, fishing, deserts and their management, air quality and its regulation, oil- and natural-gas extraction and conveyance, trail building, and so on.

3. Gilbert E. Bailey and Paul S. Thayer, *California's Disappearing Coast: A Legislative Challenge* (Berkeley: Institute of Governmental Studies, University of California, 1971), x, 1–12. The aspect of development that most alarmed the authors was the building of freeways along the shore: "The freeway may be the single biggest threat to the California coastline.... [Freeways] may destroy much of the remaining tidal and marshlands, they will scar the coast, and they are almost certain to stimulate unwise development" (33).

4. For an insightful study that profiles a group of such reformers (many of whom were engineers and business executives with graduate degrees), see Steven M. Gelber and Martin L. Cook, *Saving the Earth: The History of a Middle-Class Millenarian Movement* (Berkeley: University of California Press, 1990).

5. Stanley Scott, *Governing California's Coast* (Berkeley: Institute of Governmental Studies, University of California, 1975), 319. Revelle's entire speech is found in Edmund G. Brown, *California and the World Ocean* (Sacramento: California Office of State Printing, 1964), 10–18.

6. Ellen Stern Harris to Lieutenant Governor (Robert H.) Finch, March 20, 1967, Letters from ESH, 1960–1990s, Box 14, Folder 12, Ellen Stern Harris Papers, Collection 1287, Special Collections Department, Charles E. Young Graduate Research Library, UCLA.

7. Jared Farmer, *Trees in Paradise: A California History* (New York: W. W. Norton, 2013), 92.

8. On the Deep Ecology movement, see especially Bill Devall, "The Deep, Long-Range Ecology Movement: 1960–2000," *Ethics and the Environment* 6, no. 1 (2001): 18–41.

9. Carin Crawford, "Waves of Transformation" (master's thesis, Department of History, UC San Diego, 1993), www.lajollasurf.org/wavesof.html.

10. For example, the Surfrider Foundation, headquartered in San Clemente and eventually the nation's leading advocacy organization for surfers, was not established until 1984.

11. Peter Douglas, "Saving the Coast: A Job That's Never Done," speech delivered at the California Colloquium on Water, UC Berkeley, September 13, 2007, www.youtube.com/watch?v=fvFZ5cqH9KM.

12. Robert Dawson and Gray Brechin, *Farewell, Promised Land: Waking from the California Dream* (Berkeley: University of California Press, 1999), 191.

13. See "San Bruno Mountain" in Laura Mason, "A Salute to Bay Area Mountains on International Mountain Day," *Save the Bay Blog,* https://blog.savesfbay.org/tag/san-bruno-mountain/.

14. Carolyn Merchant, *Green versus Gold: Sources in California's Environmental History* (Washington, DC: Island Press, 1998), 361.

15. Harold Gilliam, "How the Bay Was Saved; Development Threatened to Fill It In," *SFGate,* April 22, 2007, www.sfgate.com/bayarea/article/How-the-bay-was-saved-Development-threatened-to-2564089.php.

16. Joseph E. Bodovitz, "Management and Policy Directions," an oral history interview conducted by Malca Chall in 1984, in *The San Francisco Bay Conservation and Development Commission, 1964–1973,* pp. 10–12, Regional Oral History Office, Bancroft Library, University of California, Berkeley, 1986.

17. See Peter Douglas, "Blog 2: Cancer and Saving the Sundown Coast—a Personal Story, Part One," Live Love with Cancer, June 12, 2011, http://livelovewithcancer.blogspot.com.

18. Bodovitz, "Management and Policy Directions," 14.

19. Thomas J. Osborne, "Saving the Golden Shore: Peter Douglas and the California Coastal Commission, 1972–2011," *Southern California Quarterly* 96, no. 4 (Winter 2014): 442 and n. 27.

20. *Los Angeles Times,* obituary for Melvin B. Lane, August 1, 2007.

21. Douglas, "Saving the Coast: A Job That's Never Done."

22. See Bill Kortum's account, "How It All Got Started," n.d., California Coastal Trail.info, www.californiacoastaltrail.info/cms/pages/trail/kortum.html.

23. As quoted on the website of the California Coastal Conservancy. See, specifically, AllGov, www.allgov.com/usa/ca/departments/natural-resources-agency/state_coastal_conservancy?agencyid=171.

24. Scott, *Governing California's Coast,* 7.

25. Robert G. Healy, ed., *Protecting the Golden Shore: Lessons from the California Coastal Commissions* (Washington, DC: Conservation Foundation, 1978), 9.

26. See Kortum, "How It All Got Started."

27. Ibid.

28. John Opie, *Nature's Nation: An Environmental History of the United States* (Fort Worth, TX: Harcourt Brace, 1998), 471.

29. Janet Bridgers, *Hero of the Coast—Ellen Stern Harris,* 2013, produced and directed by Janet Bridgers for Earth Alert, published on April 28, 2012, www.youtube.com/watch?v=ejWOZrJm7dA. This is Bridgers's interview of Harris on April 11, 2004.

30. Harriet Hyman Alonso, *Peace as a Women's Issue: A History of the U.S. Peace Movement for World Peace and Women's Rights* (Syracuse, NY: Syracuse University Press, 1993), 202–207.

31. See Peter Douglas, "Making Waves: Making a Difference," keynote speech at Surfrider Foundation's 15th Anniversary Event, August 28, 1999, San Diego, CA, www.beachapedia.org/Keynote_Speech_at_Surfrider_Foundation%27s_15_Anniversary_Event.

32. Peter M. Douglas and Joseph Petrillo, "California's Coast: The Struggle Today—a Plan for Tomorrow," *Florida State University Law Review* 4 (April 1976): 183n15.

33. Merchant, *Green versus Gold,* 328.

34. Keith C. Clarke and Jeffrey Hemphill, n Osborne_03_bn.docx "The Santa Barbara Oil Spill: A Retrospective," n.d., www.geog.ucsb.edu/~kClarke/Papers/SBOilSpill1969.pdf.

35. Ibid; Christine Mai-Due, "The 1969 Santa Barbara Oil Spill That Changed Oil and Gas Exploration Forever," *Los Angeles Times,* May 20, 2015.

36. David Helvarg, *The Golden Shore: California's Love Affair with the Sea* (New York: St. Martin's Press, 2013), 167.

37. Santa Barbara Wildlife Care Network and Jeffrey Hemphill, "1969 Santa Barbara Oil Spill," www2.bren.ucsb.edu/~dhardy/1969_Santa_Barbara_Oil_Spill/About.html.

38. Thomas Storke quoted in ibid.

39. President Richard Nixon quoted in ibid.

40. Osborne, "Saving the Golden Shore," 448–449.

41. See Douglas, "Making Waves: Making a Difference."

42. Peverill Squire and Stanley Scott, *The Politics of California Coastal Legislation: The Crucial Year, 1976* (Berkeley: Institute of Governmental Studies, University of California, 1984), 1.

43. Elaine Woo, "Robert T. Monagan Dies at 88; Assembly Speaker, Republican Supporter of Major Environmental Law," *Los Angeles Times,* January 8, 2009, http://articles.latimes.com/2009/jan/08/local/me-monagan8. For a clear, succinct introduction to the California Environmental Quality Act, see Planning and Conservation League of California, n Osborne_03_bn.docx"California Environmental Quality Act (CEQA)," n.d., www.pcl.org/campaigns/ceqa/.

44. The National Environmental Policy Act was signed into law on January 1, 1970. It required the federal government to "prepare detailed statements assessing

the environmental impact of and alternatives to major federal actions significantly affecting the environment." See the federal Environmental Protection Agency's website: epa.gov. The California Environmental Quality Act constituted an instance of state adoption of the statements and assessments required of federal agencies.

45. Ibid. The full legal citation is *Friends of Mammoth et al. v. Board of Supervisors of Mono County et al.,* 8 Cal.3d 247. Regarding this case, see also the Stanford Law School website: scocal.stanford.edu.

46. Planning and Conservation League, "CEQA Workshops and Information," n.d., www.pcl.org/campaigns/ceqa/ceqa-workshops-info/.

47. Scott, *Governing California's Coast,* 5–6.

48. Interview of Ellen Stern Harris (interviewer's name not given), February 16, 1977, Beverly Hills, CA, Collection 1287, Box 7, Folder 5, Ellen Stern Harris Papers, Special Collections Department, Charles E. Young Graduate Research Library, UCLA.

49. See Douglas, "Blog 2: Saving the Sundown Coast."

50. Scott, *Governing California's Coast,* 325.

51. Bridgers, *Hero of the Coast—Ellen Stern Harris.*

52. Ibid.

53. Scott, *Governing California's Coast,* 324.

54. Bridgers, *Hero of the Coast—Ellen Stern Harris.*

55. For a detailed description of all of these measures, see Scott, *Governing California's Coast,* 323–351.

56. Douglas, "Blog 2: Saving the Sundown Coast."

57. Ibid.

58. Ibid.

59. Ibid.

60. Douglas, "Blog 2: Saving the Sundown Coast."

61. Janet Bridgers, *E. Lewis Reid on Proposition 20 Campaign,* interviewed by Janet Bridgers for Earth Alert, published on December 6, 2013, www.youtube.com/watch?v=waXLwBzcIsA; Janet Bridgers, *Heroes of the Coast—the Documentary,* published on April 12, 2016, www.youtube.com/watch?v=E6RPp7vhGQE.

62. For a useful description of these measures that were drafted and defeated in the state legislature, see Squire and Scott, *The Politics of California Coastal Legislation,* 1–3.

63. Scott, *Governing California's Coast,* 13. In a slightly different account, John F. Dunlap includes Ed Z'berg and Alan Sieroty among the authors of AB 1471. See "Interview with Honorable John F. Dunlap, Office of March Fong Eu, Secretary of State, California State Archives, State Government Oral History Program," an oral history interview conducted by Carole Hicke, Regional Oral History Office, Bancroft Library, University of California, Berkeley, 1988, p. 94. A printed copy of the interview is housed at the Bancroft Library, UC Berkeley.

64. Scott, *Governing California's Coast,* 13–14.

65. Douglas, "Blog 2: Saving the Sundown Coast."

66. Ibid.

67. Fred C. Doolittle, *Land-Use Planning and Regulation on the California Coast: The State Role,* Environmental Quality Series no. 9, California Agencies paper 418 (Davis: Institute of Governmental Affairs, University of California, May 1972), 59, digitalcommons.law.ggu.edu/caldocs_agencies/418.

68. Ibid., 68.

69. Douglas, "Blog 2: Saving the Sundown Coast."

70. Janet Adams seems to have been nearly alone in thinking that Governor Reagan, though opposed to a coastal law, would have signed such a measure into operation to be politic if the legislature had passed it. Most seasoned observers of the legislature disagreed with her. See Scott, *Governing California's Coast,* 330.

71. Doolittle, "Land-Use Planning and Regulation of the California Coast," 69–70.

72. Janet Adams, "Proposition 20—a Citizens' Campaign," *Syracuse Law Review* 24, no. 3 (Summer 1973): 1032.

4. COASTAL CONSERVATION, POLITICS,
AND A NEW COMMISSION

1. Melvin Small, ed., *A Companion to Richard Nixon* (Malden, MA: Wiley-Blackwell, 2011), see chapter 15, "Nixon and the Environment"; Richard L. Revesz and Jack Lienke, "Nixon's 'Environmental Bandwagon': Richard Nixon Signed the Landmark Clean Air Act of 1970—But Not Because He Had Any Great Concern about the Environment," Salon.com, January 2, 2016 ; John Opie, *Nature's Nation: An Environmental History of the United States* (Fort Worth, TX: Harcourt Brace, 1998), 432.

2. The federal Coastal Zone Management Act of 1972 appears on the website of the National Oceanic and Atmospheric Administration; see http://coast.noaa.gov/czm/act/sections/?redirect=301ocm.

3. See Peter Douglas, "Blog 3: Saving the Sundown Coast—People Power, the People's Law: Drafting the Initiative," Live Love with Cancer, December 26, 2011, http://livelovewithcancer.blogspot.com.

4. Stanley Scott, *Governing California's Coast* (Berkeley: Institute of Governmental Studies, University of California, 1975), 322–323, 345–346; Janet Adams, "Proposition 20—a Citizens' Campaign," *Syracuse Law Review* 24, no. 3 (Summer 1973): 1022. The timing of Governor Reagan's action suggests, but does not prove, that he thought something needed to be done immediately to mollify, if possible, those demanding the creation of a statewide coastal regulatory body. Far short of such an authority, the California Comprehensive Ocean Area Plan essentially provided for inventorying coastal resources, compiling the information, and making policy recommendations.

5. Paul A. Sabatier and Daniel A. Mazmanian, *Can Regulation Work? The Implementation of the 1972 California Coastal Initiative* (New York: Plenum Press, 1983), 40, 53, 61n37.

6. Scott, *Governing California's Coast,* 349.

7. *Los Angeles Times,* May 17, 1972.

8. Douglas, "Blog 3: Saving the Sundown Coast."

9. Ibid.

10. Peverill Squire and Stanley Scott, *The Politics of California Coastal Legislation: The Crucial Year, 1976* (Berkeley: Institute of Governmental Studies, University of California, 1984), 2, note d.

11. For a useful summary of the California Coastal Zone Conservation Act of 1972, see Peter M. Douglas and Joseph E. Petrillo, "California's Coast: The Struggle Today—a Plan for Tomorrow," *Florida State University Law Review* 4, no. 2 (April 1976): 185–188; Squire and Scott, *The Politics of California Coastal Legislation,* 3.

12. See "Coastal Access Program: The California Coastal Trail," California Coastal Commission website: coastal.ca.gov; see also the website California Coastal Trail.info, www.californiacoastaltrail.info/cms/pages/trail/done.html.

13. *Los Angeles Times,* May 6, 2016; *Santa Rosa Press Democrat,* May 3, 2016. Situated amid five-hundred-year-old redwood trees and overlooking a remote and rugged coastline, the Peter Douglas Trail is especially scenic.

14. Douglas, "Blog 3: Saving the Sundown Coast." About four years later, when the state legislature was debating the Coastal Plan connected to the 1976 California Coastal Act, Douglas's boss, Chairman Charles Warren of the Assembly Natural Resources Committee, asked him to delete the controversial statement. Douglas did so reluctantly, replacing "belonging to all the People" with "is of vital and enduring interest to all the People."

15. Ibid.

16. Ibid.; Adams, "Proposition 20—a Citizens' Campaign," 1033.

17. Douglas, "Blog 3: Saving the Sundown Coast."

18. Adams, "Proposition 20—a Citizens' Campaign," 1035–1036.

19. Ibid., 1033, 1035.

20. David Helvarg, "The Savior of California's Coast," *Los Angeles Times* opinion-editorial, April 8, 2012; Thomas J. Osborne, "Saving the Golden Shore: Peter Douglas and the California Coastal Commission, 1972–2011," *Southern California Quarterly* 96, no. 4 (Winter 2014): 439.

21. Scott, *Governing California's Coast,* 357.

22. Ellen Stern Harris, testimony before the California Coastal Commission, titled "For the Record," October 8, 1996, Letters from ESH, 1960–1990s, Box 14, Folder 12, Ellen Stern Harris Papers, Special Collections Department, Charles E. Young Graduate Research Library, UCLA, hereafter Ellen Stern Harris Papers.

23. Scott, *Governing California's Coast,* 357–358.

24. Ibid., 357.

25. *Lodi News-Sentinel,* November 4, 1972.

26. Jared Orsi, "Restoring the Common to the Goose: Citizen Activism and the Protection of the California Coastline, 1969–1982," *Southern California Quarterly* 78, no. 3 (Fall 1996): 264.

27. Scott, *Governing California's Coast,* 359–361. This thoroughly researched and invaluable source contains a table listing groups for and against Proposition 20.

28. The California Coastal Zone Conservation Act of 1972 (Proposition 20), chapter 5, Interim Permit Control, Article 1, General Provisions, 27401 (c). Proposition 20, in its entirety, is posted on the California Coastal Commission website, www.coastal.ca.gov/legal/proposition-20.pdf.

29. LeRoy Chatfield, who with his wife, Bonnie, were leaders of the effort to defeat the ballot initiative, uncovered the deception. They found that voters had been falsely told by the paid signature gatherers that the main purpose of the measure—emblazoned on the signature sheets—was to "Lower Food Prices." Moreover, the Chatfields amassed considerable evidence that many of the signatures were fraudulent in that thousands of so-called signatories had never affixed their names to the petition. See LeRoy Chatfield, Proposition 22, https://libraries.ucsd .edu/farmworkermovement/essays/essays/PROP22ESSAY.pdf. Also, Daniel Cornford, ed., *Working People of California* (Berkeley: University of California Press, 1995), 395–396; Richard B. Rice et al., *The Elusive Eden: A New History of California* (New York: McGraw-Hill, 2012), 509.

30. See Douglas, "Blog 3: Saving the Sundown Coast."

31. *Washington Post,* "Everything You Need to Know about the Fairness Doctrine in One Post," August 23, 2011.

32. Robert G. Healy et al., eds., *Protecting the Golden Shore: Lessons from the California Coastal Commissions* (Washington, DC: Conservation Foundation, 1978), 12.

33. Ibid.

34. James R. Mills, former senate president pro tem, interview by author, April 11, 2011, in Coronado, CA, audio recording. Mills used the term *fat cats* to describe the special-interest spokespersons inside the Cadillac limousines trailing the bicyclists.

35. See Douglas, "Blog 3: Saving the Sundown Coast"; Osborne, "Saving the Golden Shore," 438–439.

36. Adams, "Proposition 20—a Citizens Campaign, 1041.

37. Ibid.; Douglas, "Blog 3: Saving the Sundown Coast."

38. Adams, "Proposition 20—a Citizens' Campaign," 1039.

39. This claim was made by Michael L. Fischer, a former executive director of the California Coastal Commission. See Ann Lage, typescript of oral history interview of Michael L. Fischer, conducted in 1992 and 1993, Regional Oral History Office, University of California, Berkeley, for the California State Archives, State Government Oral History Program, p. 24. Historian Todd Holmes echoed this view in his presentation "Navigating Uncharted Territory: Mel Lane and the Formative Years of the California Coastal Commission" (lecture, Bill Lane Center for the American West, Stanford University, November 18, 2015).

40. See Janet Bridgers's illuminating interview of Peter Douglas in *Heroes of the Coast—the Documentary,* July 2011, published on April 12, 2016, www.youtube .com/watch?v=E6RPp7vhGQE.

41. Douglas, "Blog 3: Saving the Sundown Coast."

42. For those whose building projects were under way when the coastal initiative passed, the California Supreme Court held that rights must have vested before November 8, 1972, in order to be exempted from the new permit regulations. Legal action was taken against one developer who neglected to obtain a permit after February 1, 1973, the mandated beginning date for the imposition of permitting requirements. That same year, the California Supreme Court held, in a four-to-three decision, that if substantial, lawful construction had been performed by that date, then a given project was legal. See Douglas and Petrillo, "California's Coast," 203–204.

43. Squire and Scott, *The Politics of California Coastal Legislation*, 3. Proposition 20 was amended in 1973 to accommodate a shift to two-year legislative sessions.

44. Transcript of Janet Bridgers's interview of Peter Douglas, 2006, part 1, for *Heroes of the Coast—the Documentary*, author's copy provided by Bridgers.

45. *Los Angeles Times*, obituary, August 1, 2007.

46. Melvin B. Lane to Ellen Stern Harris, October 24, 1973, Coastal CCC Letters, 1971–1976, Box 7, Ellen Stern Harris Papers. In this letter, Lane also said: "We have to limit our time to the things that affect thousands or millions of people on the coast. We should never have gotten involved in a teahouse or someone's porch" (in reference to a Laguna Beach neighborhood dispute concerning obstruction of ocean views).

47. Douglas, "Blog 3: Saving the Sundown Coast." Joseph E. Bodovitz, the first executive director of the statewide coastal commission, described Lane as an "even-tempered" environmentalist who was highly respected for his "decency and fair-mindedness" by those in business and politics. Bodovitz, interview by author, December 30, 2013, in Larkspur, CA, audio recording.

48. Later Harris became an outspoken critic of the Coastal Commission, scolding it for approving the San Onofre nuclear power facility and for not stemming shoreline development and assuring sufficient public access to beaches. Myrna Oliver, "Ellen Stern Harris, 76; Activist Who Helped Establish State's Coastal Conservation Act," *Los Angeles Times*, January 3, 2006, http://articles.latimes .com/2006/jan/03/local/me-harris3.

49. Ellen Stern Harris to Attorney General Evelle Younger, October 4, 1973, Box 21, CA Gov., Ellen Stern Harris Papers. Harris's papers did not indicate whether Younger acted on her request for representation.

50. Peter Douglas, "Coastal Zone Management: The Experience with a Citizens' Law in California" (unpublished manuscript prepared for the Assembly Select Committee on Coastal Zone Resources, March 1974), 5, 6, quoted in Scott, *Governing California's Coast*, 310–311.

51. Joseph Bodovitz, "Joseph Bodovitz: Founding Director of the Bay Conservation Development Commission and the California Coastal Commission," an oral history interview conducted by Martin Meeker, Oral History Center, Bancroft Library, University of California, Berkeley, 2015, p. 97. Hereafter cited as Meeker, oral history interview of Joseph Bodovitz. Coming across this revealing exchange

buried in the interior pages of the transcript of Meeker's oral history interview helped this writer see more clearly the initial differences between Douglas and Bodovitz.

52. Speech titled "The Future of Coastal Management," January 11, 1993, delivered before the Ocean Governance Study Group, Berkeley, CA, copy in Coastal/CCC—Testimony, Peter Douglas and Paper, 1994–1995, Ellen Stern Harris Papers (emphasis in the original).

53. Orsi, "Restoring the Common to the Goose," 266.

54. Douglas and Petrillo, "California's Coast," 226.

55. *Los Angeles Times,* August 6, 1973.

56. Healy et al., *Protecting the Golden Shore,* 78–79.

57. Ibid., 67.

58. The codrafters of the Coastal Plan included state staff, state commissioners, and regional commissioners and their staffs.

59. Douglas and Petrillo, "California's Coast," 184.

60. Healy et al., *Protecting the Golden Shore,* 15–16.

61. Scott, *Governing California's Coast,* 132.

62. Ibid., 16.

63. Ibid., 29–30.

64. Ibid., 33.

65. Ibid.

66. Ibid., 35.

67. Peter Douglas, "Blog 2: Cancer and Saving the Sundown Coast—a Personal Story, Part One," Live Love with Cancer, June 12, 2011, livelovewithcancer.blogspot .com.

68. For an anthology of their writings, see Eugéne Bardach, *The California Coastal Plan: A Critique* (San Francisco: Institute for Contemporary Studies, 1976). See also Osborne, "Saving the Golden Shore," 443n29.

69. Robert C. Ellickson, "Ticket to Thermidor: A Commentary on the Proposed California Coastal Plan," *Southern California Law Review* 49 (1976): 716. The entire article appears online: http://digitalcommons.law.yale.edu/cgi/viewcontent .cgi?article=4767&context=fss_papers.

70. Ibid., 717.

71. Ibid., 726.

72. Ibid., 732–733.

73. Ibid., 721–723.

74. Healy et al., *Protecting the Golden Shore,* 48.

75. Ibid., 49.

76. The so-called "coastal essence" components were included in the 1976 California Coastal Act. They included (1) a permanent statewide coastal commission with an appeals role, plan review, plan amendment, and cease and desist authority; (2) judicial review for commission and local government decisions; (3) shared jurisdiction with state and/or local government on all marine-related energy facilities; (4) protection and enhancement of marine ecology; (5) protection of remaining

wetlands, estuaries, and marshes from further development; 6) conservation of coastal-dependent farmlands; (7) preservation of biological habitat, particularly for endangered species; (8) watershed management; (9) preservation of coastal land-forms, plant life, and open space; (10) confinement of development primarily to areas where it has already occurred; (11) retention of old and acquisition of new recreation areas; (12) maximum public access to beaches and tideland areas commensurate with environmental protection; and (13) prioritization of coastal-dependent uses over those not dependent on the seaboard. See ibid. 224n171. These thirteen components are taken nearly verbatim from this source.

77. Senator David Roberti (a Democrat from Hollywood) cast the deciding vote against the bill, complaining that it did not provide public access to the beaches at Malibu and elsewhere in Los Angeles County. "If this bill is to mean anything, it must mean that people can get to the beach," he insisted. Supporters of the bill suspected, with reason, that Roberti's opposition was due at least in part to influence brought to bear on him from his contributors in the building trades. Ibid., 54.

78. On June 17, Governor Brown interrupted his campaign for the White House to say that he hoped "a very strong bill to protect the coast" could still be "patched together." Ibid., 55.

79. Bridgers's interview of Peter Douglas, July 2011.

80. Healy et al., *Protecting the Golden Shore*, 57.

81. Ibid.

82. The threat of another initiative, whose terms would not be influenced by labor unions or developers, was no idle threat. Moreover, according to a 1976 poll commissioned by the opponents of a coastal bill, public support for seaboard protection was approximately as strong as it had been when Proposition 20 passed. See ibid., 53.

83. Ibid., 58.

84. Ibid.

85. According to Michael L. Fischer, an eyewitness and soon-to-be executive director of the California Coastal Commission: "It was Jerry Brown's last minute lobbying that got the coastal act of '76 passed in the last hour in the last of the legislative session with one vote to spare in the state senate." See Lage, typescript of oral history interview of Fischer, 118.

86. California Coastal Act of 1976, SB 1277, 1975–1976 Reg. Sess., Cal. Stat., ch. 1330 (1976). My summary of the Coastal Act appearing here is drawn in some instances word for word from my article "Saving the Golden Shore," 443–444.

87. The language is from a 2012 commission press release. See www.coastal.ca .gov/40thPressRlease_Prop_20.pdf. The entire law appears on the California Coastal Commission website. www.coastal.ca.gov/coastact.pdf.

88. Douglas, "Blog 3: Saving the Sundown Coast."

89. Ibid.

90. Ibid.

91. Rasa Gustaitis, "Never Saved; Always Being Saved: An Interview with the Coastal Commission's Peter Douglas," *California Coast & Ocean* 12, no. 4 (Winter 1996–1997): 16.

92. The absence of a sustainable funding mechanism in the 1976 California Coastal Act is treated in Stanley Scott, ed., *Coastal Conservation: Essays on Experiments in Governance* (Berkeley: Institute of Governmental Studies, University of California, 1981), 20.

93. Bodovitz said he resigned as commission chief in 1978 mainly because much had been accomplished and he did not look forward to dealing with the difficulties on the horizon. For example, the Coastal Plan had been drafted, followed by passage of the Coastal Act, which had made the agency permanent. Also the upcoming challenge of putting Local Coastal Programs in place seemed "tough" and "less interesting" to him. Meeker, oral history interview of Joseph Bodovitz, 137.

94. Letter from Michael Fischer to Douglas, September 8, 1978, California Coastal Commission, Executive Director Files, Personal Correspondence, September through October 1978, California State Archives, Sacramento. From the time of Douglas's departure from Sacramento, he seems to have been held somewhat less responsible for managing the commission's routine, day-to-day relations with the state legislature. The Coastal Commission documents at the State Archives are rich and voluminous, occupying some fourteen linear feet of shelf space.

95. The full retreat schedule is found in PROPOSED AGENDA FOR RETREAT [for April 3, 1981], California Coastal Commission, Records of the Assistant Executive Director, General Correspondence Files, 1980–1981, R254.025, California State Archives, Sacramento.

96. Letter from Peter Douglas to Larry Moss, deputy secretary for resources for the State of California, March 20, 1981, California Coastal Commission, Records of the Assistant Executive Director, General Correspondence Files, 1980–1981, R254.025, California State Archives, Sacramento. In this candid letter, Douglas stated, "Our biggest enemy is . . . poor morale and a sense of frustration born of what is perceived as extensive loss of support. Virtually everyone who is visible in Sacramento has something to complain about with respect to the coastal commission and is taking shots at us. The conservative trend nationally, has filtered down to us."

97. Letter from Peter Douglas to Senator Alan Sieroty, March 25, 1981, marked "CONFIDENTIAL," California Coastal Commission, Records of the Assistant Executive Director, General Correspondence Files, 1980–1981, R254.025, California State Archives, Sacramento. Douglas confided to his mentor and close friend Sieroty: "We are being told that unless we initiate or at least participate in working out a compromise on this issue the rest of the Coastal Act will be in jeopardy this session. . . . It is frustrating and indeed depressing. I would welcome any thoughts you may have as to how we should proceed."

98. Sabatier and Mazmanian, *Can Regulation Work?* 333–334. By March 1981, the regional and state coastal commissions had approved, altogether, about 4,828 units of affordable housing in the Coastal Zone.

99. *Los Angeles Times,* July 12, 1978.

100. *Los Angeles Times,* September 29, 1980.

101. Orsi, "Restoring the Common to the Goose," 274, 278.

102. Todd Holmes, "Tides of Tension: A Historical Look at Staff-Commission Relations in the California Coastal Commission," April 15, 2016, http://west.stanford.edu/static/tides-of-tension/index.html.

103. This was reported in the Coastal Commission's newsletter, *Coastal News* 4, no. 4 (June–July 1981): 7. The bill providing for the abolition of the commission, SB 260, did not make it out of the Senate Natural Resources and Wildlife Committee, which on April 28 consigned it to interim study, a move that effectively kills a bill. Two authorities on the Coastal Commission wrote, "Given the increasingly conservative political climate in the state, the result has been continuous turmoil. Every legislative session since 1979 has witnessed the introduction of dozens of bills seeking to weaken the authority of the [regional] commissions.... [Some bills called for] the outright abolition of the [statewide] agency." Sabatier and Mazmanian, *Can Regulation Work?* 316–317.

104. Alan Sieroty, interview by author, October 8, 2013, in Los Angeles, CA, audio recording. Others who were also knowledgeable about Coastal Commission affairs agreed with Sieroty. For example, Joseph E. Bodovitz, the agency's first executive director, believed moderate Republican Melvin Lane was a salutary counterforce who helped the newly created commission contend with its "factions." Bodovitz, interview by author, December 30, 2013, Larkspur, CA, audio recording.

105. Orsi, "Restoring the Common to the Goose," 276.

106. *Los Angeles Times,* May 10, 1981, www.gpo.gov/fdsys/pkg/CZIC-ht393-c3-c35–1981/html/CZIC-ht393-c3-c35–1981.htm. Though Harris remained a critic of the Coastal Commission, the mutual respect between her and Peter Douglas remained intact. Even in the face of her later attacks on the agency for allowing too much development and assuring too little public beach access, Douglas stated publicly: "I love Ellen. I admire her tenacity, her integrity. She pushes the envelope all the time." *Los Angeles Times,* March 2, 1998.

107. See Lage, typescript of oral history interview of Fischer, pp. 141–142.

108. Fischer, oral history interview, p. 119. An email from Dr. Carlotta Mellon to the author on July 16, 2015 stated, "Gender and ethnicity were important considerations to [Governor] Jerry [Brown] in making appointments[,] along with a person's experience, ideas and philosophy as it might relate to the position for which they were being considered. [Governor] Jerry [Brown] had an impressive record in appointing women and persons of color."

109. Dr. Judy B. Rosener, interview by author, July 30, 2014, Newport Beach, CA, audio recording. Professor Rosener taught at UC Irvine's Paul Merage School of Business.

110. Letter of resignation from Naomi Schwartz to outgoing governor Edmund G. Brown Jr., December 1, 1982, California Coastal Commission, Records of the Assistant Executive Director, Appointment Files, 1979–1983, R254.027, California State Archives, Sacramento. Deukmejian's opposition to the Coastal Commission must be viewed within the larger context of his probusiness, antiregulatory outlook in general. For example, while undercutting the Coastal Commission's budget he also sought to rein in the authority of the California Labor Relations Board, which

since the 1970s had struggled to assure fair practices and the collective bargaining rights of farmworkers. *Christian Science Monitor,* June 1, 1983; *Los Angeles Times,* August 17, 1990.

5. HIGH TIDE

1. Michael L. Fischer, interview by author, March 21, 2016, Dipsea Café, Mill Valley, CA, audio recording.

2. David Rolland, "Man and the Sea: Is Coastal Commission Chief Peter Douglas an Environmental Savior, a Socialist Fanatic—or Both?" *San Diego City Beat,* October 22, 2003, www.sdcitybeat.com/sandiego/article-1023-man-and-the-sea .html.

3. Larry B. Stammer, "Coastal Panel Chooses New Leader in Time of Crisis," *Los Angeles Times,* July 10, 1985.

4. Susan McCabe, former coastal commissioner, interview by author, November 11, 2015, at McCabe's Marina del Rey, CA, office, audio recording.

5. Julie M. Hamilton, attorney and former Coastal Commission staffer, interview by author, December 30, 2015, at author's home, Laguna Beach, CA, audio recording.

6. Katherine Ellison, "Leading the Coastal Commission for 25 Years, a Crusader and Lightening Rod," *New York Times,* May 8, 2010.

7. Speech by Peter Douglas titled "Caring to Make a Difference: Environmental Activism," delivered before the Planning and Conservation League, Sacramento, April 14, 2007.

8. For Douglas, as for Campbell, a life of "bliss" was one of service to others, meaning, and fulfillment, not one of self-indulgence. Moreover, while some critics of Campbell have charged that the latter was anti-Semitic, this writer has seen no evidence that Douglas viewed the mythologist as such.

9. The reference to "radical pagan heretic" appears in the *Los Angeles Times* obituary for Peter Douglas; see Elaine Woo, "Peter M. Douglas Dies at 69; California Coastal Commission Chief," April 4, 2012.

10. Susan Jordan, founder and executive director of the California Coastal Protection Network, interview by author, September 8, 2016, Newport Beach City Council Chamber, Newport Beach, CA, audio recording.

11. Though Douglas seldom, if ever, publicly referred to himself as a socialist, when accused of being one he did not run from that label. To one critic, Wade Major of Malibu, Douglas said, "Socialist is not a nasty word in my dictionary. We have been governed in this country from fear for so long that words like 'liberal,' 'socialist' or 'community interest' have been made into derogatory terms, when in fact the community interest is what really started this country." See Rolland, "Man and the Sea."

12. Flossie Horgan, former executive director of Bolsa Chica Land Trust, interview by author, March 31, 2016, Laguna Beach, CA, audio recording.

13. Speech by Douglas, "Caring to Make a Difference." Douglas's rapier wit could sometimes be dark and self-deprecating. In 2006 he amassed a pile of dry leaves, poured gasoline on the debris, and lit the heap. He emerged from the ensuing conflagration with extensive burns on his face and hands, all of which required considerable bandaging. Douglas told his sons afterward that had the incendiary stunt gone any worse for him he could have been a candidate for a Darwin Award— a tongue-in-cheek accolade named for evolutionary scientist Charles Darwin and bestowed annually on those whose idiotic acts resulted in either self-sterilization or death, thereby removing them from and improving the human gene pool. Sascha Douglas, son of Peter Douglas, interview by author, December 30, 2013, in Larkspur, CA, audio recording.

14. The frog-and-crane-cartoon anecdote was related to the author by Vanja C. Douglas, son of Peter Douglas, interview by author, January 2, 2014, UC San Francisco Medical Center, San Francisco, CA, audio recording.

15. Alex Matthews, "A Tale of Tension at the Coastal Commission," *Sacramento Capitol Weekly,* February 4, 2016.

16. Vanja Douglas, interview by author. Former coastal commissioner Shirley Dettloff, similarly commented, "Peter [Douglas] got energized by criticism, by the fight, [though] he never lost his temper with developers." Dettloff, interview by author, August 6, 2015, at Dettloff's Huntington Beach, CA, home, audio recording.

17. See "Peter Douglas '60 on Following Your Bliss," *Stevenson Alumni Magazine* (2012): 36.

18. Dettloff, interview by author.

19. Esther C. Sanchez, former coastal commissioner, interview by author, October 13, 2015, at Sanchez's law office in Oceanside, CA, audio recording.

20. Rusty Areias, former Coastal Commission chair, interview by author, January 30, 2016, at Areias's Walnut Grove, CA, home, audio recording.

21. Gary Giacomini, former Coastal Commission chair, interview by author, November 20, 2015, at Hanson Bridgett Law Office, Larkspur, CA, audio recording; Areias, interview by author.

22. The corporate officer, who asked to remain anonymous, emailed his recollection to the author on August 28, 2015.

23. Robert H. Burnham, former city attorney for Newport Beach, interview by author, August 25, 2015, at the author's home in Laguna Beach, audio recording. Mr. Burnham believed the Coastal Commission staff at times was too focused on minutia and showed too little willingness to negotiate differences in interpreting the Coastal Act.

24. Wendy Mitchell, coastal commissioner, interview by author, June 9, 2016, Hyatt Regency Hotel Restaurant, Santa Barbara, CA, audio recording.

25. Susan McCabe, interview by author. Former commission staffer Julie M. Hamilton shared McCabe's view (Hamilton, interview by author). Ditto for commission chair Steve Kinsey (Kinsey, interview by author, January 14, 2016, at Coastal Commission meeting held at San Diego County Board of Supervisors Chamber).

26. See the transcript of Janet Bridgers's informative interview of Michael L. Fischer in *Heroes of the Coast:* "Transcript of Video Interview with Michael L. Fischer," recorded August 2012, p. 7, http://earthalert.org/hotc/wp-content /uploads/2015/08/Fischer-Michael-re-CCC.pdf. Bridgers is executive director of Earth Alert!

27. Mary K. Shallenberger, former Coastal Commission chair, interview by author, May 12, 2016, Radisson Hotel Restaurant, Newport Beach, CA, audio recording.

28. Douglas's successor as executive director, Dr. Charles F. Lester, affirmed that Douglas fully realized that he served at the pleasure of the coastal commissioners, who collectively were his boss. Lester, interview by author, December 15, 2015, at the Santa Cruz Coastal Commission office, audio recording.

29. Sara Wan, email to author, November 12, 2015.

30. Douglas's oldest son, Sascha Douglas, interview by author; Robert H. Burnham, interview by author. Coastal commissioner Mary K. Shallenberger, agreed, describing Douglas as "extraordinarily ethical" (Shallenberger, interview by author).

31. Kenneth Frank, former city manager of Laguna Beach, interview by author, August 20, 2015, Laguna Beach, CA, audio recording.

32. "Extended Biography and Personal Comments: Peter Douglas, California Coastal Commission Executive Director, 1985–2011," California Coastal Commission website, n.d., p. 2, www.coastal.ca.gov/pd-bio-comments.pdf.

33. Jared Orsi, "Restoring the Common to the Goose: Citizen Activism and the Protection of the California Coastline, 1969–1982," *Southern California Quarterly,* 78, no. 3 (Fall 1996): 279.

34. California Coastal Commission, "California Coastal Commission Budget Funding History," in *Governor's Proposed Budget Governor's Budget for FY 2014– 2015,* March 28, 2014, http://documents.coastal.ca.gov/reports/2014/4/W6b-4- 2014.pdf.

35. The figure for Douglas's salary comes from Larry B. Stammer, "Coastal Panel's Director Keeps Job . . . ," *Los Angeles Times,* July 20, 1991.

36. In 1980 the Coastal Commission staff numbered 212. From then until 2010 that number was reduced to 125. Ellison, "Leading the Coastal Commission for 25 Years, a Crusader and Lightening Rod."

37. Author's interview of Dettloff.

38. Jeffrey Rabin, former Coastal Commission staffer, interview by author, March 17, 2015, at Rabin's home in Long Beach, CA, audio recording.

39. "Extended Biography and Personal Comments," p. 3.

40. Gary Giacomini, interview by author.

41. Rusty Areias, interview by author.

42. Dr. Charles F. Lester, second in command (as senior deputy director) under Douglas, stated that his boss and mentor did not micromanage staff (Lester, interview by author). Former commission staffer Julie M. Hamilton, agreed strongly with Lester's view (Hamilton, interview by author).

43. Fischer, interview by author.

44. Douglas quoted in "Extended Biography and Personal Comments," 3.

45. Jeffrey Rabin, interview by author.

46. Susan McCabe, interview by author.

47. "Extended Biography and Personal Comments," 3.

48. Douglas quoted in ibid.

49. Rolland, "Man and the Sea."

50. 483 U.S. 825 (1987). A clear, brief overview of the case can be found in Eric T. Freyfogle, "Nollan v. California Coastal Commission," in *The Oxford Guide to United States Supreme Court Decisions,* ed. Kermit L. Hall and James W. Ely Jr., 2nd ed. (New York: Oxford University Press, 2009), www.oxfordreference.com /view/10.1093/oi/authority.20110803100236785.

51. Timothy Beatley, David J. Brower, and Anna K. Schwab, *An Introduction to Coastal Management,* 2nd ed. (Washington, DC: Island Press, 2002), 148–149.

52. The five justices constituting the conservative majority included William Rehnquist, Byron White, Lewis F. Powell Jr., Sandra Day O'Connor, and Antonin Scalia. The four justices comprising the liberal minority included Thurgood Marshall, William J. Brennan Jr., Harry Blackmun, and John Paul Stevens.

53. For an incisive legal analysis in support of the Supreme Court's majority decision, see Andrew P. Valentine, "Property Rights—the Effect of Nolan v. California Coastal Commission on Land Use Permits: A Proposed Constitutional Analysis," Comment, *Santa Clara Law Review* 32, no. 4 (1992): 1174–1176. These pages offer a clear explanation of "essential nexus." In defense of the Coastal Commission, several members of the court minority held that the majority should not have gone beyond requiring "just a loose, rational connection between harm and remedy." Essential nexus, in other words, was too narrow of a legal standard. Freyfogle, "Nollan v. California Coastal Commission."

54. David G. Savage, "High Court to Decide Beach Access Question: Ventura Homeowner Challenging Coast Panel's Rule Keeping Private Frontage Open to Public," *Los Angeles Times,* March 29, 1987.

55. David W. Myers, "High Courts Leave Mark on Industry: 1987 Decisions Bring New Rules for Real Estate-Related Matters, *Los Angeles Times,* January 10, 1988.

56. *San Francisco Chronicle,* June 27, 1987.

57. See Pacific Legal Foundation, "A Legacy of Freedom Victories in the Courts," n.d., www.pacificlegal.org/page.aspx?pid=4407.

58. Peter Douglas, "The Loss of Community Environmental Values: An American Tragedy" (speech presented before the California Chapter of the American Planning Association, Monterey, CA, October 13, 1997), Georgetown Environmental Law and Policy Institute website, www.gelpi.org/gelpi/current_research/documents /RT_Pubs_Other_Douglas.pdf.

59. Also in 1987, after the Nollan decision, several additional U.S. Supreme Court rulings were made that strengthened the rights of property owners while reining in the authority of government to condition permits for development. For example, in the case of *First English Evangelical Lutheran Church v. Los Angeles, CA,* 482 U.S. 304 (1987), the court majority ruled for the first time that when a

government agency is found guilty of a "taking," monetary damages are payable to the property owner during the interim period from the time an administrative action was taken until the time that a "taking" is court-determined. Consequently, if the Coastal Commission ran afoul of the Nollan case, that already underfunded agency could suffer severe financial consequences. The threat of this would inhibit the commission from robust enforcement of the Coastal Act. See Chicago-Kent College of Law at Illinois Tech, *First English Evangelical Lutheran Church v. Los Angeles, CA*, 482 U.S. 304 (1987), Oyez, www.oyez.org/cases/1980–1989/1986/1986_85_1199. In a second case, *Dolan v. City of Tigard*, 512 U.S. 374 (1987), the court majority held that when governmental agencies condition building permits, the conditions must be in rough proportionality to the impacts of the project. So even if an "essential nexus" exists between a conditioned permit and a project's impacts, the permitting agency would have to show that the benefits to the public justified the required conditions. Chicago-Kent College of Law at Illinois Tech, *Dolan v. City of Tigard*, Oyez, www.oyez.org/cases/1990–1999/1993/1993_93_518.

60. See case of *City of Malibu et al., Plaintiffs v. California Coastal Commission et al.,* Defendants and Respondents, B171650, 05 C.D.O.S. 3468, 2005 DJDAR 4723, Court of Appeal of the State of California (April 25, 2005), p. 2.

61. Chris Dixon, "Geffen Agrees to Public Access at Beachfront Malibu Home," *New York Times,* April 17, 2005, www.nytimes.com/2005/04/17/us/geffen-agrees-to-public-access-at-beachfront-malibu-home.html.

62. Kenneth R. Weiss, "Geffen to Reimburse $300,000," *Los Angeles Times,* April 16, 2005, http://articles.latimes.com/2005/apr/16/local/me-geffen16.

63. Dixon, "Geffen Agrees to Public Access at Beachfront Malibu Home."

64. Ibid.

65. *City of Malibu et al., Plaintiffs v. California Coastal Commission et al.,* Defendants and Respondents, Facts, p. 7.

66. Martha Groves, "Resistant Malibu Homeowner Finally Opens Pathway to 'Billionaires' Beach,'" *Los Angeles Times,* July 3, 2015.

67. Hans Laetz, "Beach Access Next to Geffen's Home Opened," *Malibu Times,* June 1, 2005, www.malibutimes.com/news/article_68d596e6-5ad2-51bf-9b24-c2264996f48b.html.

68. Dixon, "Geffen Agrees to Public Access at Beachfront Malibu Home."

69. See Jonathan Club website, www.jc.org/Default.aspx%3Fp%3DDynamicM odule%26pageid%3D358611%26ssid%3D266616%26vnf%3D1.

70. Common sense would suggest that Douglas's Jewish heritage, especially his and his family's traumatic World War II experiences in Germany (chapter 1), figured into his determination to force a nondiscriminatory membership policy on the Jonathan Club. Still, this writer has come across no documentary evidence explicitly linking his Jewish heritage to the position he, and by inference the commission, took regarding the permitting of the Jonathan Club's expansion plans.

71. See transcript of California Coastwalk's *Stories of the Coast* series on the fortieth anniversary of Proposition 20, titled "The Jonathan Club," 2012. Robin

Pressman was the host and interviewer. Public Radio Exchange made access to this series possible, www.prx.org/pieces/87666/transcripts/198807.

72. Lyndon Stambler, "Membership Policy Probe Asked: Expansion Plan by Jonathan Club OKd," *Los Angeles Times,* January 10, 1985, http://articles.latimes.com/1985-01-10/news/we-9329_1_membership-policies.

73. "The Jonathan Club," transcript.

74. Ibid.

75. Ibid.

76. Ibid.

77. Dorothy Townsend, "Jonathan Club Told to Observe Anti-Bias Rule," *Los Angeles Times,* October 22, 1985, http://articles.latimes.com/1985-10-22/local/me-12339_1_jonathan-club.

78. "The Jonathan Club," transcript.

79. Anthony Summers, who argued the case for the State of California, speculated that perhaps some of the judges may have been members of exclusive social clubs themselves and, for that reason, may not have wanted to adjudicate the case on its merits. Ibid.

80. Robert W. Stewart, "Jonathan Club Loses Appeal to High Court on Bias Ruling," *Los Angeles Times,* October 12, 1988, http://articles.latimes.com/1988-10-12/local/me-3132_1_jonathan-club.

81. "The Jonathan Club," transcript.

82. Douglas and some other sources claimed that nearly a dozen attempts were made to fire him. Former coastal commissioner Susan McCabe, however, strongly disagreed, telling the author that not more than a few such attempts were mounted. Susan McCabe, interview by author. Most of the others this author interviewed said Douglas's estimate of firing attempts was too high. The record clearly shows that at least two major attempts were made (in 1991 and 1996) to remove him. At this time the available evidence is unclear as to how many more such efforts were made.

83. Rolland, "Man and the Sea."

84. Ibid.

85. Ibid. Gary Giacomini confirmed this account, adding that Nathanson and Malcolm received "bags of money" from developers in payment for their votes in favor of coastal development permits. Gary Giacomini, interview by author.

86. Larry B. Stammer, "Coastal Panel's Director Keeps Job: Environment: State Commission Votes 10–0 to Retain Peter Douglas; the Decision Follows Weeks of Maneuvering by Two Members to Oust Him," *Los Angeles Times,* July 20, 1991, http://articles.latimes.com/1991-07-20/news/mn-2177_1_peter-douglas.

87. Ibid.

88. Mark Gladstone, "Coastal Chairman Faces Stormy Fight over Job," *Los Angeles Times,* July 19, 1991, http://articles.latimes.com/1991-07-20/news/mn-2177_1_peter-douglas.

89. Roland, "Man and the Sea"; Orsi, "Restoring the Common to the Goose," 280. Madelyn Glickfeld, a former coastal commissioner, suspected there were additional instances of corruption—without specifying what they may have been.

Glickfeld, interview by author, December 19, 2013, at UCLA's Institute of the Environment and Sustainability, Westwood, CA, audio recording. Glickfeld added in the interview that unlike some of the politically appointed panelists, the commission "staff was never captured" by the interests it regulated.

90. *Marine Forests Society v. California Coastal Commission* (2005). For a remarkably judicious and informative summary of the facts and legal reasoning involved in this case, see Emily Plett-Miyake, "California Coastal Commission's Authority Upheld," National Sea Grant Law Center (University of Mississippi), n.d., http://nsglc.olemiss.edu/SandBar/SandBar4/4.3california.htm.

91. David Haldane, "Coastal Commission Rejects Permit for Reef Built 9 Years Ago," *Los Angeles Times,* April 12, 1997.

92. Peter Douglas, "Marine Forests Ignores the History, Purpose of State's Separation of Powers Clause," Coastal Catch, *Los Angeles Daily Journal,* June 15, 2001.

93. Article III, Section 3, of the Constitution of the State of California reads, "The powers of state government are legislative, executive, and judicial. Persons charged with the exercise of one power may not exercise either of the others except as permitted by this Constitution." See *The Constitution of the United States of America and the Constitution of California,* 2003–2004 ed., published by the California Legislative Assembly, n.d., 166.

94. Carl Ingram, "Davis Urged to Act on Coastal Panel," *Los Angeles Times,* January 3, 2003.

95. *Marine Forests Society v. California Coastal Commission,* 2005 Cal. LEXIS 6846 at 29 (Cal. June 23, 2005).

96. Ibid., at 32.

97. "U.S. Supreme Court Declines to Hear Coastal Commission vs. Marine Forests Case," *Malibu Times,* November 2, 2005. Readers wanting to know more about the legal basis on which plaintiff attorney Zumbrun appealed the California Supreme Court ruling against Marine Forests should consult his article "What Can You Do When the State Supreme Court Trashes Your Case?" appearing in the *Sacramento Daily Recorder,* August 8, 2005, 1–4. Essentially, Zumbrun contended that the court's ruling deprived Marine Forests of its "experimental habitat" (a taking of private property prohibited under the Fourteenth Amendment) without providing "just compensation" and "due process of law."

98. Dennis Pfaff and Hudson Sangree, "Court OK's Coastal Commission," *San Francisco Daily Journal,* June 24, 2005, 2.

99. Ibid.

100. Ibid., 1–2.

101. Woo, "Peter M. Douglas Dies at 69; California Coastal Commission Chief."

102. The only book-length account of the Bolsa Chica Wetland controversy is David M. Carlberg's *Bolsa Chica: Its History from Prehistoric Times to the Present* (Huntington Beach, CA: Amigos de Bolsa Chica, 2009). Carlberg's highly informative book focuses largely on the efforts and activities of the Amigos de Bolsa Chica, a preservationist group for which he had served as president. To the book's credit, it

recognizes the critical importance of the Bolsa Chica Land Trust's legal proceedings against the Coastal Commission.

103. Philip L. Fradkin and Alex L. Fradkin, *The Left Coast: California on the Edge* (Berkeley: University of California Press, 2011), 90.

104. The area had been degraded by Standard Oil Company's drilling operations beginning in the 1920s and by the U.S. military's building of bunkers and emplacement of gun turrets during World War II.

105. *Los Angeles Times,* January 12, 1996.

106. Fradkin and Fradkin, *The Left Coast,* 89. According to Philip Fradkin, Peter Douglas made this point regarding the impossibility of barring all housing in the lowlands at a meeting with members of the Amigos de Bolsa Chica. See also James A. Aldridge, ed., *Saving the Bolsa Chica Wetlands* (Fullerton: California State University, Fullerton, Oral History Program, 1998), 252. Fradkin cited the Aldridge account as his source for Douglas's view, and Aldridge relied on the oral history statement of Chuck Nelson, former president of the Amigos. The Amigos meeting with Douglas that Nelson describes took place in the summer of 1994. Given the fact that the Coastal Commission could be sued for financial damages if a law court found that a "taking" had occurred (see note 59), Douglas's view that environmentalists would have to accept some residential development in the Bolsa Chica lowlands seems understandable.

107. Dan Morain, "Speaker to Give Coast Panel Its First Republican Majority," *Los Angeles Times,* May 21, 1996; Jeffrey L. Rabin and Deborah Schoch, "Coastal Panel to Consider Firing Top Director," *Los Angeles Times,* July 2, 1996.

108. Rabin and Schoch, "Coastal Panel to Consider Firing Top Director."

109. Jeffrey L. Rabin, "Key Official Backs Firing of Coastal Panel's Director," *Los Angeles Times,* July 4, 1996. Secretary Wheeler objected to Douglas's refusal to support the Koll Real Estate Group's project, endorsed by the Orange County Board of Supervisors, to build thirty-three hundred homes on land both abutting and near the Bolsa Chica Wetland.

110. Rabin and Schoch, "Coastal Panel to Consider Firing Top Director."

111. Jeffrey L. Rabin, "Coastal Crusader in Deep Water," *Los Angeles Times,* July 11, 1996.

112. Louis R. Calcagno, former Coastal Commission chair, interview by author, February 14, 2016, at Calcagno's Moss Landing, CA, home, audio recording. Calcagno told this writer that the 1996 firing episode was perhaps the most stressful experience in his life. He said he had to be escorted out of the Huntington Beach meeting venue by armed police for his protection from Douglas supporters.

113. Rabin, "Key Official Backs Firing of Coastal Panel's Director."

114. Calcagno, interview by author.

115. Alan G. Sieroty, former California legislator and employer of Peter Douglas, interview by author, October 8, 2013, at Sieroty's office in downtown Los Angeles, audio recording.

116. Rolland, "Man and the Sea"; Alex Barnum, "Coastal Chief Keeps His Job— for Now," *SFGate,* July 13, 1996, www.sfgate.com/green/article/Coastal-Chief-Keeps-His-Job-For-Now-2974383.php.

117. Rabin, "Coastal Crusader in Deep Water."

118. Eric Bailey, "A Political Survivor Finds His Life's Work," *Los Angeles Times,* March 2, 1998.

119. Calcagno, interview by author. Calcagno thought the Wilson spokesperson was the governor's chief of staff. To obtain more information and seek political balance, this writer repeatedly sent emails to Bob White, Governor Wilson's then chief of staff, but these communications went unanswered. The same is true for this writer's emails to a former assembly Speaker, Kurt Pringle.

120. Barnum, "Coastal Chief Keeps His Job—for Now."

121. Bailey, "A Political Survivor Finds His Life's Work." Assessing Douglas, Steinberg added: "He's a terribly effective communicator. On the surface he seems conciliatory, like you're going to your clergyman or analyst. But he is a political animal. His policies are hard-nosed."

122. Speech by Ellen Stern Harris titled "The Future of the California Coast," delivered at a joint meeting of the Friends of the Irvine Coast and the Laguna Canyon Conservancy, November 18, 1996, Tivoli Terrace restaurant, Laguna Beach, CA, Ellen Stern Harris Papers, Collection 1287, Box 7, Coastal CCC—Letters to/from 1987–2002, Special Collections Department, Charles E. Young Research Library, UCLA.

123. Ralph Faust, email interview by author, May 23, 2016.

124. *Bolsa Chica Land Trust et al., Petitioners v. The Superior Court of San Diego County,* Respondent; *California Coastal Commission, Real Party in Interest v. The Superior Court of San Diego County,* Respondent; Bolsa Chica Land Trust et al., Real Parties in Interest, nos. D029461, D030270, April 16, 1999.

125. Sierra Club, Press Room, Angeles Chapter, "Bolsa Chica Campaign: A Success Story," http://angeles.sierraclub.org/pressroom/FS_BolsaChica.asp.

126. Apropos the commission's defeat in the Bolsa Chica lawsuit, Douglas later remarked, "While the Commission has prevailed in well over ninety percent of cases brought against or by it, when it has lost a case the result has often been an unanticipated strengthening of the law—transforming the 'loss' into a 'win.'" See Douglas's blog, http://livelovewithcancer.blogspot.com/2011_06_01archive.html. Steve Ray, executive director of the Banning Ranch Conservancy, related to the author on June 12, 2013, at the California Coastal Commission meeting in Long Beach, CA, that in late March 2012 Douglas told him that the commission's court defeat was the best thing that could have happened, because the Coastal Act was upheld. See also *Half Moon Bay Review,* August 12, 1999, for Peter Douglas's statements voicing approval of the court verdict against the Coastal Commission, hmbreview.com.

127. Charles Lester, "CZM in California: Successes and Challenges Ahead," *Coastal Management Journal* 41, no. 3 (2013). Dr. Lester emailed the author a copy of his article; page numbers were not indicated in the online version: tandf.com.

128. Flossie Horgan, interview by author.

129. Frank Clifford, "Will San Simeon Coast Become a Playground?" *Los Angeles Times,* January 11, 1998.

130. Todd S. Purdum, "Environmentalists and Hearst Heirs Locked in Battle at San Simeon," *New York Times,* January 15, 1998.

131. Clifford, "Will San Simeon Coast Become a Playground?"; Bettina Boxall, "State Deal with Hearst over Coastal Land Closes," February 19, 2005.

132. Rasa Gustaitis, "Showdown at Hearst Ranch," *California Coast & Ocean* 14, no. 1 (Spring 1998): 7, 9.

133. All of the quotations appear in Frank Clifford, "Coastal Panel Rejects San Simeon Resort Plan," *Los Angeles Times,* January 16, 1998.

134. Clifford, "Will San Simeon Coast Become a Playground?"

135. Richard Jackoway, "Why the Coastal Commission Had Such an Easy Time Voting against the Hearst Resort," *Monterey County Weekly,* January 22, 1998.

136. Clifford, "Will San Simeon Coast Become a Playground?"

137. Clifford, "Coastal Panel Rejects San Simeon Resort Plan."

138. The two environmental groups were the California Rangeland Trust and the American Land Conservancy.

139. Lisa Leff, "Historic Land Deal between Hearst Corp. and California Made Final," *St. Augustine (FL) Record,* February 20, 2005, http://staugustine.com/stories/022005/nat_2900722.shtml#.VU_G_utUz9A.

140. "Saving Crystal Cove," KRCB-FM "Radio 91," aired on November 9, 2012. This program episode was the last of a three-part series of radio interviews titled *Stories of the Coast—How the California Coast Was Saved.*

141. "The Rescue of Crystal Cove," *Los Angeles Times,* February 18, 2001. For most of the Crystal Cove residents the cottages were second homes the occupants had rented for years at a modest price in a state park. While Merrilees focused on stopping the resort development, she also gave serious thought to saving the cottages and more. Accordingly, she arranged for Dr. Knox Mellon, California's state historic preservation officer, to speak at a Laguna Beach event in early 2001 about the California State Department of Parks and Recreation Resources codes 5024 and 5024.5 mandating that the majority of the Crystal Cove cottages had to stay given their historical importance. Beyond saving the cottages, Merrilees urged planning for the future of the park. See *Laguna Coastline News,* March 16, 2001.

142. Jeannette Merrilees, "Crystal Cove Historic District Plans Mid-July Workshops Likely," *Village Laguna Newsletter,* June 2000.

143. *Orange County Register,* January 31, 2001, and February 10, 2001.

144. Jeannette Merrilees, "State Abandons Crystal Cove Resort," *Village Laguna Newsletter,* February 2001.

145. "Saving Crystal Cove," KRCB-FM.

146. Michael A. Kahoe, "States' Role in OCS [Outer Continental Shelf] Development: The California Model," undated manuscript, Environmental Affairs Agency, California Coastal Commission Files (1981–1988), Coastal Zone Management Program, California State Archives, Sacramento.

147. Gilbert E. Bailey and Paul S. Thayer, *California's Disappearing Coast: A Legislative Challenge* (Berkeley: Institute of Governmental Studies, University of California, 1971), 37–38. In 1970, 1,879 offshore oil wells stood within the state's three-mile zone. In federal waters offshore, California had some 166 wells, all in the Santa Barbara Channel.

148. The executive branch's harsh criticism of the Coastal Commission is evidenced in the agency's response to a lengthy report issued by the Office of Ocean and Coastal Resource Management, a component of the National Oceanic and Atmospheric Administration, which is under the aegis of the U.S. Department of Commerce. See California Coastal Commission Response to the Draft Evaluation of the California Coastal Management Program Prepared by the Office of Ocean and Coastal Resource Management, September 17, 1987, Environmental Affairs Agency, California Coastal Commission Files (1983–1987), Correspondence, California State Archives, Sacramento. Also, see *Los Angeles Times,* November 25, 1987.

149. Bailey and Thayer, *California's Disappearing Coast,* 41.

150. State of California Natural Resources Agency, "Oil and Gas," in *California's Ocean Resources: An Agenda for the Future* (State of California Natural Resources Agency, July 1995), http://resources.ca.gov/ocean/html/chapt_5e.html.

151. Paul Rogers, "Despite Protests, Offshore Oil Drilling Remains Unlikely for Golden State," *San Jose Mercury News,* April 15, 2009, www.mercurynews.com /ci_12149244. According to this source, the federal government estimated that some 10.5 billion barrels of oil lay untapped beneath California's coast.

152. Kenneth R. Weiss, "Oil Firms File Offshore-Drilling Suit," *Los Angeles Times,* July 8, 2004, http://articles.latimes.com/2004/jul/08/local/me-offshore8.

153. Jane Kay, "51% of Californians Back Offshore Drilling," *SFGate,* July 31, 2008, www.sfgate.com/green/article/51-of-Californians-back-off-shore-drilling-3202868.php.

154. Rogers, "Despite Protests, Offshore Oil Drilling Remains Unlikely for Golden State."

155. Ibid.

156. Weiss, "Oil Firms File Offshore-Drilling Suit."

157. As indicated in chapter 4, the federal Coastal Zone Management Act (1972) empowered the state to review federally authorized or conducted activities seaward of the three-mile limit for consistency with the federally approved Coastal Management Program of California. The state's Coastal Management Program initially derived its authority from the California Coastal Zone Conservation Act of 1972 and other state laws. Similarly, after passage of the Coastal Act of 1976, the commission's authority to conduct consistency reviews derived from that law and other California statutes. Consequently, Douglas and the commission used the commission's consistency-review power to exercise the agency's regulatory authority in specified instances in federal waters. See "Memorandum Regarding the Commission's Authority with Respect to Emissions from Outer Continental Shelf Activities," prepared by Ralph Faust Jr., chief counsel, and Carolyn Small, staff counsel, June 6, 1986, Environmental Affairs Agency, California Coastal Commission Correspondence, California State Archives, Sacramento. For a primer on consistency review, consult "Federal Consistency in a Nutshell," coastal.ca.gov.

158. Rogers, "Despite Protests, Offshore Oil Drilling Remains Unlikely for Golden State."

159. Weiss, "Oil Firms File Offshore-Drilling Suit."

160. See California Environmental Protection Agency, Air Resources Board, website: arb.ca.gov.

161. See California Energy Commission website, www.energy.ca.gov/lng/.

162. California Coastal Commission, *Staff Report and Recommendation (Th7a)*, (State of California Resources Agency, February 20, 2007), pp. 2–3. The applicant is listed as BHP Billiton LNG International. See http://documents.coastal.ca.gov /reports/2007/4/Th7a-4-2007.pdf.

163. Scott Hadly and Charles Levin, "LNG Decision Charts New Territory in Regulations," *Ventura County Star,* April 15, 2007.

164. Jordan's network conducted an investigation of BHP Billiton and found that it had spent $1.8 million lobbying in California alone, plus more money at the national level to influence Congress and the White House on its LNG terminal project. See Janet Bridgers's informative 2007 *Heroes of the Coast* video interview with Jordan: *Susan Jordan—CA Coastal Activist Extraordinaire,* interviewed by Janet Bridgers for Earth Alert, published on Jun 26, 2015, www.youtube.com /watch?v=JSFVDQrLSM4.

165. Frank D. Russo, "Lesson from Offshore LNG Siting Decision: Winning Election in 'Down Ticket' Races Has Consequences," *California Progress Report,* April 11, 2007, www.californiaprogressreport.com/site/lesson-offshore-lng-siting-decision-winning-elections-down-ticket-races-has-consequences.

166. Hadly and Charles Levin, "LNG Decision Charts New Territory in Regulations."

167. Ibid.

168. California Coastal Commission, *Staff Report and Recommendation (Th7a);* California Planning and Development Report, "Global Warming Regulation Is Suddenly Hot," May 22, 2007, www.cp-dr.com/node/1662.

169. Hadly and Charles Levin, "LNG Decision Charts New Territory in Regulations."

170. California Planning and Development Report, "Global Warming Regulation Is Suddenly Hot."

171. In a letter to the U.S. Maritime Administration, the governor said, "Any LNG import facility must meet the strict environmental standards California demands to continue to improve our air quality, protect our coast and preserve our marine environment." Governor Schwarzenegger's letter made no mention of global warming. See Marc Lifsher, "Governor Vetoes Liquefied Gas Proposal," *Los Angeles Times,* May 19, 2007, http://articles.latimes.com/2007/may/19/business /fi-lng19

172. Poseidon Resources specializes in developing and financing water infrastructure projects, particularly seawater desalination and water treatment plants. See Carlsbad Desalination Project information at carlsbaddesal.com.

173. Carlsbad Desalination Project, http://carlsbaddesal.com/coastal-commission-staff-recommends-denial-of-request.

174. Editorial Board, "For Coast Commission, a Little History Is in Order," *San Diego Union-Tribune,* August 12, 2014.

175. Quoted in Michael Burge, "Proposal for Carlsbad Desalination Plant Rejected," *San Diego Union-Tribune,* November 2, 2007, http://legacy.utsandiego.com/news/northcounty/20071102–2148-bn2desal.html.

176. Michael Burge, "Poseidon Ordered to Offset Marine Deaths," *San Diego Union-Tribune,* November 17, 2007, http://legacy.sandiegouniontribune.com/news/northcounty/20071117–9999–6m17desal2.html.

177. Burge, "Proposal for Carlsbad Desalination Plant Rejected."

178. Ibid.

179. See Recommended Revised Findings Coastal Development Permit Application, Application File No. E-06–013, p. 5, http://documents.coastal.ca.gov/reports/2008/6/Th17a-6–2008.pdf.

180. See letter (dated September 20, 2007) over the signature of Joe Geever, California Policy Coordinator, Surfrider Foundation to California Coastal Commission, State Lands Commission, State Water Resources Board, and San Diego Regional Water Quality Control Board. The opposing organizations are all listed in alphabetical order. Peter Douglas was copied on the letter. See www.bvaudubon.org/PositionPapers/CDP.sign-on.FINAL.pdf.

181. Michael Burge, "Desalination Project Needs Another Panel's Approval," *San Diego Union-Tribune,* November 16, 2007, http://legacy.utsandiego.com/news/metro/20071116–9999–1m16desal.html.

182. Burge, "Poseidon Ordered to Offset Marine Deaths."

183. Ibid., and *San Diego Union-Tribune,* editorial, May 10, 2009, www.completecampaigns.com/Sitebuilder/CarlsbadDeSal/news.aspx?id=226.

184. The TCA was established in Orange County in 1986, when explosive housing, population, and economic growth seemingly necessitated a larger, regional, vehicular transportation system. To design, finance, and build such a system, the county and fifteen cities signed a joint powers agreement. Claiming that federal and state public highway building funds were unavailable, the TCA secured private investment monies through bond sales to build toll roads. The bonds were to be defrayed by toll road revenues. See the TCA website, www.thetollroads.com/.

185. These issues, and especially their legal handling, are covered in Joel R. Reynolds and Damon K. Nagami, "Lines in the Sand: Contrasting Advocacy Strategies for Environmental Protection in the Twenty-First Century," *UC Irvine Law Review* 1, no. 4 (December 2011): 1128–1142.

186. The Save San Onofre Coalition, founded in 2005, comprised more than a million members. It lobbied officials at all levels of government, constructed a joint website, initiated lawsuits, wrote opinion-editorials and letters to newspaper editors, prepared press releases, and much more. Participating groups included Audubon (California), California Coastal Protection Network, California State Parks Foundation, Defenders of Wildlife, Endangered Habitats League, Laguna Greenbelt, Natural Resources Defense Council, Orange County Coastkeeper, Sea and Sage Audubon, Sierra Club, and Surfrider Foundation. Ibid., 1129n12, 1132–1133, 1141.

187. Chad Nelsen, CEO and national environmental director of Surfrider Foundation, interview by author, May 15, 2014, at Nelsen's home in Laguna Beach,

audio recording. Wild Coast, a binational nonprofit organization headquartered in San Diego and led by Serge Dedina, mobilized its surfer and other marine environmentalist members by assisting Surfrider in opposing the 241 Toll Road. See Serge Dedina, *Wild Sea: Eco-Wars and Surf Stories from the Coast of the Californias* (Tucson: University of Arizona Press, 2011), 101–114.

188. Douglas's remarks on February 6, 2008, appear on YouTube at www .youtube.com/watch/v=8wzr4TzaNjo.

189. In the Toll Road controversy, the TCA was required to obtain approvals from several federal agencies, thereby triggering the Coastal Commission's "consistency review" power under the Coastal Zone Management Act. In this instance, the commission decided that the Toll Road project was "inconsistent with multiple Coastal Act policies." Per the CZMA, the TCA appealed the commission's consistency review decision to the U.S. Secretary of Commerce, who upheld the commission's verdict. See Lester, "CZM in California."

190. *OC Weekly,* October 16, 2008.

191. Chad Nelsen, interview by author; *San Diego Union-Tribune,* September 23, 2008.

192. Polls commissioned by the California State Parks and conducted in 2007 and 2008 by the nonpartisan David Binder Research firm found in 2008 that when informed that the new toll road would go through San Onofre State Beach and come close to Trestles Beach, support dropped markedly—from 51 percent supporting in 2007 to 33 percent in 2008. http://californiaprogressreport.com/site /new-poll—orange-county-voters-remain-strongly-opposed-toll-road-through-state-park.

193. Reynolds and Nagami, "Lines in the Sand," 1142–1144.

194. Peter Douglas, guest on Warren Olney's *Which Way, LA?* KCRW, February 7, 2008, kcrw.com.

6. EBB TIDE

1. Douglas said "starting to smoke" was one of his poor decisions. *We Live in a Political World,* blog; "187/Peter Douglas: The WHY to Live," blog entry by Gary Patton, July 7, 2010, www.gapatton.net/2010/07/187-peter-douglas-why-to-live .html.

2. Lloyd Billingsley, "Coastal Commission Holds Sacto Lovefest," Cal Watchdog, June 24, 2011, http://calwatchdog.com/2011/06/24/coastal-commission-seeks-fining-power/. As the title of this article suggests, Billingsley, affiliated with the Pacific Research Institute, was a critic of both the Coastal Commission and Peter Douglas's leadership of the agency. Regarding this underreported conference, Billingsley complained about the admiration shown Douglas and the commission by prominent state figures in attendance, such as California Resources secretary John Laird, former assemblyman and Coastal Commission chair Rusty Areias, former assemblyman Pedro Nava, and others.

3. See chapter 4.

4. Steve Kinsey, Coastal Commission chair, interview by author, January 14, 2016, Coastal Commission meeting held at San Diego County Board of Supervisors Chamber, audio recording.

5. Peter Douglas, "Visiting Churches," *Peter Douglas's Journal,* October 31, 2011, www.caringbridge.org/visit/peterdouglas/journal/index/2/0.

6. "Peter Douglas, Marin Resident and Fierce Protector of California's Coast, Dies," *Marin Independent Journal,* April 3, 2012, www.marinij.com/general-news/20120403/peter-douglas-marin-resident-and-fierce-protector-of-californias-coast-dies.

7. Douglas, "Visiting Churches." Regarding Douglas's camping in the Anza-Borrego Desert, see Paul Rogers, "Peter Douglas, Champion of the California Coast, Dies at 69," *San Jose Mercury News,* April 3, 2012, www.mercurynews.com /ci_20316247/peter-douglas-champion-california-coast-dies-at-69.

8. Robert H. Burnham, former city attorney for Newport Beach, interview by author, August 25, 2015, at the latter's home in Laguna Beach, CA, audio recording.

9. Peter Douglas, "Latest from Retirement Land," *Peter Douglas's Journal,* November 27, 2011, www.caringbridge.org/visit/peterdouglas/journal/index/2/0.

10. Ibid.

11. Douglas, "Visiting Churches." In a 2009 letter to the San Luis Obispo Board of Supervisors, Douglas wrote, "In our headlong rush for renewables, I respectfully urge you ... to hit pause, step back, take stock of our human and environmental condition, and envision what we will have saved for the seventh generation of our kin.... I have no doubt, that if the proposed industrial solar projects are built on the Carrizo Plain [located in southeastern San Luis Obispo County] the essence of this National Monument will be destroyed." The letter is excerpted in *Mojave Desert Blog: Advocating for the Preservation of Desert Wildlands,* "Peter Douglas," unsigned blog entry, April 4, 2012, www.mojavedesertblog.com/2012/04/peter-douglas.html.

12. See chap. 1; *We Live in a Political World,* blog; "187/Peter Douglas: The WHY to Live."

13. Peter Douglas, "Caring to Make a Difference: Environmental Activism," speech delivered before the Planning and Conservation League, Sacramento, April 14, 2007, www.pcl.org/projects/2007symposium/proceedings/Douglas-keynote.pdf.

14. Peter Douglas, "Still Hugging Trees," *Peter Douglas's Journal,* October 17, 2011, www.caringbridge.org/visit/peterdouglas/journal/index/2/0.

15. Douglas, "Caring to Make a Difference."

16. Ibid.; Peter Douglas, "Keep Fighting for Gaia," *Peter Douglas's Journal,* October 11, 2011, www.caringbridge.org/visit/peterdouglas/journal/index/3/0.

17. Janet Bridgers, *Hero of the Coast—Peter Douglas—July 2011 Interview,* interviewed by Janet Bridgers for Earth Alert, published September 6, 2011, www .youtube.com/watch?v=byzjG5SqHto. Bridgers is executive director of Earth Alert! Another instance of Douglas referring to the coast as "California's geographic soul," is found in Peter Douglas, "Blog 2: Cancer and Saving the Sundown Coast—a Personal

Story, Part One," Live Love with Cancer, June 12, 2011, http://livelovewithcancer
.blogspot.com/.

18. "Extended Biography and Personal Comments: Peter Douglas, California
Coastal Commission Executive Director, 1985–2011," California Coastal Commission website, n.d., www.coastal.ca.gov/pd-bio-comments.pdf. The comment was
made in 2011 on the eve of Douglas's retirement in November of that year. The
quotation also appears in Congresswoman Jackie Speier's speech in the House of
Representatives, "In Recognition of Peter Douglas," April 19, 2012, *Congressional
Record,* vol. 158, no. 57 (Washington, DC: U.S. Government Publishing Office,
2012), E599–E600.

19. Peter Douglas's speech, "The Future of Coastal Management," January 11,
1993, delivered before the Ocean Study Governance Group, Berkeley, CA, Coastal/
CCC Testimony, Peter Douglas and Paper, 1994–1995, Ellen Stern Harris Papers,
Collection 1287, Box 7, Special Collections Department, Charles E. Young Research
Library, UCLA.

20. Quoted in Rogers, "Peter Douglas, Champion of the California Coast, Dies
at 69."

21. *We Live in a Political World,* blog; "187/Peter Douglas: The WHY to Live."
According to the *Merriam-Webster* online dictionary, the term *kakistocracy* is
defined as "government by the worst people."

22. *Stevenson Alumni Magazine,* "Peter Douglas '60 on Following Your Bliss"
(2012): 36.

23. Peter Douglas, "Latest from Retirement Land, Questions I No Longer (have
to) Ask," *Peter Douglas's Journal,* October 8, 2011, www.caringbridge.org/visit/peter
douglas/journal/index/2/0.

24. David Helvarg, *The Golden Shore: California's Love Affair with the Sea* (New
York: St. Martin's Press, 2013), 188. Helvarg attended the gathering.

25. Susan Jordan, founder and executive director, California Coastal Protection
Network, interview by author, September 8, 2016, Newport Beach City Council
Chamber, Newport Beach, CA, audio recording.

26. Christiane Maria Douglas, sister of Peter Douglas, interview by author,
December 21, 2013, at her home in La Quinta, CA, audio recording.

7. FOOTPRINTS IN SAND

1. Elana Leone and Quito Tsui, "A Closer Look at Local Coastal Programs: A
Case Study of the North Central Coast," Bill Lane Center for the American West,
Stanford University, October 19, 2015, https://west.stanford.edu/research/works
/closer-look-local-coastal-programs-case-study-north-central-coast.

2. Elaine Woo, "Peter M. Douglas Dies at 69; California's Coastal Commission
Chief," *Los Angeles Times,* April 4, 2012.

3. Dennis Hevesi, "Peter Douglas, Sentry of California's Coast, Dies at 69," *New
York Times,* April 8, 2012.

4. "Peter Douglas: Commission Director," *Washington Post,* April 4, 2012, www.washingtonpost.com/local/obituaries/notable-deaths-peter-douglas/2012/04/04/gIQAsmYrvS_story.html?utm_term=.9dc541bf271f.

5. "Peter Douglas Dies, Crusaded for State's Coasts," *San Francisco Chronicle,* April 4, 2012, www.sfgate.com/news/article/Peter-Douglas-dies-crusaded-for-state-s-coasts-3457291.php.

6. Paul Rogers, "Peter Douglas, Champion of the California Coast, Dies at 69," *San Jose Mercury News,* April 3, 2012, www.mercurynews.com/2012/04/03/peter-douglas-champion-of-the-california-coast-dies-at-69/.

7. Obituary, *Sacramento Bee,* April 3, 2012, http://blogs.sacbee.com/capitol alertlatest/2012/04/longtime-coastal-commission-director-peter-douglas-dies.html.

8. Obituary, *San Diego Union-Tribune,* April 3, 2012.

9. John Howard, "Coastal Commission's Peter Douglas to Step Down," *Malibu Times,* August 17, 2011, www.malibutimes.com/news/article_524bb243-2ee6-5729-9c73-6a8b1cb5b098.html.

10. "Peter Douglas Announces Retirement," *Carmel Pine Cone,* August 12, 2011, www.pineconearchive.com/110812PCA.pdf.

11. Surfrider Foundation Blog; "Coastal Preservation," blog entry by Chad Nelsen, April 2, 2012, www.surfrider.org/coastal-blog/entry/peter-douglas-1942–2012.

12. Obituary, *Huffington Post,* June 3, 2012, www.huffingtonpost.com/2012/04/03/peter-douglas-dead-califo_n_1400665.html.

13. Quoted in Hevesi, "Peter Douglas, Sentry of California's Coast, Dies at 69."

14. Janet Bridgers, "Peter Douglas, Thomas Jefferson to the Coast," Obituaries, *Berkeley Daily Planet,* April 5, 2012. John Laird, California's secretary of natural resources, compared Douglas favorably to Sierra Club cofounder John Muir. See Paul Rogers, "Peter Douglas, Longtime Champion of the Coast, Hands Over Power," *San Jose Mercury News,* October 29, 2011. Similarly, Michael Sutton, vice president of the Monterey Bay Aquarium, averred: "There's no doubt Peter will go down in the history books alongside the likes of John Muir and other great champions of our environment." See Rogers, "Peter Douglas, Champion of the California Coast, Dies at 69."

15. Sara Wan, former Coastal Commission chair, interview by author, October 22, 2013, Malibu, CA, audio recording.

16. Toni Iseman, former coastal commissioner and Laguna Beach councilwoman, interview by author, January 27, 2015, at her Laguna Beach, CA, home, audio recording.

17. Shirley Dettloff, former coastal commissioner, interview by author, August 6, 2015, at her Huntington Beach, CA, home, audio recording.

18. Paul C. Horgan, lead attorney on precedent-setting case successfully suing Coastal Commission, interview by author, March 9, 2016, at the latter's home in Huntington Beach, CA, audio recording.

19. "Executive Director Lester Statement on the Passage of Peter Douglas," California Coastal Commission website, n.d., www.coastal.ca.gov/ExecDirTributeto-Peter.pdf.

20. National Oceanic and Atmospheric Administration website, "NOAA Announces Walter B. Jones Awards for Coastal and Ocean Management Excellence," June 26, 2012, www.noaanews.noaa.gov/stories2012/20120626_walterjonesaward .html.

21. Jason Hoppin, "After 40 Years of Coastal Activism, Coastal Commission Chief Peter Douglas to Retire," *Santa Cruz Sentinel News,* August 11, 2011.

22. Woo, "Peter M. Douglas Dies at 69; California's Coastal Commission Chief."

23. *Eye on the News* blog; "Legacy of Zealotry," blog entry by Lloyd Billingsley, June 28, 2012, www.city-journal.org/2012/cjc0628lb.html.

24. Hoppin, "After 40 Years of Coastal Activism, Coastal Commission Chief Peter Douglas to Retire." As critical as Beard had been, he acknowledged that Douglas was "an extremely successful leader . . . [of] probably the most powerful land use agency in the United States." Paul Beard II, former Pacific Legal Foundation attorney, interview by author, January 29, 2016, at his law office in Sacramento, CA, audio recording.

25. Wendy Mitchell, coastal commissioner, interview by author, June 9, 2016, Hyatt Regency Hotel Restaurant, Santa Barbara, CA, audio recording.

26. For one of the clumsiest and most blatant examples, see the website for a film documentary titled *Sins of Commission,* by Richard Oshen, which attacks Douglas's self-avowed paganism. One blog post reads, "Viewing the leader of the California Coastal Commission, through the prism of paganism, one can begin to see why people, especially people with families are held in such low regard. . . . [We] can understand how an omnipotent organization, all three branches combined is in essence omnipotent lead *[sic]* by an unelected person with an *[sic]* very *different* from mainstream American, philosophical beliefs, *could have* created a system out of proportion with human rights." The emphasis and errors in grammar are all in the original statement. See the website Sins of Commission, www.sinsofcommission .com/California-Coast/tag/peter-douglas/.

27. Lisette Ackerberg, owner of a large beachfront home built with a conditioned permit requiring a public beach access way, battled Douglas and the Coastal Commission for years, refusing to honor the easement she and her husband had previously accepted. Court decisions in 2012 and 2013 forced her acquiescence to opening the pathway to the shore, which was dedicated in 2015. See Ann O'Neill, "Billionaire's Beach Just Got a Lot Less Exclusive," *CNN,* July 17, 2015, cnn.com.

28. For a good synopsis of the fight to reopen Martins Beach, see Dan Morain, "Despite Environmental Efforts, Billionaire Faces Martin's Beach Access Fight," *Sacramento Bee,* August 24, 2014, www.sacbee.com/opinion/opn-columns-blogs /dan-morain/article2607606.html.

29. Laylan Connelly, "Crystal Cove Cottages Approved for Final Phase of Renovation," *Orange County Register,* March 9, 2017; "Awakening the Cove," *Newport Beach Magazine,* October 11, 2013, newportbeachmagazine.com.

30. Charles Lester, "CZM in California: Successes and Challenges Ahead," *Coastal Management Journal,* 41, no. 3 (2013). Page numbers are not indicated in the online version: tandfonline.com.

31. Ibid.

32. John Krist, "Bolsa Chica Saga Proves Wetlands Are for the Birds," *California Planning and Development Report* 17, no. 1 (January 2002), www.cp-dr.com /node/994.

33. Judith Kildow and Charles S. Colgan, *California's Ocean Economy: Report to the Resources Agency, State of California* (Sacramento: California Resources Agency Report, 2005), 1, 8, www.opc.ca.gov/webmaster/ftp/pdf/docs/Documents_Page /Reports/CA_Ocean_Econ_Report.pdf. The economic sectors studied included construction, living resources, minerals (oil and gas exploration/production), ship and boat building, tourism and recreation, and transportation. Because certain economic sectors were excluded from the report (the government sector, fisheries-harvesting employment, marine science and education, real estate, and corporate investment) for specified, technical reasons, the figures given for California's ocean/coastal economy should be regarded as very conservative.

34. Ibid., 18.

35. The quotation from Peter Douglas appears in his keynote speech, "Making Waves: Making a Difference," delivered at Surfrider Foundation's 15th Anniversary Event, August 28, 1999, www.beachapedia.org/Keynote_Speech_at_Surfrider_Foundation%27s_15_Anniversary_Event. See also the similar commentary by former coastal commissioner and then UC Irvine professor Judy B. Rosener, "Legacy of State's Coastal Act Can Be Seen by What's Not There Now," *Los Angeles Times,* April 13, 1989. Rosener wrote, "The legacy of the Coastal Act is not easy to assess. It is as much measured in the development you don't see as in the quality of development you do see. It is as much measured in the views and public access you enjoy as in the citizen participation that made the views and access possible. It is as much measured in changed attitudes about protecting the environment as in seeing how public-private partnerships have been forged to protect coastal resources. As we anticipate the reaction that will come when the hotels, roads and houses begin to sprout along the Irvine coast, we should remind ourselves of what might have been!" This author conducted an interview with Dr. Rosener, a much-referenced authority on the California Coastal Commission, July 30, 2014, at her Newport Beach, CA, home, audio recording.

36. David Helvarg, "The Savior of California's Coast," opinion-editorial, *Los Angeles Times,* April 8, 2012.

37. According to UCLA law professor Jonathan Zasloff, an acknowledged expert on the Coastal Commission: "The commission is the single most powerful land use authority in the United States." This quotation appears in a highly informative newspaper article titled: "In California, Coastal Commission Wields Vast Power," by Jennifer Steinhauer, *New York Times,* February 23, 2008. A former coastal commissioner and now political consultant on Coastal Commission issues, Susan McCabe, holds that the state agency is "the most powerful land use body in the world because of Peter Douglas and his expansive view of the Coastal Act" (McCabe, CEO of McCabe & Company, government affairs consulting, Sacramento, former coastal commissioner, interview by author, November 11, 2015, at her Marina del Rey office, audio recording).

38. Chapter 4 of this work detailed his primary roles in the drafting of Proposition 20 (1972) and the California Coastal Act (1976). Additionally, as noted in appendix B, Douglas helped draft regulations implementing the federal Coastal Zone Management Act (1972).

39. "Extended Biography and Personal Comments: Peter Douglas, California Coastal Commission Executive Director, 1985–2011," www.coastal.ca.gov/pd-bio-comments.pdf; Alan G. Sieroty, former California legislator and employer of Peter Douglas, interview by author, October 8, 2013, at Sieroty's business office in downtown Los Angeles, audio recording.

40. A few weeks after Peter Douglas's death, Dedina surfed in the early morning hours at Trestles. On that occasion a sense of gratitude welled up within the wave rider/coastal activist. "It was fortuitous that I happened to be at Trestles that morning," he recalled. "Because if Peter had not lived and dreamed of a coastline in California that belonged to us all, there just might not be a San Mateo Creek or surf at Trestles." Serge Dedina, "Peter Douglas: California Coastal Crusader," *The Inertia* (April 25, 2012), www.theinertia.com/environment/remembering-peter-douglas-californias-coastal-crusader/.

41. Mark A. Massara, attorney specializing in coastal issues, interview by author, March 9, 2016, at a restaurant across the street from the Santa Monica Civic Auditorium, Santa Monica, CA, audio recording.

BIBLIOGRAPHY

ARCHIVAL AND MANUSCRIPT COLLECTIONS

San Diego State University, Special Collections Archives

California Proposition 20, Coastal Initiative Collection.

State Archives of California

California Coastal Commission. Environmental Affairs Agency. Coastal Zone Management Program, 1981–1989, Box 1.

California Coastal Commission. Environmental Affairs Agency. Correspondence, 1978–1990, R284.7–R284.8.

California Coastal Commission. Executive Director Files. Personal Correspondence, March through August, September through October 1978, R254.020.

California Coastal Commission. Records of the Assistant Executive Director. Appointment Files, 1979–1983, R254.027.

California Coastal Commission. Records of the Assistant Executive Director. General Correspondence, Files 1980–1981, R254.025.

UC Berkeley, Bancroft Library

Michael L. Fischer Papers.
Sierra Club Papers.

UCLA Special Collections Department, Charles E. Young Graduate Research Library

Ellen Stern Harris Papers.

MASTER'S THESES AND DOCTORAL DISSERTATIONS

Byrne, Travis Arthur. "Bill Devall's Deep Ecology: Simple in Means, Rich in Ends." Master's thesis in sociology, Humboldt State University, 2011.

Crawford, Carin. "Waves of Transformation." Master's thesis, Department of History, UC San Diego, 1993. www.lajollasurf.org/wavesof.html.

Nelsen, Chad Edward. "Collecting and Using Economic Information to Guide the Management of Coastal Recreational Resources in California." PhD diss., UCLA, 2012.

Reineman, Dan. "The Human Dimensions of Wave Resource Management in California." PhD diss., Stanford University, 2015.

Rosener, Judy B. "Citizen Participation in an Administrative State: Does the Public Hearing Work?" PhD diss., Claremont Graduate School, 1979.

WEBSITES CONSULTED

Adelman, Kenneth, and Gabrielle Adelman. California Coastal Records Project. 2002–2015. californiacoastline.org. This is an aerial photographic survey of the California coastline.

Banning Ranch Conservancy. "Banning Ranch Park and Preserve: A Vision for the Future." March 20, 2014. banningranchconservancy.org.

Biel, Daniela. "Inventing the Beach: The Unnatural History of a Natural Place." *Smithsonian,* June 23, 2016. Smithsonianmag.com.

Billingsley, Lloyd. "Coastal Commission Holds Sacto Lovefest." Cal Watchdog, June 24, 2011. http://calwatchdog.com/2011/06/24/coastal-commission-seeks-fining-power/.

Blank, Elizabeth. "Burdens on Public Access." *Sea Grant Fellows Publications,* paper no. 63, 2013. http://docs.rwu.edu/law_ma_seagrant/63.

Bridgers, Janet. *E. Lewis Reid on Proposition 20 Campaign.* Interviewed by Janet Bridgers for Earth Alert. Published on December 6, 2013. www.youtube.com/watch?v=waXLwBzcIsA.

———. *Heroes of the Coast—the Documentary.* Interviewed by Janet Bridgers for Earth Alert. Published on April 12, 2016. www.youtube.com/watch?v=E6RPp7vhGQE.

———. *Hero of the Coast—Ellen Stern Harris.* Produced and directed by Janet Bridgers for Earth Alert. Published on April 28, 2012. www.youtube.com/watch?v=ejWOZrJm7dA.

———. *Hero of the Coast—Peter Douglas—July 2011 Interview.* Interviewed by Janet Bridgers for Earth Alert. Published September 6, 2011. www.youtube.com/watch?v=byzjG5SqHto.

———. *Susan Jordan—CA Coastal Activist Extraordinaire.* Interviewed by Janet Bridgers for Earth Alert. Published on June 26, 2015. www.youtube.com/watch?v=JSFVDQrLSM4.

————. "Transcript of Video Interview with Michael L. Fischer." Recorded August 2012, p. 7. http://earthalert.org/hotc/wp-content/uploads/2015/08/Fischer-Michael-re-CCC.pdf.

California Climate Change Center. *The Impacts of Sea-Level Rise on the California Coast: Final Paper,* 2009. http://pacinst.org/app/uploads/2014/04/sea-level-rise.pdf.

California Coastal Commission. www.coastal.ca.gov.

————. "California Coastal Commission Budget Funding History." In *Governor's Proposed Budget Governor's Budget for FY 2014–2015,* March 28, 2014. http://documents.coastal.ca.gov/reports/2014/4/W6b-4-2014.pdf.

————. *Sea Level Rise Policy Guidance,* adopted unanimously August 12, 2015. www.coastal.ca.gov/climate/slrguidance.html.

California Coastal Commission Project, Stanford University. Historical and Empirical Analysis Components. 2016. http://west.stanford.edu/projects/california-coastal-commission-project.

California Coastal Records Project, an Aerial Photographic Survey of the California Coastline. www.californiacoastline.org.

California Coastal Trail. "Big Sur: Sanctuary of the Spectacular." KCET. KCETLink.

Center for Marine Sciences, Cal Poly, San Luis Obispo. "History of the Pier." N.d. www.marine.calpoly.edu/history-pier.

Demographia, "Coastal County Population: 1900–2010." N.d. www.demographia.com/db-coastalco.pdf.

Douglas, Peter. "Blog 2: Cancer and Saving the Sundown Coast—a Personal Story, Part One." Live Love with Cancer, June 12, 2011. http://livelovewithcancer.blogspot.com.

————. "Blog 3: Saving the Sundown Coast—People Power, the People's Law: Drafting the Initiative." Live Love with Cancer, December 26, 2011. http://livelovewithcancer.blogspot.com/.

————. "Caring to Make a Difference: Environmental Activism." Speech delivered before the Planning and Conservation League, Sacramento. April 14, 2007. www.pcl.org/projects/2007symposium/proceedings/Douglas-keynote.pdf.

————. "Making Waves: Making a Difference." Keynote speech at Surfrider Foundation's 15th Anniversary Event, August 28, 1999, San Diego, CA. www.beachapedia.org/Keynote_Speech_at_Surfrider_Foundation%27s_15_Anniversary_Event.

————. "Saving the Coast: A Job That's Never Done." Speech delivered at the California Colloquium on Water, UC Berkeley, September 13, 2007. www.youtube.com/watch?v=fvFZ5cqH9KM.

————. *We Live in a Political World,* blog; "187/Peter Douglas: The Why to Live." Blog entry by Gary Patton, July 7, 2010. www.gapatton.net/2010/07/187-peter-douglas-why-to-live.html.

Fine, Jason. "The Beach Boys' Last Wave." *Rolling Stone,* June 21, 2012. www.rollingstone.com/music/news/the-beach-boys-last-wave-20120621.

Holmes, Todd. "Navigating Uncharted Territory: Mel Lane and the Formative Years of the California Coastal Commission." Lecture, Bill Lane Center for the American West, Stanford University, November 18, 2015. west.stanford.edu.

———. "Tides of Tension: A Historical Look at Staff-Commission Relations in the California Coastal Commission." http://west.stanford.edu/static/tides-of-tension/index.html.

Kortum, Bill. "How It All Got Started." California Coastal Trail, n.d. www.californiacoastaltrail.info/cms/pages/trail/kortum.html.

Leone, Elana, and Quito Tsui. "A Closer Look at Local Coastal Programs: A Case Study of the North Central Coast." Bill Lane Center for the American West, Stanford University. October 19, 2015. https://west.stanford.edu/research/works/closer-look-local-coastal-programs-case-study-north-central-coast.

Malibu Complete. "Malibu Development: 1950s–1960s." N.d. www.malibucomplete.com/mc_history_dev_1950s-60s.php.

Marisol Malibu. "The Beach Boys' Malibu Beach House." Blog Home, November 29, 2012. http://marisolmalibu.com/en/about/blog/beach-boys-malibu-beach-house/.

Mason, Laura. "A Salute to Bay Area Mountains on International Mountain Day." *Save the Bay Blog.* https://blog.savesfbay.org/tag/san-bruno-mountain/.

McConahey, Meg. "Sea Ranch: Coastal Legacy." *Sonoma* magazine, September 10, 2014. www.sonomamag.com/sea-ranch-coastal-legacy/#.VM_Jt1pUz9B.

NASA. "New Satellite Animation Shows 'Pineapple Express' Bringing Rains to California." February 10, 2014. www.nasa.gov/content/new-satellite-animation-shows-pineapple-express-bringing-rains-to-california/#.VL6ro1pUz9B.

National Park Service, Point Reyes National Seashore, California. "Geologic Activity." Last updated November 21, 2016. www.nps.gov/pore/naturescience/geologicactivity.htm.

Oceanside Small Craft Harbor District. "Profiles of Special Districts in San Diego County." Service Review and Sphere of Influence Data Summary, Local Agency Formation Commission, 2007. www.sdlafco.org/Agendas/Aug2007/Draft%20District%20Profiles%20Harbor.pdf.

Orange County Parks and Recreation. "History." N.d. http://ocparks.com/beaches/salt/history.

Pacific Legal Foundation, "A Legacy of Freedom Victories in the Courts." N.d. www.pacificlegal.org/page.aspx?pid=4407.

Paddison, Joshua, and University of California. "1921–Present: Modern California—Migration, Technology, Cities." Calisphere, University of California, 2005. www.calisphere.universityofcalifornia.edu/calcultures/eras/era6.html.

Planning and Conservation League of California. "California Environmental Quality Act (CEQA)." N.d. www.pcl.org/campaigns/ceqa/.

———. "CEQA Workshops and Information." N.d. www.pcl.org/campaigns/ceqa/ceqa-workshops-info/.

Revesz, Richard L., and Jack Lienke. "Nixon's 'Environmental Bandwagon': Richard Nixon Signed the Landmark Clean Air Act of 1970—but Not Because He Had Any Great Concern about the Environment." Salon.com, January 2, 2016.

Santa Barbara Wildlife Care Network and Jeffrey Hemphill. "1969 Santa Barbara Oil Spill." www2.bren.ucsb.edu/~dhardy/1969_Santa_Barbara_Oil_Spill /About.html.

UC San Diego, "Campus Timeline." N.d. http://ucsd.edu/timeline/.

Venice Historical Society, "On the Toss of a Coin: Our Story." www.venicehistorical .org.

We Live in a Political World, blog. "187/Peter Douglas: The WHY to Live." Blog entry by Gary Patton, July 7, 2010. www.gapatton.net/2010/07/187-peter-douglas-why-to-live.html.

NEWSPAPERS CONSULTED

Carmel Pine Cone
Christian Science Monitor
Daily Breeze (South Bay, Los Angeles)
Eureka Times-Standard
Half Moon Bay Review
Huntington Beach Independent
Laguna Beach Independent
Lodi News-Sentinel
Los Angeles Daily Journal
Los Angeles Times
Malibu Times
Marin Independent Journal
Monterey County Weekly
Napa Valley Register
New York Times
OC Weekly
Orange County Register
Sacramento Bee
Sacramento Capitol Weekly
Sacramento Daily Recorder
San Diego Union-Tribune
San Francisco Chronicle
San Francisco Daily Journal
San Jose Mercury News
Santa Barbara Independent
Santa Barbara News-Press
Santa Cruz Sentinel
Santa Rosa Press Democrat
St. Augustine (FL) Record
Ventura County Star
Washington Post

Adams, Janet. "Proposition 20—a Citizen's Campaign." *Syracuse Law Review* 24, no. 3 (Summer 1973): 1019–1046.

Aldridge, James A. *Saving the Bolsa Chica Wetlands.* Fullerton: California State University, Fullerton Center for Oral and Public History and Amigos de Bolsa Chica, 1998.

Alonso, Harriet Hyman. *Peace as a Women's Issue: A History of the U.S. Peace Movement for World Peace and Women's Rights.* Syracuse, NY: Syracuse University Press, 1993.

Bailey, Gilbert E., and Paul S. Thayer. *California's Disappearing Coast: A Legislative Challenge.* Berkeley: Institute of Governmental Studies, University of California, 1971.

Bakken, Gordon Morris, and Brenda Farrington, eds. *Environmental Problems in America's Garden of Eden: The American West.* New York: Garland Publishing, 2001.

Bakker, Elna, S. *An Island Called California: An Ecological Introduction to Its Natural Communities.* 2nd ed. Berkeley: University of California Press, 1984.

Bardach, Eugéne. *The California Coastal Plan: A Critique.* San Francisco: Institute for Contemporary Studies, 1976.

Beatley, Timothy, David J. Brower, and Anna K. Schwab. *An Introduction to Coastal Zone Management,* 2nd ed. Washington, DC: Island Press, 2002.

Bergel, Kurt, and Alice R. Bergel, eds. and trans. *Albert Schweitzer and Alice Ehlers: A Friendship in Letters.* New York: University Press of America, 1991.

Bodovitz, Joseph E. "Management and Policy Directions." In *The San Francisco Bay Conservation and Development Commission, 1964–1973.* Regional Oral History Office, Bancroft Library, University of California, Berkeley, 1986.

Brown, Edmund G. *California and the World Ocean.* Sacramento: California Office of State Printing, 1964. This volume contains the proceedings of the conference held at the California Museum of Science and Industry in Los Angeles, January 31 to February 1, 1964.

Caldwell, Margaret, et al. *Pacific Ocean Synthesis: Scientific Literature Review of Coastal and Ocean Threats, Impacts, and Solutions.* Stanford, CA: Woods Center for the Environment at Stanford University, 2009.

California Coastal Commission. *California Coastal Access Guide.* 7th ed. Oakland, CA: University of California Press, 2014.

———. *California Coastal Resource Guide.* Berkeley: University of California Press, 1987.

Carlberg, David M. *Bolsa Chica: Its History from Prehistoric Times to the Present.* Huntington Beach, CA: Amigos de Bolsa Chica, 2009.

Chiang, Connie Y. *Shaping the Shoreline: Fisheries and Tourism on the Monterey Coast.* Seattle: University of Washington Press, 2008.

Chiles, Frederic Caire. *California's Channel Islands: A History.* Norman: University of Oklahoma Press, 2015.

Corbin, Alain. *The Lure of the Sea: Discovering the Seaside in the Western World, 1750–1840*. Translated by Jocelyn Phelps. Penguin: New York, 1995.

Cornford, Daniel, ed. *Working People of California*. Berkeley: University of California Press, 1995.

Dawson, Robert, and Gray Brechin. *Farewell, Promised Land: Waking from the California Dream*. Berkeley: University of California Press, 1999.

Dedina, Serge. *Wild Sea: Eco-Wars and Surf Stories from the Coast of the Californias*. Tucson: University of Arizona Press, 2011.

Devall, Bill. "The Deep, Long-Range Ecology Movement: 1960–2000." *Ethics and the Environment* 6, no. 1 (2001): 18–41.

Deverell, William, and David Igler, eds. *A Companion to California History*. Malden, MA: Wiley-Blackwell, 2008.

Doolittle, Fred C. *Land-Use Planning and Regulation on the California Coast: The State Role*. Environmental Quality Series no. 9, California Agencies Paper 418. Davis: Institute of Governmental Affairs, University of California, May 1972. digitalcommons.law.ggu.edu/caldocs_agencies/418.

Douglas, Christiane M. *All My Children: The Life Story of Paula Elisabeth Vetter*. Privately printed, 1997. Copy shelved at Pilgrim Place Library, Claremont, CA.

Douglas, Peter M. Unfinished, unpublished, and undated typescript of autobiography. Author's copy.

Douglas, Peter M., and Joseph E. Petrillo. "California's Coast: The Struggle Today—a Plan for Tomorrow." *Florida State University Law Review* 4, no. 2 (April 1976): 179–230.

Ellickson, Robert C. "Ticket to Thermidor: A Commentary on the Proposed California Coastal Plan." *Southern California Law Review* 49 (1976).

Engstrand, Iris. *San Diego: California's Cornerstone*. San Diego: Sunbelt Publications, 2005.

Erlandson, J. M., M. L Moss, and M. Des Lauriers. "Life on the Edge: Early Maritime Cultures of the Pacific Coast of North America." *Quaternary Science Reviews* 27 (2008): 2232–2245.

Fagan, Brian M. *Before California: An Archeologist Looks at Our Earliest Inhabitants*. Walnut Creek, CA: AltaMira Press, 2003.

Farmer, Jared. *Trees in Paradise: A California History*. New York: W. W. Norton, 2013.

Fischer, John Ryan. *Cattle Colonialism: An Environmental History of the Conquest of California and Hawai'i*. Chapel Hill: University of North Carolina Press, 2015.

Fradkin, Philip L., and Alex L. Fradkin. *The Left Coast: California on the Edge*. Berkeley: University of California Press, 2011.

Fredrickson, Angie. "The California Coastal Act and Ports: The Unintended Environmental Justice Implications of Preserving California's Coastline." *Coastal Management Journal* 41, no. 3 (2013): 258–271.

Gamble, Lynn H. *The Chumash World at European Contact: Power, Trade, and Feasting among Complex Hunter-Gatherers*. Berkeley: University of California Press, 2008.

Gelber, Steven M., and Martin L. Cook. *Saving the Earth: The History of a Middle-Class Millenarian Movement.* Berkeley: University of California Press, 1990.

Gillis, John R. *The Human Shore: Seacoasts in History.* Chicago: University of Chicago Press, 2012.

Griffin, L. Martin. *Saving the Marin-Sonoma Coast: The Battles for Audubon Canyon Ranch, Point Reyes, and California's Russian River.* Healdsburg, CA: Sweetwater Springs Press, 1998.

Griggs, Gary. *Introduction to California's Beaches and Coast.* Berkeley: University of California Press, 2010.

———. *Our Ocean Backyard: Collected Essays.* San Bernardino, CA: CreateSpace Independent Publishing Platform, 2014.

Griggs, Gary, Kiki Patsch, and Lauret Savoy, eds. *Living with the Changing California Coast.* Berkeley: University of California Press, 2005.

Griggs, Gary, and Deepika Shrestha Ross. *California Coast from the Air: Images of a Changing Landscape.* Missoula, MT: Mountain Press, 2014.

Gustaitis, Rasa. "Never Saved; Always Being Saved: An Interview with the Coastal Commission's Peter Douglas." *California Coast & Ocean* 12, no. 4 (Winter 1996–1997): 10–18.

———. "Showdown at Hearst Ranch." *California Coast & Ocean* 14, no. 1 (Spring 1998): 7, 9.

Hayes, Miles O., Jacqueline Michel, and Joseph Holmes. *Coast to Explore: A Coastal Geology and Ecology of Central California.* Columbia, SC: Pandion Books, 2010.

Healy, Robert G., et al., eds. *Protecting the Golden Shore: Lessons from the California Coastal Commissions.* Washington, DC: Conservation Foundation, 1978.

Helvarg, David. *The Golden Shore: California's Love Affair with the Sea.* New York: St. Martin's Press, 2013.

Hogan, Richard. *The Failure of Planning: Permitting Sprawl in San Diego Suburbs, 1970–1999.* Columbus: Ohio State University Press, 2003.

Ingram, B. Lynn, and Frances Malamud-Roam. *The West without Water: What Past Floods, Droughts, and Other Climatic Clues Tell Us about Tomorrow.* Berkeley: University of California Press, 2013.

Jacobs, John. *A Rage for Justice: The Passion and Politics of Phillip Burton.* Berkeley: University of California Press, 1995.

Jeffers, Robinson. *The Selected Poetry of Robinson Jeffers.* Palo Alto, CA: Stanford University Press, 1966.

Kildow, Judith, and Charles S. Colgan. *California's Ocean Economy: Report to the Resources Agency, State of California.* Sacramento: California Resources Agency Report, 2005. www.opc.ca.gov/webmaster/ftp/pdf/docs/Documents_Page/Reports/CA_Ocean_Econ_Report.pdf.

Killion, Tom, with Gary Snyder. *California's Wild Edge: The Coast in Poetry, Prints, and History.* Berkeley: Heyday Books, 2015.

Kripal, Jeffrey J. *Esalen: America and the Religion of No Religion.* Chicago: University of Chicago Press, 2007.

Lester, Charles. "CZM in California: Success and Challenges Ahead." *Coastal Management Journal* 41, no. 3 (2013): 219–244.

"Locked Out: Why the Key to Black's Beach Is One of the Most Coveted and Elusive Objects at UCSD." *The Guardian* (University of California, San Diego), May 30 2006.

Lotchin, Roger W. *Fortress California, 1910–1961: From Warfare to Welfare.* New York: Oxford University Press, 1992.

Lyndon, Donlyn, and Jim Alinder. *The Sea Ranch: Fifty Years of Architecture, Landscape, Place, and Community on the Northern California Coast.* New York: Princeton Architectural Press, 2014.

May, Kirse Granat. *Golden State, Golden Youth: The California Image in Popular Culture, 1955–1966.* Chapel Hill: University of North Carolina Press, 2002.

McPhee, John. *Assembling California.* New York: Farrar, Straus & Giroux, 1993.

Meldahl, Keith Heyer. *Rough-Hewn Land: A Geologic Journey from California to the Rocky Mountains.* Berkeley: University of California Press, 2011

———. *Surf, Sand, and Stone: How Waves, Earthquakes, and Other Forces Shape the Southern California Coast.* Oakland, CA: University of California Press, 2015.

Merchant, Carolyn, ed. *Green versus Gold: Sources in California's Environmental History.* Washington, DC: Island Press, 1988.

———, ed. *Major Problems in American Environmental History.* Lexington, MA: D. C. Heath, 1993.

Miller, Char. *Not So Golden State: Sustainability vs. the California Dream.* San Antonio, TX: Trinity University Press, 2016.

National Research Council et al. *Sea-Level Rise for the Coasts of California, Oregon, and Washington: Past, Present, and Future* (Washington, DC: National Academies Press, 2012). Nap.edu.

O'Hara, Susan Pritchard, and Gregory Graves. *Saving California's Coast: Army Engineers at Oceanside and Humboldt Bay.* Spokane, WA: Arthur H. Clark, 1991.

Opie, John. *Nature's Nation: An Environmental History of the United States.* Fort Worth, TX: Harcourt Brace, 1998.

Orsi, Jared. "Restoring the Common to the Goose: Citizen Activism and the Protection of the California Coastline, 1969–1982." *Southern California Quarterly* 78, no. 3 (Fall 1996): 257–284.

Osborne, Thomas J. *Pacific Eldorado: A History of Greater California.* Malden, MA: Wiley-Blackwell, 2013.

———. "Saving the Golden Shore: Peter Douglas and the California Coastal Commission, 1972–2011." *Southern California Quarterly* 96, no. 4 (Winter 2014): 433–464.

Panetta, Leon, with Jim Newton. *Worthy Fights: A Memoir of Leadership in War and Peace.* New York: Penguin Books, 2014.

Pilkey, Orrin H., and Rob Young. *The Rising Sea.* Washington, DC: Island Press, 2009.

Queenan, Charles F. *The Port of Los Angeles: From Wilderness to World Port.* Los Angeles: Los Angeles Harbor Department, 1983.

Reynolds, Joel R., and Damon K. Nagami. "Lines in the Sand: Contrasting Advocacy Strategies for Environmental Protection in the Twenty-First Century." *UC Irvine Law Review* 1, no. 4 (December 2011): 1128–1142.

Rice, Richard B., William A. Bullough, Richard J. Orsi, and Mary Ann Irwin. *The Elusive Eden: A New History of California*. New York: McGraw-Hill, 2012.

Ricketts, Edward F., Jack Calvin, and Joel W. Hedgpeth. *Between Pacific Tides*. 5th ed. Revised by David W. Phillips. Palo Alto, CA: Stanford University Press, 1985.

Rosener, Judy B. "Intergovernmental Tension in Coastal Zone Management: Some Observations." *Coastal Zone Management Journal* 7, no. 1 (1980): 95–109.

———. "Involvement of Concerned Citizens." In *Proceedings of the Southern California Coastal Zone Symposium, Fullerton, California, March 17–18, 1972*. Fullerton: California State University, Biology Department, 1972.

Rosener, Judy B., et al. *Environmentalism vs Local Control: A Study of the Voting Behavior of Some California Coastal Commissioners*. Los Angeles: John Randolph Haynes and Dora Haynes Foundation, 1977.

Sabatier, Paul A., and Daniel A. Mazmanian. *Can Regulation Work? The Implementation of the 1972 California Coastal Initiative*. New York: Plenum Press, 1983.

Schoenherr, Allan A., *A Natural History of California*. Berkeley: University of California Press, 1992.

Schoenherr, Allan A., C. Robert Feldmeth, and Michael J. Emerson. *Natural History of the Islands of California*. Berkeley: University of California Press, 1999.

Schulz, Florian. *The Wild Edge: Freedom to Roam the Pacific Coast*. Seattle: Mountaineers Books, 2015.

Scott, Stanley, ed. *Coastal Conservation: Essays on Experiments in Governance*. Berkeley: Institute of Governmental Studies, University of California, 1981.

———. *Governing California's Coast*. Berkeley: Institute of Governmental Studies, University of California, 1975.

Sharpsteen, Bill. *The Docks*. Berkeley: University of California Press, 2011.

Small, Melvin, ed. *A Companion to Richard Nixon*. Malden, MA: Wiley-Blackwell, 2011.

Sollen, Robert. *An Ocean of Oil: A Century of Political Struggle over Petroleum off the California Coast*. Juneau, AK: Denali Press, 1998.

Squire, Peverill, and Stanley Scott. *The Politics of California Coastal Legislation: The Crucial Year, 1976*. Berkeley: Institute of Governmental Studies, University of California, 1984.

Starr, Kevin. *Golden Dreams: California in an Age of Abundance, 1950–1963*. New York: Oxford University Press, 2009.

Stevenson Alumni Magazine. "Peter Douglas '60 on Following Your Bliss." (2012): 36.

Turner, Tom. *David Brower: The Making of the Environmental Movement*. Oakland: University of California Press, 2015.

Tyrrell, Ian. *True Gardens of the Gods: Californian-Australian Environmental Reform, 1860–1930*. Berkeley: University of California Press, 1999.

Valentine, Andrew P. "Property Rights—the Effect of Nolan v. California Coastal Commission on Land Use Permits: A Proposed Constitutional Analysis." Comment. *Santa Clara Law Review* 32, no. 4 (1992): 1174–1176.

Virga, Vincent. *California: Mapping the Golden State through History; Rare and Unusual Maps from the Library of Congress.* Guilford, CT: Morris, 2010.

Wellock, Thomas Raymond. *Critical Masses: Opposition to Nuclear Power in California, 1958–1978.* Madison: University of Wisconsin Press, 1998.

Winchester, Simon. *Pacific: Silicon Chips and Surfboards, Coral Reefs and Atom Bombs, Brutal Dictators, Fading Empires, and the Coming Collision of the World's Superpowers.* New York: HarperCollins, 2015.

Wollenberg, Charles. *Marinship at War: Shipbuilding and Social Change in Wartime Sausalito.* Berkeley: Western Heritage Press, 1990.

INDEX

The abbreviation *PD* in index entries refers to Peter Douglas.

Corona Del Mar, 123, 125
Coronado Island, 29
Costa, Jim, 129
Council of Carpenters, 68
counterculture, 41, 42–44
County Line Beach, 37
County Supervisors Association of California, 48, 58
Crocker Land Company, 45
Crowley, John F., 69
Crystal Cove, 123–127, 152, 161, 194n141
Crystal Cove Alliance, 125, 126
Crystal Cove Historic District, 126

Dana Point Harbor, 35–36
Darwin Award, 186n13
Davick, Laura, 124, 125, 126
Davis, Gray, 113, 161
Davoren, William T., 55
DDT, 62
Dedina, Serge, 149, 156, 161, 204n40
Deep Ecology, 43–44
Denham, Jeff, 129
Dennis the Menace (comic strip), 71
desalination: Point Loma desalination plant, 32; Poseidon desalination plant, 132–135, 162
Dettloff, Shirley, 97
Deukmejian, George, 91, 92, 97, 99, 159–160
Devall, Bill, 44
Diablo Canyon project, 35
Dickson, Edward, 105
Dixon, John, 97
Djerba, 11
Donna O'Neill Land Conservancy, 136
Dora, Mickey "Da Cat," 44
Douglas, Christiane (sister), 1–3, 6, 7, 140, 146, 166n12
Douglas, Donald W., Jr., 7
Douglas, Peter: accomplishments and honors, 163; Aquarium of the Bay celebration, 144–145, 145*fig.*, 162; California Coastal Act, 84–86, 86*fig.*; childhood and youth, 1–14, 31–32, 165n1; commissioner interactions, 94–96; commissioners attempt to fire PD (1991), 109–111; commissioners

attempt to fire PD (1996), 116–118; creative leadership of, 93–95, 106–109; death of, 144, 146, 162; declining health of, 139–140; ecological consciousness, 41, 43, 44; environmental legislative aide to Alan Sieroty, 12–14, 13*fig.*, 39–40, 55–59; integrity and frugality of, 96–97; legacy of, 151–156; love of the sundown coast, 7–8, 58, 94*fig.*, 120; philosophy and politics of, 49, 56–58, 93–95, 141–144; retirement, 140–141; tributes to, 147–151. *See also* California Coastal Commission (CCC); litigation and key CCC battles
Douglas, Rotraut Schmidt "Roe," 9, 10–12, 14, 56
Douglas, Sascha, 96, 186n13
Douglas, Vanja, 95, 96
Dreebin, Bert H., 3, 4–5*fig.*, 6
Dunlap, John, 47–48, 57, 117

Earth Day, 52, 158
Ehlers, Alice (grandmother), 3, 8, 9, 142, 166nn14, 15
Ehlers, Maria (mother), 1–3, 4–5*fig.*, 6, 165n1
Ehlers, Peter Michael. *See* Douglas, Peter
Elkhorn Slough, 117
Ellickson, Robert C., 81–82
El Niño Southern Oscillation events, 23–24, 23*fig.*, 169n22
environmental impact reports (EIRs), 53
environmentalism in California: California Environmental Quality Act (1970), 52–53; COAAST and the Coastal Alliance, 47–48, 70, 157; emergence of (1960s and 1970s), 41, 173n2; left coast and counterculture, 41, 42–44; San Francisco Bay Conservation and Development Commission (1965–1969), 44–47; Santa Barbara oil blowout (1969), 48–49, 50*fig.*, 51–52; statewide coastal commission and AB 1471, 56–59; statewide coastal commission evolution, 53–55
environmentally sensitive habitat areas, 119–120, 136–137, 161

equal protection, 106–109
Esalen Institute, 34

failure avoidance, 62
Fairness Doctrine and FCC regulations,
    70–71
Farallon Islands, 22, 26, 27*fig.*
Farallon Plate, 16, 17
Farr, Fred, 55
Faust, Ralph, 118
Federal Communications Commission,
    70–71
Feinstein, Diane, 128
Firestone, Brooks, 118
*First English Evangelical Lutheran Church
    v. Los Angeles, CA*, 188n59
Fischer, Michael L., 89, 90, 91, 92, 96, 159,
    179n39
flooding, Central Valley (1861), 24
Ford Ord, 31
Fradkin, Philip L., 38
Franciscan Complex, 17, 22
Frank, Kenneth, 96–97
Freed, Michael, 125, 126
Friends of Mammoth case, 53
Friends of the Earth, 35
Fuller, Buckminster, 34

Gaia, 142–143
Garamendi, John, 131
Geffen, David, 103–105, 162
geological origins and events, 16–17, 18*fig.*,
    19–22, 20*fig.*
George, Ronald, 113
Get Oil Out, 52, 157
Giacomini, Gary, 95, 98, 110
Gidget (film), 37, 102
Golden Gate Bridge, 30
Governor's Advisory Commission on
    Ocean Resources, 43
gray whales, 21
Griggs, Gary, 19, 22–23, 25, 169n21
Grossman, Marshall, 107, 108
Gughemetti, Joseph, 116
Gulick, Esther, 45, 157
Guthrie, Woody, 144

Hahn, Ernest W., 36
Half Moon Bay, 21

Halprin, Lawrence, 33
Hann, Kathi, 131
Harris, Ellen Stern: California Coastal
    Act, 87; criticizes effectiveness of CCC,
    91, 180n48, 184n106; need for statewide
    coastal management agency, 48, 54, 157;
    on "People Power" and support for PD,
    118; Proposition 20 campaign, 68;
    public beach access, 54–55, 71, 102;
    serves as commissioner, 75
Hartley, Fred L., 48–49
Hearst, George, 122
Hearst, Patricia Bell, 122
Hearst, William R., II, 122
Hearst, William Randolph, 121, 148
Hearst Ranch and Highway 1, 120–123, 161
Heidt, John M., 104
Heidt, Mary Ann K., 104
Hemingway, Ernest, 29
Henning, John, 85, 86
Heston, Charlton, 71
Highway 1 landslide, 23*fig.*
Holmes, Frank E., 129
Horgan, Flossie, 94, 120
Horgan, Paul C., 119
Hotel Coronado, 29
Hotel Del Monte, 29
Hoye, Steve, 103
Humboldt State University, 44
Huntington, Henry, 29
Huntington, Henry Edward, 105
Huntington Beach: Bolsa Chica Wetland,
    114–116, 119–120, 119*fig.*, 153; oil devel-
    opment, 30; surf culture, 21
Huntington Beach Tomorrow, 119

*The Impacts of Sea-Level Rise on the Califor-
    nia Coast* (California Energy Commis-
    sion), 26
independent, quasi-judicial agency, 63
Ingomar Club, 75
Irvine Company, 35, 68, 124
Iseman, Toni, 150

Jackson, Herbie, 72
Jonathan Club, 105–109, 160, 189n70
Jordan, Susan, 93, 122–123, 126, 131, 137,
    146, 161